PERSONALITY
ASSESSMENT
THROUGH
MOVEMENT

PERSONALITY ASSESSMENT THROUGH MOVEMENT

MARION NORTH

*Head of the Movement and Dance Department,
Goldsmiths' College, University of London
Director of the Art of Movement Studio,
Addlestone, Surrey*

Publishers   PLAYS, INC.   Boston

© Macdonald and Evans Limited 1972

First U.S. edition published by
PLAYS, INC. 1975

Library of Congress Cataloging in Publication Data

North, Marion.
    Personality assessment through movement.

    Includes bibliographical references.
    1. Movement, Psychology of. 2. Personality assessment.
I. Title [DNLM: 1. Kinetics. 2. Movement. 3. Personality
assessment. BF698 N866p 1972]
BF295.N67 1975   155.2'8   74-13127
ISBN 0-8238-0173-X

Printed in Great Britain

PREFACE

This book is an attempt to describe and validate a technique of movement observation which, I believe, has a contribution to make to the assessment of personality. It is intended to be read by the general reader as well as the professional practitioner. Some knowledge of current movement theory and practice is assumed, but most readers interested in the educational and therapeutic use of the arts should find that the book has something to offer them.

The book is written in three sections. Part One, which may present the most difficulty for the general reader, is an account of the theory upon which the argument of the rest of the book is based. Some readers may prefer to read the account of the application of movement observation in Parts Two and Three first, and to study the theory in the earlier chapters and Appendix I after their first reading of the assessments. It is important, however, that the basic symbols of movement notation be mastered at an early stage; they will be found on pages 4 and 5. The more technical details of the theory will be found in Appendix I.

The assessments,* which form a large part of the descriptive material in the book, are always written in a manner which will make them easily readable for the particular recipient (teacher, parent, employer, therapist). Readers who wish to make more detailed links between interpretation and the movements which gave rise to them should always consult the detailed material in Appendix I. Students of movement might find that it is an interesting exercise to study an assessment and, by reference to Appendix I, "work out" what the original observations must have been.

The book deals with some of the research into, and the application of, Laban's ideas about human movement. His original teachings were given to me practically and verbally over a period of ten years; some of the work was seen and approved by him and much has been developed since his death. I now feel that there are certain aspects of his discoveries which should be available in written form, if only to interest others in the possibility of using this means of observation and analysis to help diagnose personality traits, and to

* All names of the children studied and used in the assessments are fictitious.

draw attention to the therapeutic value of experience through movement. I have had to develop ways in which the knowledge I gained
could be used for various purposes, and to this extent I have used my
own experience and ideas; this account is therefore my personal
understanding and development of his work, and in this sense is
not original, but at all times I have tried to relate back to the movement principles which Laban discovered. There is a need for a great
deal of consistent and thorough research, and to this end I am
training a small group of students in the work. I hope that they in
their turn will further the application and knowledge of assessment of
personality through movement, develop movement therapy as an
accepted aid for the maladjusted, and that they will find that the
greater understanding of movement can lead to increased personal
awareness.

It is very valuable that the differences between the work of various
movement practitioners be pointed out. Mostly the differences are
due to individuals finding a particular need to explain and express an
aspect of movement in their own way. There is certainly room for all
these experiments, suggestions and changes, though it is a pity when
the same notation signs are used by different people to mean different
things, for this inhibits communication between workers in the
various areas of study. All the signs used in this book are those
developed together with Laban in his last years of active work. Some
of them are slightly different from those used in his early work
Effort.

Apart from the notation signs, more fundamental areas of disagreement become clear in the description of movement itself. I have
become convinced that we should try to retain the concept of *movement* study (including, as a central study, the body itself, with all its
manifestations of effort and space rhythms and patterns) rather than
effort-shape or *effort/space/body* concepts. Analysing the movement
into its component parts is essential and helpful only when the total
movement experience has been "grasped." Observing movement requires just this subjective, skilful assessment, and recognition, supported by accurate and precise analysis.

I wish to illustrate a technique which is not meant to be a statement of a philosophy (although in the later chapters where examples
of personality assessments are given, my personal opinions regarding
future training or treatment will reflect something of my own philosophy). This, however, should not be confused with the movement
observation, interpretation and assessment itself. Many aspects of

Laban's work have been omitted, including some which have been most personally helpful. I have not yet assimilated certain of his most advanced ideas, and often those which I have made my own are not strictly relevant to this immediate study, and are therefore excluded.

I believe that the reports included in this book are a valuable record of the development of the work in movement assessment since Laban's death, even though my style of presentation is now somewhat more refined. Inevitably, with greater experience, changes of attitude and outlook occur, and in addition further information is accumulated (for example, of movement development in babies and young children). I should now give greater emphasis to the art of movement (as distinct from movement practice) and avoid words of such overall sentimental generality as "harmony," "integration" and "cure" when discussing education or therapy. Nevertheless, the principles of movement and the interpretations remain essentially the same.

M.N.

November 1971

ACKNOWLEDGMENTS

My debt to Rudolf Laban is acknowledged throughout the book, and I hope that I have done some degree of justice to his ideas and inspiration.

I should also like to thank Hen van de Water, who helped me over a considerable period of time, especially in formulating Appendix I; Keith Richards, who read through the whole book at manuscript stage and made some very valuable suggestions; all those students and colleagues who have allowed me to experiment with ideas in classes and courses; and the children, parents, teachers, patients and workers who have helped me to develop my theories.

M.N.

CONTENTS

Part One: The Theory of Personality Assessment through Movement

CHAPTER 1

THE STUDY OF MAN THROUGH MOVEMENT

The contribution of Laban

It is probably true to say that Laban "lived before his time"—that his ideas and discoveries will be understood in the years ahead better than they have been by his contemporaries. Yet in many ways he was very much a man "of his time." He was interested in the human personality, the human psyche, human behaviour and human experience. He was interested in the artistic and practical endeavours of man, and he studied rituals, folk-lore, mythology, architecture, dancing and painting in his search for the understanding of modern man. His unique contribution was to see the link through all aspects of life as a dynamic movement and pattern. He saw movement everywhere—in seemingly static crystals, in changing melody and harmony, or in word or colour patterns. He was able to help others gain a real experience of the richness of dynamic movement—alone, when we relate our body movement to our inner world, and in groups, when we make a genuine relationship through our body movement to one or more other human beings. As Laing* points out so clearly, "A personal relationship is not only transactional, it is transexperiential and therein is its specific human quality. Transaction alone, without experience, lacks specific personal connotations." This is exactly what Laban expressed in his own terms so often, and it is the basis upon which he built his therapeutic and recreational work; it was an attempt to gain and recover "the wholeness of being human through the relationships between them"† (in this case the therapist and patient).

During Laban's life in England, he worked in many spheres: with factory workers and managers, with young people seeking vocational guidance, with sick children and adults, with students, teachers, doctors and artists. He invented a system of movement notation which is now used throughout the world ‡ and it is probably for this he is

---

* *The Politics of Experience*, R. D. Laing (Penguin Books).　　　† *Ibid.*
‡ *Principles of Movement and Dance Notation*, Rudolf Laban (Macdonald & Evans).

most widely known at present. He recognised that movement could
be described either in terms of its spatial pattern (for example, a
gesture of the right arm might describe a complete circle in front of
the body, widely extended) or in terms of its rhythm and accent,
which he called "effort" (for example, this circular gesture might
start suddenly, impulsively and freely, but gradually become restrained
and tense as the arm comes full circle). For a full description,
both aspects are necessary, just as in understanding a musical phrase
both the rhythm and melody must be taken into account, not as two
separate units but in their inter-relationship. Similarly, a painting can
be recognised in both its form and pattern, and its colour and texture.

Movement vocabulary

The development of a simple, quickly written "shorthand" of
movement meant that it was possible to capture and record how a
person moves. Before the symbols could be invented, it was necessary to understand how to look at the movement itself, and still
today this is the biggest hurdle for a student observer. It is not
possible to describe exactly in words what the different "effort"
qualities of movement are. It is easier to describe the spatial directions and patterns, as these areas are outside the body, and we have
adequate and specific vocabulary—forward, upward, round, angular
and so on. Laban had to analyse the "effort" qualities, and give them
names approximate to their content—for there are no exact ready-
made words. Gradually, an accepted terminology has been evolved,
but it will be readily appreciated that if words are borrowed or
coined it is not possible to use them exclusively for transmitting
understanding about movement—the word makes sense only if the
movement is experienced and recognised.

In the following chapters I have used symbols and words vari-
ously, hoping that one or other will convey a meaning to the reader.
These eight symbols, the basis of all movement notation, are shown
below and a detailed explanation is given in Appendix I, p. 231 *et
seq.*

        ↓   Light movement

        ⌠   Strong movement

        ╱   Sustained movement

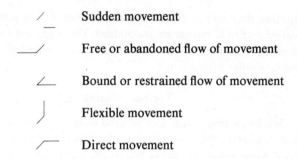

Sudden movement

Free or abandoned flow of movement

Bound or restrained flow of movement

Flexible movement

Direct movement

The accent sign / is always present, denoting "effort." Not only is it quicker to write in symbols than in words, but in practice it is easier to interpret, and at the stage of analysing the symbols this is important.

The use of film

A person talking or working makes a multitude of movements with different parts of the body in quick succession. It might be thought that a film would be a valuable tool, so that it could be played back, and no movement would be missed. In fact, film, while being very useful for some purposes, is not the whole answer to the problem. Apart from the question of mechanical and technical difficulties, and expense, some of the subtlety of movement is "ironed out" and the two-dimensional picture of movement loses the richness of the original. Certainly a great deal can be taken from a film, and no doubt this will become more frequently used, perhaps in training observers—at least we could thereby guarantee an exact repetition of a movement, which is difficult for anyone to produce consciously.

Movement observation

In observing a person's movement patterns it is not necessary, however, to notate every single movement—anyway it is impossible! Over a period of, say, twenty to thirty minutes, the same patterns of movement will be repeated, and a good observer will be able to write down, for example, every fourth or sixth movement. Provided that the person is in a situation where he is provoked to varied responses (such as an interview), his full range will be noted. (As will be described later, it is necessary to arrange for this more specifically with children.) Experiments have been made observing for a long period, perhaps an hour and a half, and then observing the person at another time and in different circumstances, to test whether a more varied record of movement is obtained. The range was found to be the same for both periods, and with the different kinds of phrases appearing in similar proportion.

The body "speaking"

We know that words can be used in many ways: to say what we mean, what we think we mean, what we think we ought to mean, what we deliberately do not mean and so on. Movement, as revealed in our gestures, unconscious movements ("shadow" movements), body carriage and our working actions, is always "ourselves." It always speaks honestly, or by its counter-actions of superimposed phrases reveals that an act (conscious or unconscious) is being put on. The assessor of movement recognises the difference between habitual and temporary actions, for it should be remembered that even these "acquired" momentary actions still belong to the person.

The body speaks clearly, and is usually understood and recognised at a non-verbal level—much of our communication and relationships depend upon this. Perhaps we lose some of our early recognition by and through the body as we acquire language. Young children respond spontaneously to the movement of another person—they "see" or "feel" or "experience" the person as a whole, through their whole being with a kinaesthetic sense, without analysing or verbalising, and, of course, we are told that primitive peoples still have this faculty strongly developed. It is also recognisable in mass meetings —a sort of "effort contamination."

This is a fascinating study of man through his movement, and a study of the world of movement in which man has his unique place.

CHAPTER 2

MOVEMENT AND PERSONALITY

What can be seen in movement

The main part of the assessment work as described in this book is based on "effort" observation, how the body uses "effort" and how it is related to space and shape patterns of movement. G. W. Allport describes in some detail the use which has been made by psychologists of expressive behaviour observations, that is, observations of "one's manner or style of behaving," which are concerned with "the oblique mirroring of personal traits."* Both he and Laban point out the distinction between "expressive and coping behaviour," though realising that "every single act a person performs has both its expressive and its adaptive (coping) aspects, sometimes more of one, sometimes more of the other."

Allport further states:

"The fact that expression tends with growing maturity to become confined to limited regions of the body has important consequences for personality assessment. For one thing, it means that various features of expression are of unequal significance in different people. Some faces are open books; some are 'poker-faces.' For some people, gestures are merely conventional; for others, highly individual. Sometimes the style of clothing and the handwriting seems 'just like' the person; in other cases, entirely non-expressive. One person reveals himself primarily in his speech; another, in his posture and gait; a third, in his style of clothing or ornamentation. As a promising hypothesis, we suggest that every person has one or two leading expressive features which reveal his true nature. If this is so, it is somewhat futile to study all people by the same ones, *e.g.*, voice, eyes or handwriting. The cue that is revealing for one person is not necessarily revealing for another.

"Every child is exposed to standard forms of expression which

* *Pattern and Growth in Personality*, G. W. Allport (Holt, Rinehart & Winston, 1961).

tend to limit his individual impulses in movement. He learns to write from a standard model, to play the piano or to dance according to rules. As Klages says, he tends to break away in part (but only in part) from the models. His handwriting acquires 'graphic maturity,' his musical interpretation and his dancing steps are his own.

"Even the stenographer in time modifies her system of shorthand, and the physician, when no longer an intern, comes to practise his art in his own manner. But all people remain conventional to some degree. What is important is the extent to which they break through the prescriptions of training and convention, and develop their own stamp of individuality. As we have said, the stamp may be more apparent in some expressive features than in others."

What I hope to show in this study is that however conventional gestures appear to be, however "poker-faced" an expression or seemingly "ordinary" a posture or gait, a human being reveals through the accumulation and variety of his movements his own personality. As previously stated, it is impossible for a normal person so to cover his inner life that a skilled and trained observer cannot see the difference between his basic movement patterns and his acquired or "cover up" patterns. (The possible exceptions to this are perhaps the paralysed person, or the severely mentally sick who withdraw almost completely into static immobility. I have not enough experience of these extreme cases to judge this.)

The observer

A comment must be made about the objectivity of the movement observations. A great deal of the training and experience of the student observer is directed towards his being able to observe accurately the subtle variations of movement patterns described later. It is necessary to be able to move oneself in a richly varied way in order to recognise the patterns of others. At the beginning, a student almost invariably observes those movements which are either very obviously most stressed or nearest to his own personal patterns. Gradually, he is led to extend his own range, and to be able to see a wider range, through his own kinaesthetic experiences. When three or four observers all independently see the same pattern, one begins to believe that a degree of objectivity has been achieved.

Laban's view of "expressive" movement

Shortly before Laban's death we discussed the idea of "expressive" movement. I had previously accepted as self-evident that movement behaviour was a direct reflection of the inner state of mind of the person, and that it could give, correctly observed and interpreted, a picture of the personality. The view which Laban advanced was a result of his years of experience and wisdom, and showed me a different understanding. Movement, he held, is not an automatic reflection: it has a definite function, either in objective work or, even more frequently, in operating in one's own inner being. Objective work is often conscious (though skilled and habitual actions can become automatised in repetition); subjective movement is most frequently unconscious.* Laban, in one of his lectures, said:

"Movement is in both of its aspects not a language, but a building process in which many and varying operations and actions are compounded. Language, on the contrary, is a means of depicting things and ideas and to bring them in various degrees of clarity into consciousness. One can for the sake of understanding depict also movement, or at least its characteristics."†

Movement as "building processes"

In trying to build a picture of a personality, we observe not only those movement patterns which are conscious and voluntary but also those habits of movement which a person has developed in general or particular circumstances. Applying the above idea, it seems that in life a person uses his own wide range of movement patterns, both subtle and crude, in gestures and "shadow" movements, in order to try to balance his own inner vibrations and attitudes. If we observe, say, a person who is angry, what we are really seeing in his movement is an attempt to establish an inner balance—a fight with an inner emotional state, and not the emotion itself. If the person is conscious of his movements to regain control—"self-conscious"— he is already to some degree acting a part; and if he tries to convey to others that he is suffering, or angry or whatever emotion is

* It is implicit in the idea of movement as an agent for therapy that it is possible to train and influence unconscious movement patterns within certain limits. This influence can only be effective if developed through non-conscious, spontaneous movement experience.

† Laban. Quotations are from my notes of talks and discussions and from personal letters.

appropriate to the situation, he becomes more an actor of a part which he imagines himself to be playing. The actor, mime or dancer uses such devices, and deliberately trains himself to "express" these emotions, and, as we know from experience, this ability for movement mastery is by no means sure to be transferred to his inner life.

An experienced observer distinguishes between movement patterns which are genuine "building processes" and those which are deliberate mime or imitation: for example, he would be alerted by seeing two contrasting rhythms appearing simultaneously. This might be an example of an imitative movement—although, of course, it could be an expression of a split inner attitude. It is possible, of course, that a movement pattern which starts as imitation may be absorbed and become part of a genuine "building process": for example, with children, copying is a way of learning which is frequently absorbed. In writing down phrases, sequences and whole processes of movement, the observer must be detached from emotional involvement and deliberately resist any attempt at simultaneous interpretation which could cloud the clear patterns. Interpretation of the observations comes later.

Laban recognised the appearance of all kinds of discordant body tensions and rhythms in people who for some reason lacked social adaptation and personal well-being. He observed the definite connection between these disharmonious rhythms, muscular tensions and emotional conflicts. He told me of experiments which showed that prolonged practice of discordant movement sequences could produce distress and discomfort, which he said was "near akin to emotional conflict." It interested me to hear from him that, in those people who had some capacity for resisting such distress, such an experience could be a valuable strengthener, but for those whose capacity for resistance is below a certain level, it could be destructive.

We all have a certain balance of resistance; none of us is completely "all round," some are lop-sided, and if we avoid a certain range of body tensions and rhythms, this could signify a relative lack of resistance in a definite direction. The use of movement practice, either individually or in a group, can help towards some degree of harmonising and stimulating inner activity. Sometimes it can be observed that movement activity (in rhythm or muscular tension) follows the inner activity; sometimes the emotion or inner stir follows the movement; at other times they are simultaneous. Also movement may seem completely suspended, as in deep thought. In pictures and sculptures, the artist frequently captures this moment of "frozen" movement, for we can see easily that the person is thinking by his body attitude. In life also, we would rarely confuse a sleeping man with a thinking one, however relaxed the body appeared in the thinker, and usually there are intermittent shadow movements or body adjustments which indicate mental activity. It is a mistake to conclude that the mind and body are separate, because of such definable movements of seeming separation; they are relatively infrequent.

CHAPTER 3

ASPECTS OF MOVEMENT FOR ASSESSMENT

Movement observation in daily life

If we accept that the way people sit, walk and make gestures has any relevance to how they are thinking and feeling, then it is only a short step towards the idea that a more subtle and deep analysis of the composition of the movement can lead towards a greater understanding of the personality.

It is common knowledge that we are all observers of movement, and that we all draw conclusions from our observations of other people. I do not think that we ever observe the emotion or attitude of another directly (although this is a view held by some psychologists); I think that we observe the resulting bodily action, both in posture (or body attitude) and in shadow movements of the face, shoulders, eyes, arms and feet, and make a quick assessment, based on our previous experience and kinaesthetic awareness. Some conclusions are more accurate and others are less accurate, according to varied experience or simply a gift for intuitive assessment. The example was given in a lecture I attended that a child might be angry or irritated and make exactly the same movement, and yet the observer would know whether it was anger or irritation which stimulated the action—"he would just know this." I believe that this "know" is based on a more subtle movement observation than the lecturer was aware of, for, although the movement might superficially appear to be the same in both circumstances, it would not in fact be so. The rhythm, intensity, degree of extension, accompanying facial movements and body attitude would all reveal subtle differences. It is not such a mysterious affair after all!

Movement in education

The inter-relationship of body and mind is thus revealed, and it has from ancient times been accepted that there is educational value in the artistic practice of movement—in dance, mime and drama. Special help has been appreciated by those using movement therapy with maladjusted children, and by the few practitioners working with adult patients. The effect of movement on our attitudes and temporary feelings can easily be demonstrated, and indeed we have incorporated into our language many admonitions to move: "Pull yourself together," "Chin up" and so on. Influences on a more habitual attitude can also be obtained in many cases, but this obviously requires a longer, deeper and more subtle form of movement treatment, usually with other forms of therapy. It is quite useless, and may even be dangerous, when recognising a disharmony, to attempt to correct it by practising a specific pattern of movement as compensation. The whole pattern of movement must be understood before any special section can be related to the whole.

Movement observation and the subsequent evaluation and assessment resulting from the observations are concerned with the actions and responses which human beings make in life. Each human being has his own personal colour, mixture and variations on the basic human actions and responses which are possible to all of us. It can be discerned which are actions and responses, and which are only temporary or momentary influences on the fundamental action.

Practical application of this understanding of movement has been made to various fields of activity. Most outstandingly, perhaps, as mentioned above, the education of children has been influenced by the recognition of the effect of creative movement on the growing personality as well as the body.* (Detailed assessments of young children are given later, in Chapters 5 and 6.)

Some uses of movement assessment

Vocations

It is possible to make selection and placement of manual and executive workers in industry and commerce, based on the revealed characteristics of an applicant as observed by a movement expert. (Examples of such assessments are given in Chapters 8 and 9.) Similarly, vocational guidance and help in training can be based on movement evaluation of young people when their potential and latent abilities are discovered, as well as their more obvious achievements and attitudes. (For examples *see* Chapter 7.)

* *Modern Educational Dance*, Laban (Macdonald & Evans). *Modern Dance in Education*, Russell (Macdonald & Evans). *An Introduction to Movement Study and Teaching*, North (Macdonald & Evans). *A Handbook for Modern Educational Dance*, Preston (Macdonald & Evans).

Therapy

The mentally sick always reveal in their movement characteristics and habits very definite variations and distortions from the range of "normality." There is still a great deal of research to be made in co-operation with doctors and psychiatrists, to discover just how much help might be given in diagnosis, and subsequent movement treatment. (One example of a mentally sick patient and her treatment is described in Chapter 10.)

Recreation

Recreative movement through dance and drama also is based on the same principles of movement, though here the aim is to provide a more general recovery and recreative vitality through the experience of individual and group activity.

Movement make-up of an individual

Many different aspects of movement must be considered when we make a comprehensive observation of a person's movement make-up. These aspects can be divided broadly into three:

(a) The use of the body, *i.e.* the nature of its actions.

(b) Where the body moves in the surrounding space, *i.e.* the shape and direction of its movements.

(c) How the body moves: general style, and quality of movement (with what accents, stress and rhythm, *i.e.* the effort which is used).

Greater detail of one or other of (a), (b) or (c) will be required according to the ultimate purpose of the observations—for example, assessment for treatment, vocational guidance, education, drama or dance.

The use of the body

To look first at the body actions, we can discern which part (or parts) of the body moves, the different actions which are made in gestures, in steps or in body carriage. A gesture can be an isolated movement of the hand in pointing, a shrug of the shoulder or a wriggle of the foot. A step is a movement resulting in a changed position of the body, that is, a changing of weight from one foot to the other. A movement of the body carriage changes the posture or attitude of the body, for instance, in sitting, or in drawing oneself up from a sagging to an upright position. Other aspects which must be taken into account include: the range of movement, or its restrictions, in bending, stretching and twisting; the counter-movements in different parts of the body at the same time (such as sitting down with careful precision and, at the same time, gesticulating with both hands); the differentiation of movements developing through the body successively from one part to the next (such as the gradual unfolding of a pointing gesture, starting in the elbow, going through the wrist and into the hand and fingers), and its contrast in movement which is simultaneously achieved by all parts moving together (as, for instance, a similar pointing gesture with elbow, wrist and hand participating all at the same time).

It is also important to observe where any movement originates in the body. For instance, in the example above of drawing oneself up from a sagging to an upright position, did the movement start in the shoulders and upper part of the body, and gradually include the lower spine, or did it originate at the bottom of the spine and work upwards? It can also be observed whether the parts of the body touch or join other parts, such as fingertips touching, legs crossing, hands gripping, as well as which parts move while others are held in position; for instance, the head can be held still upright and backward, while the eyes dart from side to side.

The above briefly indicated body actions must be speedily observed and written down, but of themselves they only tell us a small part of a person's movement in special situations. Naturally all kinds of intuitive interpretations are made spontaneously when we see these various actions, but in a movement analysis no action will be considered in isolation, and no conclusion drawn from the body action alone. Only when we can see where the action is made, and with what effort or rhythm, can we begin to understand it.

The body and its use of space

Where does the body action take place in the space surrounding the body? If we imagine a light attached to the hand, for instance, and a gesture describing the size of a large balloon is made by the person, the pathway of the light through the air could be seen to be circular. Now imagine a light attached to each part of the arm, or the head or the shoulders, and every time a movement is made, a series of pathways is shaped through the air. The recognition of the shapes which each person habitually uses gives us another clue to his movement configuration. Are these shapes zig-zag, or angular, that is, shapes which have an immediate change of direction at a corner? Or are these shapes rounded, where the movement continues around one centre, or around a moving centre? Or are they twisted, like a figure eight or letter S? Or most probably, are they a mixture of two or three in quite complicated patterns? The size and extension of these shapes—normal, reduced or exaggerated—are significant. Here, of course, racial variations can be seen to be important. The Italians are reputed to be generous and expansive in gesture size, the English, restrained and narrow. We would also observe where the shapes of the gestures are placed in relation to the body, high, across or to the open side of the body, in front or behind. Detailed observation can be made of the different directions to which a gesture or movement is orientated.*

The study of the directions of movements in space is a highly complicated and fascinating study of the harmony of movement and it is interesting to note that relationships of inclinations in space can be compared with the relationships of tones in music harmony.

Style of movement

In relating these first two aspects of movement (the body actions and the shapes made by the movements of the body into different directions in space), we can observe whether the movements are more "spoke-like," that is, centrally moving from the body to an outer object or position; more "edge-like," that is, travelling around the body and never coming to the centre, or between the two and "passing-by" the body in more transverse movements.

Two fundamental movements can be discerned: that of gathering towards oneself, or its contrast of scattering away from oneself. As will be seen in the later examples, the habitual use of one or the other gives a clue towards the development and attitude of a person towards his environment. Babies will usually use gathering and grasping movements, and it is a sign of development when such movement shapes reverse their direction on some occasions, and become scattering and outwardly orientated, as a balance to inward flow.

Shapes and patterns are often found to be blurred, directions indistinct and the line of the movement broken and only half completed. Some people will start in a muddle and finish clearly—some will start clearly and finish vaguely. (An interesting comparison here is in handwriting, which shows each individual's variations on basic forms and shapes of the letters and words.)

* *Choreutics*, Rudolf Laban (Macdonald & Evans).

Each one of us has a particular style of movement, which can be understood in the same way as our voice having a tendency towards soprano, tenor, mezzo-soprano or contralto-bass. In some people the type is very marked and easily discerned, giving a significant style to all of their movements, while in others there is a rather "in-between" style. The high mover has a natural tendency to lift in space, to prefer light, buoyant movement and to stress an erect body carriage. The high mover also seems to prefer shaped and clearly defined patterns of gestures. A gifted classical ballet-dancer will always be a high mover. The contrasting deep mover has a natural tendency to stress the downward direction in space, will prefer stamping and crouching where the body carriage is rounded or curved, or a sinking, falling attitude. The rhythmic qualities of action will probably be more pronounced than formal shaping ability. The medium mover uses predominantly more or less horizontal shape, enjoys perhaps leaning, swinging, lilting movements and uses the body in either an open expansive way or a closed protective way.

It will be noticed that the description of such a style of movement takes into account:

(a) the body shape assumed—erect; crouched; open or closed;
(b) where the person moves in the space—high, low or medium level;
(c) the inner quality of the movement—buoyant flight; rhythmic active; lilting swing.

It is not the physical build which determines the style; a heavily built, stocky person may be a high mover. However, there would often be a relationship between, for instance, tall slender build and a high mover. It becomes apparent through observation that mental and emotional attitudes play at least as great a part as physical structure in determining which type of movement will predominate in a person. Human beings are never categorised so easily, many of us are mixtures, and it is possible to discern all kinds of combinations of predominant styles, as well as those people who conveniently fit into one category. I have observed one person who was at one time high and buoyant, and at another deep and rhythmic—both with equal efficiency, but never medium and swinging. This combination of extremes is much less usual than high and medium, or medium and deep. When a very dominant style is evident in a person, this can give an indication of one aspect of his personal make-up, and would therefore be specifically mentioned.

Quality of movement, *i.e.* effort

The other aspect of movement which is considered is the "effort" (energy, timing and rhythmical phrasing), which is peculiarly our own. No two people ever move with exactly the same accents, timing and phrasing, although there are occasionally some small similarities in gesture, carriage and stance between children and parents, or between identical twins.

The following chapters will deal mainly with this aspect of movement, because many of the subtle variations of each human being's personality, and therefore movement patterns, can be observed through the rhythms and phrases which he or she habitually uses. From an analytical study point of view, it is necessary to take each detail of "effort" and look at it in isolation and in combination with other details. It cannot be emphasised often enough, however, that it is the inter-related movement patterns and rhythm which reveal personality traits. The exact knowledge of isolated parts can never give a whole. It would be like describing a picture as being three parts blue, one part red, four parts white and two parts mixed colours. It tells us nothing of the picture itself, of its composition and its meaning. After the analytical part of Chapter 6 onwards, I shall attempt to give the wholeness of personality its rightful importance.

It has been stated that movement cannot be understood and learned purely intellectually. In recognising movement patterns, it will be seen that different aspects of movement are naturally related one to another; for instance, firmness and strength is most easily experienced in deep sinking movements, and these movements are related in the body mainly to the centre of gravity, which is the lower part of the trunk. It is perhaps in recognising and understanding these relationships that movement has to be experienced and learned by more than the intellect. It is also truly stated that in observing others it is easier to see those movement characteristics which are like our own! This means that anyone hoping to develop the skill of movement observation must be prepared to experience, practise and recognise many other patterns outside his own natural range of movement. This is not necessarily energetic leaping about, but it is certainly active and requires time, patience and the absorption of the whole body and mind.

Body, shape and effort

We will now summarise those aspects of movement which have to be considered in making an all-round study of the "body-mental" efforts of an individual.

1. The body:

(a) Defining the part used in the body actions—

(i) gesture;
(ii) steps;
(iii) carriage.

(b) The body function (and restrictions) in bending, stretching and twisting, and the range of the movement—the measurable angle of the movement.

(c) Counter-movements in different parts of the body at the same time.

(d) Movements which develop successively through the body from one part to the next, contrasted with a simultaneous movement.

(e) Where the movement originates in the body.

(f) The touching or joining of different parts.

(g) Simultaneous observation also of the body parts which are held in stillness while another part moves.

2. Shape and space:

(a) Simple shape discernment and their relationship to each other—

(i) zig-zag—angular;
(ii) rounded;
(iii) twisted—simple or complex (1, 2, 3 times, etc.).

(b) Size—normal, reduced or exaggerated.

(c) Placement—in the zone around the body—

(i) above or below;
(ii) to the open side or closed side;
(iii) in front or behind.

(d) Differentiated in kind—linear, plane or plastic (1-, 2- or 3-dimensional).*

* This is outlined by Laban in *Modern Educational Dance* (Macdonald & Evans).

(e) Direction of the shape—

    (i) orientated to points 1 to 12 in icosahedron;*
    (ii) orientated dimensionally ⎫ and combinations
    (iii) orientated diagonally ⎰ of these.

(f) Towards and away from the body—

    (i) in central movement (spoke-like);
    (ii) in transverse movement (passing by);
    (iii) in peripheral movement (edge).

(g) Towards and away from the body—

    (i) in gathering;
    (ii) scattering shapes.

(h) Counter-directions of the body at the same time or in sequence (*chordic*), or following a changing direction, *i.e.*, drawing shape in the air (*melodic*, or *complex-melodic* when more than one shape is drawn simultaneously).

(i) Clarity or blurredness of drawn shapes—continuous or with breaks.

(j) High, medium or low mover.

3. Stress (or effort) (the reader is also referred to the outline of effort theory in Appendix I):

(a) Motion factors—weight, time, space, flow.

(b) Elements (in exaggeration, blurred or lessened degrees)—

opposites of light and strong;	The replacement
sustained and sudden;	of one element
flexible and direct;	by a near
free and bound flow	element

(c) Combination of elements and motion factors, where the main stress is—

(i) Of two	Weight and time (4 variations)	
	Weight and space (4 variations)	Inner states
	Time and flow (4 variations)	of mind or
	Time and space (4 variations)	inner attitudes
	Space and flow (4 variations)	

* *Modern Educational Dance* (Macdonald & Evans).

(*ii*) Of three   Time, weight, space (8 variations) ⎫
                Time, weight, flow (8 variations) ⎪
                Time, flow, space (8 variations) ⎬ Drives
                Weight, flow, space (8 variations) ⎭
(*iii*) Of four   Time, weight, space, flow
                (complete movement)

(*d*) Phrases—the kinships and relationships between each combination—

    (*i*) Lengths
    (*ii*) Developments—pauses (increases, decreases, resiliency and evenness)
    (*iii*) Rhythms—accents (simple and combined)
                —impact: impulse
                —regularity: irregularity
                —preparation: recoveries
    (*iv*) Patterns —leading into and out of different combinations, *i.e.*, routes of mental movement

All the different movement aspects mentioned above—*i.e.* body actions; shape and space; stress or effort—must be considered as a unity, and it is only for study purposes that an analysis is made. In some movements one or the other aspect will appear most important or stressed, but it will always be modified by the others.

CHAPTER 4

MAKING AND INTERPRETING THE OBSERVATIONS

Movement phrases

Their importance

Movement occurs in phrases, that is, in sequences of elements, inner attitudes and drives. The changing order of appearance of these movement happenings reveals a person's characteristic routes of mental and emotional activities, or the individual's "coping style." Over a period of time, a large number of different sequences or phrases appear. The variety of route gives an indication of the richness of personal responses and actions, the more limited the range—the more routine and predictable, the greater the variety—the richer is the potential field of response. Movement can thus be likened to music in that it is recognisable, not in individual notes, but in the phrases and sequences of notes and pauses. Equally, the richness itself may be an asset to a person only if he can select and apply appropriately and if the quality and patterns have been mastered adequately.

The difficulty of charting the phrases

Although this chapter deals with the most vital aspect of movement, that it appears in sequences in time, and not in movements that can be captured in a still photograph and represented by a single element notation, it is much more difficult to chart or analyse, because the variety is literally infinite. The lengths of phrases or sequences may be short or long; "simple" (as a simple sentence) and complete in itself, or "complex" or "compound" (phrased by a pause of longer or shorter duration, and during which any movement element may be retained), thus:

Held with bound flow

Held with directness and free flow

Held in light agitation

EXAMPLES

(a) The short intensive phrase may denote an immediate re-action with little preliminary activity:

(b) The longer developing phrase, which swings along, gener-ally gives an indication of a more feeling, emotional response:

Both (a) and (b) may be of fairly short duration, but the inner attitude is entirely different.

(c) The broken, divided, or even phrase tends to appear with considered, thoughtful mental action (in this case, a considered response leading to a decisive, impactive statement):

The individual and his movement style

Basic phrases and movement elements

The basic rhythm of a phrase can be simplified into:

increasing impetus; or

decreasing impetus;

or, what is more usual, combinations of these. The increasing, building-up phrase might be typical of a response or action which has a slow and cautious beginning, but builds up to a climax (often impactive); the decreasing, dying-away phrase is typical of a response which has an initial attack, but dies away (impulsive).

Many differing movement elements can be included in such phrases, and according to these, the individual's "colour" or style would be observable. Although most normal people use both phrases, chosen according to circumstances and challenge, it is usual that one or other is more frequently used in a particular individual's movement make-up. A mental and emotional disturbance may be partly revealed in a frequent and concentrated use of one or other phrase, or a violent swing from one to the other. It is generally recognised that the impactive, forceful ending is a more masculine trait, and the impulsive beginning, dying away (although it may be recharged over and over again), is a more feminine trait.

A third type is the even, unemphasised and regular phrase which neither increases nor decreases and has a steadiness and lack of variety. It could, according to the movement elements involved in the phrase, reveal attitudes ranging from calm, detached imperturbability, to routine, mechanical repetitiveness.

Constant strength		Constant directness and focus	
Constant lightness		Constant flexibility	
Constant haste		Constant restraint	
Constant calm } Sustainment }		Constant ease	

In the movement phrases of a mature adult, any combination of these kinds of phrases may occur, though certain personal preferences will begin to emerge, as sufficient examples of movement responses are observed. Variety will be seen in complicated mixtures of two or more elements, increasing and decreasing, and changing at different times and in different placements within varied lengths of phrases.

Thus:

or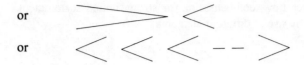

or

Such phrases can be the result of an increase or decrease in one element or combined elements:

such as strength becoming stronger:

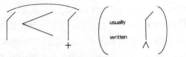

or free flexibility becoming exaggerated:

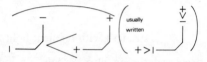

or they can be the result of a complete change of inner attitude: for instance, light bound flow developing into sudden strength:

or sudden strong flexibility dying away to light free flow:

Most normal action phrases have the simplified pattern of

     preparation   action   recovery

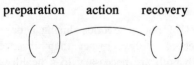

and the elements used in a good preparation and recovery (shown in brackets) are opposites or contrasts, in some way, to the main action. This may be seen as an opposite use of the same elements:

quick, light, free flow, compensating for strong bound sustainment, or as contrast by use of different elements:

$$\left(\substack{\text{---} \\ \text{---}} \right) \; \vdash \; \left(\substack{\text{---} \\ \text{---}} \right)$$

or

$$\cdot \left(\substack{\text{---} \\ \cap} \right) \cdot$$

(Here, the strong sustainment of the preparation and recovery merges together, when the action is repeated.)

A slightly different kind of recovery is seen if a movement phrase has a rebound or resiliency; for instance, dynamic resiliency (a kind of bounciness) might be characteristic for some people (revealing a mental resiliency too), as:

$$\cdot \; \downarrow \; \cdot$$ strength with resilient lightness.

A person's preferred timing also reveals his individual way of mental and physical recovery. Some people make short phrases, with resilient or intermittent recoveries, frequently repeated, others tend to continue one action-phrase over a considerable period, and then "recover" for a relatively long period. (This would give clear indication for or against certain job capacities if vocational guidance were being considered.)

Relaxation, as popularly understood to be a physical giving-in, resting and so on, is one kind of recovery which is necessary for our movement repertoire; usually this will be seen to be an indulging in the neutral states of motion factors, as here:

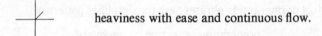   heaviness with ease and continuous flow.

However, most of our recoveries during a day are active and positive recharges of energy, rather than absence of movement altogether, though both are necessary to a healthy person. Mental and emotional disturbances are always revealed in inadequate recoveries from, and preparations for, action. Some patients are too relaxed, most are too tense, to make adequate phrases of movement relating to their inner and outer needs. Transitions from one movement to the next appear without recovery factors (perhaps then become jerky and disconnected) or the recovery factors appear to

overlap into the action phrase itself, clouding the clarity and effectiveness of the movement itself:

perhaps a general "vagueness" appears

or general inhibition

or general agitation

any of which movements may be efficient recovery elements if
limited to momentary transitions.

The variety of movement patterns

If we look at the variety and range of patterns and rhythms of the
movement of many people, we find that each configuration is personal, individual and different. This can again be likened to music
and sound sequences: there is no end to melodies and rhythms. There
are, however, forms and sequences of sound which we call scales,
which, numerous as they are, can be systematically studied and
mastered, in order to enrich our mastery and knowledge. Similarly,
there are scales of movement sequences which have a definite pattern
and form and serve to give the body and mind of the moving person
an experience beyond his own preferred choice of movement. Standard forms and "ideal" patterns are an abstraction, and are not
human, though it is possible to see that one rhythm or phrase is more
appropriate for a particular purpose than another. Ten people doing
the same job efficiently will all make individual variations on the
basic pattern required for success (a minimum requirement is necessary). Those people who do not complete the job satisfactorily either
will not have the minimum requirement or will have too many in-
truding elements to allow for efficiency.

Racial and sexual characteristics

Racially we can observe certain characteristics; also nationally, or
even in districts and counties, some differences seem to be generally
accepted: hence, "the inscrutable oriental," "the rhythmic Negro,"
"the volatile Italian," "the reserved Englishman," "the canny Scot,"
"the stolid Northcountryman," "the quick-witted Cockney" and so
on. No doubt these qualities are those which are accepted and desired
in the particular groups, and developed in the children from an early
age, either emphasising the child's tendency in this direction or
developing what potential he has to its maximum. The many people
who do not acquire such local characteristics probably show either

the weakness of the environmental pressure, or the lack of the tendency in their basic make-up.

The different sexes have clearly observable movement and rhythmical tendencies, just as much as physical differences. So much so, that a man is dubbed "effeminate" and a woman "masculine" if too many of their dominant movement characteristics, and behaviour tendencies, belong more naturally to the other sex. This is not to say that one movement phrase is exclusively masculine and another feminine, for we all should have mastery and experience of both. But our different roles in life necessitate the more frequent use of one or the other, while achieving a balance through recovery in the other. Rhythm, change and recovery can only occur between opposites.

Individual movement patterns and basic inner attitudes

People vary within a very large range according to the number and type of combinations of movement which they have at their disposal; certainly this is partly due to inheritance (as with intelligence, physique and colouring), and partly the result of the effect of environment on their inherited characteristics. Babies have quite distinct differences in their movement patterns from birth. In later years, it can be discerned that different individuals have movement patterns based on as few as one or as many as five inner attitudes. These are as follows (the reader is also referred to Appendix I, p. 231 for details of the basic theory).

1. A limited range

This may be only one inner attitude (a combination of two elements) which is used over and over again at the expense of the five others, while some of the remaining five are used infrequently or so rarely as to be almost absent for practical purposes. This group, however, is rare, and one wonders why such an exaggeration has occurred, why the potential inner life has not been developed; it is possible that such a person is, or will become, mentally ill in the lack of compensation and recovery.

2. A continuous movement between two inner attitudes

This is also in one sense limited, but compensatory recovery is available and if we take into account the possible variations within the two states, some degree of richness appears. However, the person who has established a well-worn and predictable reaction pattern will be fairly limited with such an endowment.

The two attitudes may be "akin," and therefore have one motion factor or element of it in common:

Time   /   which appears in

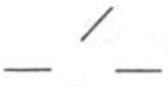

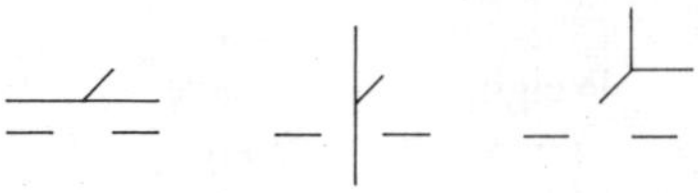

Flow    which appears in

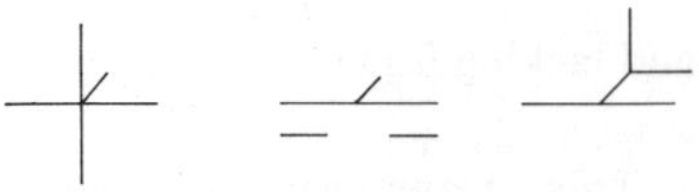

Weight    which appears in

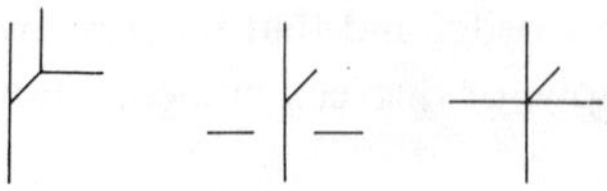

Space    which appears in

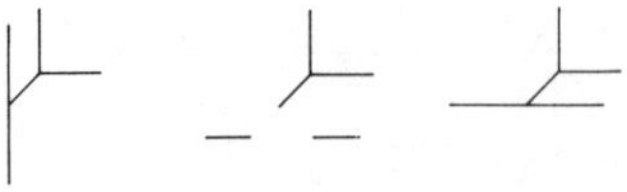

(*See* Diagram 3, p. 250.)

In these cases, the person is relying on active recovery through degrees of the same element, or of one other element only.

Alternatively, the two attitudes may be opposites, and in this case the person will tend to be working on an axis, which could give a kind of resilient recovery, thus:

and

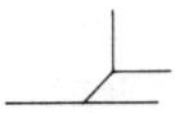

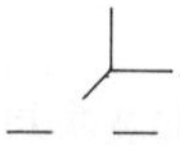

and

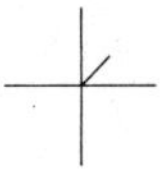

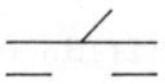

and

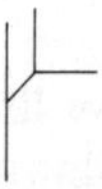

3. A continuous change between three attitudes

Three attitudes (two elements combined) are akin because they are around one drive (*i.e.* a combination of three elements); each attitude is on a different axis. (*See* Diagram 4, p. 250.)

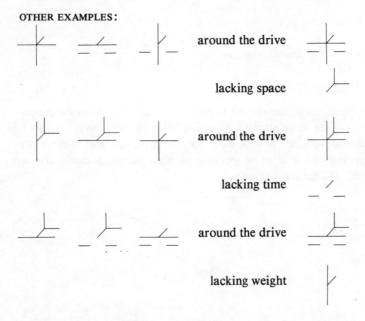

around the drive

Weight	Space	Space	Space
Time	Weight	Time	Weight
			Time

and lacking flow

This means that there will be little or no recovery on an axis opposite, and that most recovery will be with either a single element, flow, or degrees of elements within its own range.

OTHER EXAMPLES:

around the drive

lacking space

around the drive

lacking time

around the drive

lacking weight

Just as the above links can be seen in terms of a lacking motion factor, so this following group will be seen to be linked by the presence of one element in all three attitudes:

Linked by time

Linked by flow

Linked by space

Linked by weight

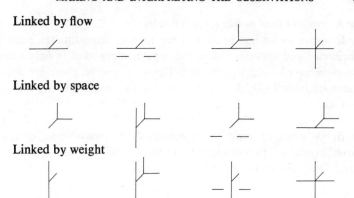

Each inner attitude is on a different axis. (*See* Diagram 3.)

These groups of three attitudes have two inner attitudes connected by the same axis (that is, opposites), and the other is a linking combination.

Hence:

and ⎯ linked by one of the following

or

and ⎯ linked by one of the following

or

and ⎯ linked by one of the following

or

4. A group of four or five inner attitudes

It seems to be less usual to have four or five attitudes equally developed and utilised; indeed this would be expected in only a few cases of exceptional ability. Sometimes, of course, there are three inner attitudes highly developed, with one or two others only slightly less so.

In all cases, it must be remembered that each inner attitude (combination of two elements) has four possible active variations, apart from the neutral states; for instance:

flow and time

has these four active variations:

as well as those incorporating a neutral state:

It is clear, therefore, that greater subtlety is observable than there are words to describe. If we say that this inner state is one of mobility, adaptability and changeability, then this has to be modified in each case according to the particular variation. How can a simple statement describe all this? It can therefore be realised that the notation symbols are more expressive of the real content, to those who can read them and understand, than any verbal description can be.

Observation and analysis of drives

Regarding a person's preferred drive configuration (combination of three elements), it can be observed that any one of the four action drives may be dominant—and any one or more lacking or rarely used. As in all observations, it is necessary to observe under what circumstances each is chosen for use:

has

Each drive has three inner attitudes which are inherent in it:

Any one of the three can be dominant; for instance, the above action might be:

mainly stable ⊦— with rhythmical —⊦ and alert practical sup-

port ⊥ ; or

mainly rhythmical —⊦ with ⊦— and ⊥ support; or

mainly practical ⊥ with ⊦— and ⊦ support.

Each movement would have a distinct flavour and difference of achievement, better or worse according to its appropriateness. Very often it is immaterial which stress is given, and the job is completed differently and still efficiently. But sometimes one approach is more efficient than another; for instance, an action needing strong rhythmical awareness might be hindered by a stable overstress of the action. This will equally apply for practical action, and for mental and emotional action (which serves an inner function).

The more intense, active man will have more movements with drive content (three combinations) than a less intense and less active man; again this applies equally to physical and mental activity.

A particular example
An example of how this pattern can change in a particular person was seen some years ago. A man who managed and owned a factory had an almost excessive intensity and drive for action, both physical and mental. Assessment at this time showed a high proportion of drives in relation to inner attitudes appearing alone. In the course of the next two years, this intensity was not given its necessary recovery and balance (warning of this had been given at the time of original assessment) either in short-term recovery actions or in long-term

ones. An assessment two and a half years later showed a striking difference of proportion of drives to inner attitudes. Patterns, rhythms, phrases and intensity were much the same, but the drives were relatively few, and all kinds of jerky and uneven transitions (which were there previously) had been emphasised. The man had almost "burned himself out," and an immediate and long rest was necessary to complete some sort of recovery. Certain distortions and lack of recovery rhythms showed that another such build-up could reoccur unless a more balanced rhythm of life was undertaken, but could he do this alone? His intensity and drive would tend to turn him away from the very aspects which would provide his recovery, and, combined with this, a stress of directness and lack of flexibility would make it difficult for him to accept or envisage any view except his own. This attitude to life would need considerable therapy before any change could result.

Personality revealed in movement

To return full circle to the first chapters, it is the combined *effort patterns, shape and space elements*, together with *body attitudes*, which reveal personality characteristics. For instance, *leadership ability* can be of many different kinds:

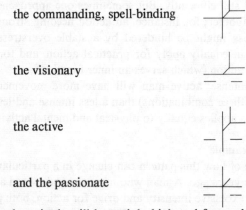

the commanding, spell-binding

the visionary

the active

and the passionate

The body attitude will be mainly high and forward, showing outgoing co-operation, and aspiration. Weight and time might reveal human understanding and the phrases used could be starting with space and flow (envisioning) with flow and time (mobility) following into space and time (practical) action. There would be a certain weight and space, forward steadfastness, and a lack of exaggerations. Shapes and patterns in gestures would probably be clearly defined.

Similarly, with the *capacity for research*, we would expect to find many opposite effort pairs, both in action combinations and in incomplete efforts. There would be a well-developed space and flow combination, as well as flow and time; the one being an abstract, isolating factor, the other a mental mobility. Almost certainly there would be long developing phrases, and a certain evenness and care shown in movement rhythms. Shape and space patterns would be well developed.

The *practical, outdoor type* would probably show frequent weight and time combinations, a good number of table plane and horizontal spreading gestures, and a predominance of action sequences— weight, time and space. By contrast, the *mechanical type*, while stressing action sequences of weight, time and space also, would show frequent use of time alternations, both mechanically and expressively, and would of necessity have a clear precise spatial sense, and shaping ability.

It is impossible to say either that a particular movement equals a special quality or that a particular quality equals one movement pattern plus a certain shape or space characteristic. Only generalisations can be made, because a movement assessment is made by the meticulous study of observed movement patterns, and the gradual building-up of a "portrait" of the person. This reminds me of the description given of how, for example, to improve one's awareness of a picture:

"Suppose you try the experience with a painting you like. Notice the lines and the drawing apart from the objects painted and the colours; for example, trace the outlines of the main figures and observe the pattern they form. Examine the pattern formed by the *empty spaces* between the outlines of the main objects. See the pattern produced by each colour in turn—abstract the patch of blue, of yellow, of red. If the picture gives an illusion of three dimensionality, follow the receding planes—the pattern of the foreground, of the middle-ground, of the background. Trace out the pattern of lights and shadows. Note the way that material is indicated by the texture of the brush strokes. Last of all, look at the story or scene portrayed, for this is where most people *begin* to look at a painting and *become fixed*.

"If you do as suggested and have liked the painting to start with, you will find that it suddenly begins to swim toward you with a new beauty and fascination. All kinds of new relations among the parts suddenly seem 'inevitable' or 'just right.' You will begin to partake of some of the *constructive* joy of the artist. Now you will be aware of the painting with spontaneous concentration—the details and their unity will be evident without painfully taking them apart and putting them together. This *single*, immediate grasp of the differentiated unity means you are in contact with the painting.

"Try the same experiment with a piece of music. If not musically trained, and if you regard yourself as unmusical, notice first how difficult it is for you to keep in contact with the music at all; the sounds soon degenerate into chaos and you into trance. In this case, abstract first the appearances of a single instrument. Then pay attention to the rhythm only; the timbre only. Detect what seems to be the melody and what the accompaniment. Often you will find that there are other 'inner' melodies that you had not expected. Abstract the harmony as you feel it; that is, notice when the harmony seems unresolved, seems to call for something more to come after it, and when, on the contrary, it seems to resolve and 'close.' Provided you do this seriously, suddenly all music will come alive for you."*

It seems to me that a similar process happens in building a portrait of a person—the important aspects become clear, those of lesser importance cluster round, and contrary or minor elements appear in relation to the whole picture. It is a dynamic art.

---

* *Gestalt Therapy. Excitement and Growth in the Human Personality*, F. Peels, R. L. Heffer and Paul Goodman (Delta Books, 1965).

Part Two: Movement Assessments

CHAPTER 5

ASSESSMENT OF CHILDREN

Development of individual movement patterns

Most psychologists now seem to agree that there is a core of individuality in each human being—a core which might change or be changed through circumstances over a period of time, but which is basically the characteristic pattern or personal responses, which occur in similar situations. Laban said that movement is man's "outward expression of living energy within." Even very young babies reveal their individuality in the way they imitate and respond to situations—one is more energetic and restless, another more placid and accepting, another more withdrawing and tentative and so on. Exactly how early these varied characteristics appear would be a valuable field for future research, but certainly by the time a baby is some months—or even weeks—old, he is a "personality." Perhaps, still generalised and ill-defined, his gross motion activity and undifferentiated action are still predominating, but his rhythms and quality of movement are discernibly his own, in spite of the fact that we can state generally that young babies use mainly strong kicking and sucking actions, wringing avoiding actions, and alternations of bound and free flow. The degrees and variations of these actions soon become known to the mother—his cry (the result of his body movement) is recognised both in pitch and in rhythm, and early voice sounds have an individuality which in later development becomes characteristic of the adult. (*See* Preface.)

As the child grows, greater differentiation of movement is achieved. Whole body excitement remains through childhood, gradually becoming restrained to the facial expressions, hand expressions and the slight body movements of the excited adult. Where an adult reveals his agitation by quicker breathing, clenching fists, beetled brows, tense shoulders, tense hips, tapping foot, a healthy young child will have his whole body vibrating in jumping, stamping, banging movement; he leaves no doubt about his mood. An adult will often derive great satisfaction from the fact that he believes he can mask his reactions, and not show his irritation, annoyance or boredom, but an astute observer can see small, usually involuntary, movements (shadow movements) which "speak" more clearly than words. This masking or inhibiting of freely expressed emotion through motion (or rather, as discussed in Chapter 1, a person's dynamic coping with the emotion) is, of course, useful socially. It is necessary for an observer to differentiate between the two layers of movement; the non-conscious and involuntary, and the conscious and voluntary masking.

Some young children learn to mask their reactions frighteningly early, but usually, in healthy children, we are concerned to keep alive the spontaneity and richness of kinaesthetic experience. This means that we should discourage too early specialisation (of any sort) which leads to a lop-sided capacity for movement. The human being's infinite variety and complexity of movement has been described in earlier chapters: the opposing alternatives, the similar or "akin" choices, the extensive range of degrees, all abound within a growing child, and the healthy "tension" of choice which must gradually be brought under control. This is a dynamic balance of ever-changing action, and not a rocklike stability. Just as the old idea of "posture" was a static, rigidly held position, we now recognise that an adjustable, mobile, changeable, dynamic, *appropriate* positioning of the body is "good posture."

Greater refinement and precision of movement develop as structural and nervous functions of the body become more specialised. Young children can experience opposites clearly, black and white, strong and light, sudden and sustained. Subtleties of degrees of "greys" in strength and time are gradually acquired, as the kinaesthetic sense develops sensitivity. All the developing senses of the child help to promote greater differentiation of experience, and varied experiences help the subtleties of the developing awareness.

Piaget, in *The Psychology of Intelligence*,* writes:

"Rhythms, regulations and grouping constitute the three phases of the developmental mechanism which connects intelligence with the morphogenetic potentialities of life itself. Rhythm characterises the functions which are at the junction between organic and mental life. Likewise, rhythm is at the root of all effector functions, including those which constitute motor habit."

This is what Laban called "effort" rhythm, and it is what a growing child is gradually mastering; the transitions, contrasts and shades of expression, which are appropriate in ever-changing situations.

* Published by Routledge & Kegan Paul, 1950.

The shapes which are made as the body or parts of the body move through space have "space rhythms" or patterns which are equally unique to the individual.

In observing a child, therefore, there is no "norm" from which we can say that anyone deviates in this or that way. The norm for each individual will gradually appear as his own best use of his capacities, his mastery over them and his ability to "choose" as appropriate. Even within a socially restricted environment which we all experience, the child must, for healthy growth, realise his own potential as a person, and not be expected to become a conforming part of a predetermined machine. *The discovery of himself, belonging to a group*—this could be the statement of aim in both educational and therapeutic teaching.

Uses of movement assessment

The assessment of the pattern of a child's present capacities can be helpful for teachers and psychologists. No reference is made to the reasons for the pattern as it is seen at the time of the observations. Obviously, an understanding of the family and environmental influences will help in the understanding of the child, and will be essential in making decisions for his education and guidance. An assessment through movement can give some indication of the areas in which the child has coped with his development problems, and those in which he has been overwhelmed. If frequent observations are made of faulty transitions, exaggerations and extremes, lack of co-ordination and lop-sided development of some aspects at the expense of others, it is fairly obvious that help is needed in these ways. The assessment carries within it guidance for treatment (if any is needed). The methods of guidance are varied and numerous. Individual work may be required by some, work in small groups by others, in larger groups by others. It is essential to aim for a whole and co-ordinated movement pattern, rather than to pinpoint a deficiency or disbalance and work on that; indeed this may well cause a rebound into a deeper state of distress.

Practical aspects of assessment

This approach to the study of temperament and personality means that some system of notating movement is essential. The symbols used in earlier chapters are simple to master, clear to read and understand, and give a visual pattern which facilitates interpretation.

Further symbols are also borrowed from Labanotation when indications of direction or levels of movement are required, and the symbols for body parts are used in a simple manner. (Details of the symbols are outlined in Appendix I.)

Clearly, speed of writing is essential, and so minimum signs are used for notating observations.

During the period of observation—usually twenty to thirty minutes—the observer must accurately observe and record. It is not recommended that any conclusion or implication of the observations is attempted during this time. Accuracy is essential and concentration must be intense to record the never-ceasing flow of movement. With young children and adolescents, it is preferable to have a situation where a knowledgeable person provokes movement responses from them; a class or small group of children is preferred. In this way, three or four may be observed during any one period, by an experienced observer. If it is not possible to have such a devised situation, a much longer period of observation will be required, as a child might not utilise one or other aspect of his make-up, in the particular activity he is undertaking. This is clearly uneconomical use of an assessor's time.

The movement "lesson" will take a form whereby the child is given the opportunity to use to the full his or her movement possibilities, and where his capacity to respond to teaching and coaching can be observed.

Many different stimuli are given for the child to respond with movement phrases. There are those aspects dealing with movement elements singly; can the child move lightly, strongly, directly, etc., and does he do this in a mechanical way, or is his whole body and mind related to the movement. If there is difficulty, where and why does it occur? Similarly, he is stimulated to perform combinations of movement elements: lightness with directness; strength with directness; free flow with suddenness; and so on. Again, he will have mastered some of these combinations, and not others, and this reveals his characteristic mental and physical make-up. The other combination possibilities of three and four elements are provoked and observed. In all situations the observations are made not only crudely but also in degrees of exaggeration or reduced quality. It may be found that although one element, for instance, lightness, is quite a common movement experience for a child, he may always use it in combination with another particular element or elements, say, free flow and sustainment, and never with bound flow or suddenness, although bound flow and suddenness are mastered by him in relation to strength.

Note is made of how the child moves his body—whether it responds easily to his mentally chosen movement decisions, and if not, why, and where is the hold-up? Is it a physical deformity or incapacity, or is it an inability to translate into co-ordinated movement? Is there an ability to move but a difficulty in controlling the body during the movement, or a difficulty in stopping when required. (Children can be told to stop or encouraged to decide when to stop. Some children can do one and not the other.) Note would also be made of voice and speech rhythms, as these are also a result of movement, and reflect the person's general effort style.

Movement using spatial patterns is stimulated: angular, round, twisted, and the mixture of these; movement far from the body in extension, movement near to the body; movement into different directions, high, low, backward and forward, as well as diagonal, off-balance movements. A group of children is always useful for the class, responses can be noted in movement terms, to leadership, working with a partner, following a lead and so on.

It is interesting that the movements of a child in such a class (provided it is well taken) reveal his natural phrases and responses, usually in a slightly exaggerated degree. I have done a good deal of work in checking observations made during a lesson, with observations of the same child in a classroom, playground or a home situation, and always there have been revealed quite distinctly the same patterns of behaviour as during the thirty-minute lesson.

Assessment I*

An illustrative example

One example of an assessment of a child is given here—in Part Three there are more.

I find usually that during the completion of the analysis of movement as shown on the report sheet, the synthesis begins to take shape; those aspects of movement which are particularly significant and revealing of the child become the *central idea or core of ideas* and other implications cluster around this centre. For instance, the central aspects of one child might be his divided and non-co-ordinated attitudes; his lack of ability to relate to his body centre; and the

---

* Assessments are numbered I–XVIII throughout Part Two.

reduced quality of most of his effort actions. For another, his main aspects might be his inturned body attitude of withdrawal; the exaggerated quality of his effort actions; his rich and varied potential of effort combinations, which lack transitions and ability to externalise. The features of another child might be poise and balance; good transitions from one movement to another and sensitive liveliness.

The following assessment was made at the request of parents, because of their concern about the boy's progress. He was only seen for about one hour altogether, before, during and after an arranged class session. In making suggestions to help the particular child, his environment must be taken into account, so that although ideally we might like all the children to have movement sessions (both from an educational and therapeutic point of view) it is pointless suggesting this to a parent living in an area where this is not available. These particular parents were intelligent, and interested in the method of evaluation; therefore much more reference was made to movement than will be seen in later assessments.

Derek: aged eight

Derek is a gifted boy, showing a wide range of movement potential. Much of this potential cannot yet be positively used, for various reasons discussed below.

He has a lively and original mind; he responds quickly and sometimes unexpectedly, taking most ideas and translating them in his own way. He is bodily agile, and enjoys the sensation of moving for its own sake. He shows no real sign of a bodily lack of co-ordination. The disharmonies which he has are still not so firmly established that they are causing body distortion, though perhaps this will not be much longer delayed unless certain habits are eased. The first area likely to be affected is that of the shoulders, neck and chest. These are closely connected with habits of inflowing bound flow together with excess strength, when he tries to control his own surging explosions of free flow.

This rather wild free flow is always outgoing, the tense bound flow, inwardly orientated. This means that he does not utilise positively the control which he has, and wastes it in a kind of rigidity which he cannot hold very long. This could be the result of his trying to control his emotional surges by his intellect. He needs help in self-mastery other than through the intellect. Much of his outgoing free flow activity is involuntary, and this purposeless movement needs channelling and organising, not repressing.

Associated with the outgoing free flow is suddenness, and with the inflowing bound flow, directness, sometimes with strength and sometimes with lightness. This results in excessive external mobility contrasted with a kind of hypnotic inner paralysis interspersed at intervals. This mobility is his outstanding characteristic, and has both positive and negative aspects. Positively, it gives him an ability for mental and physical adaptability; negatively, changeability and a lack of concentration. Sometimes, he manages to produce both states of mobility and rigidity at once in different parts of the body—a most uncomfortable situation of a split attitude.

His make-up is typified by contrasting states and attitudes similar to those discussed above, and there is a lack of transitions between movement phrases, even more pronounced than usual with a child this age.

A most positive gift is in his momentary sensitive-sustained movement combination. He concentrated over a period of time with fine touch together with both directness and flexibility, showing ability for delicate action. This gives an indication for future development. The concentration was cut across by a destructive free flow strength which faded away at the end, as interest flagged. He seems to have some ability in small practical actions. His larger actions are less directed—he showed an enjoyment for at least a limited time, in the security of mechanically repeated actions. Through such means he could be helped a little to experience and discern transitions and simple rhythmical phrases. This enjoyment is in direct contrast with his individual and spontaneous movement most of the time.

A present weakness in his movement vocabulary is in stability—the combination of weight and space. The only aspect which he shows, and this rarely, is in light flexibility, but this soon changes to heaviness with free flow. At present he compensates for this lack with bound flow (as mentioned previously), but this fails to provide him with a stable centre on which action can be based, and therefore he collapses as soon as he tries to move or act from it. This will relate to mental activity as clearly as to the physical. Bodily, he reverts to almost infantile methods to gain control of his body which should come from stability, using deep and sinking movements, almost excluding elevation. His positive sensitive flow (both bound and free) showed his only security with elevation.

His confidence in moving freely in space is contrasted with his lack of shaping ability when using large areas of space. The first shows a fairly well-developed sense of himself (for his age) in relation to the external world, the second a weakness in shaping the external world to his own needs. It appears likely that this could cause, if it has not already, retardation academically and in relationships, and probably a good deal of distress and frustration to the boy himself.

The time quality of suddenness—spontaneity and liveliness—is over-developed at the expense of sustainment. The two attitudes towards time are not used in relation to each other, and therefore he cannot really experience rhythm in the time sense, though he has an accurate awareness of variations of strength and lightness. This rhythmic development would help his self-mastery, though it is important to point out that any work in this area must be through a real time sense appreciation, not mechanical beat. Given this development, he would be able to use his intuitive powers with confidence, whereas at the moment they are too overlaid with emotional feelings.

He can pay precise attention and make a quick, vital response. It is in paying attention that his directness is evident. In actions, it is rarely utilised (usually in small movements if at all), and flexibility is mostly used whether appropriate or not.

There is a definite split between his intellectual activities and his emotional drives; his body acts as the vehicle for this conflict, and is therefore subjected to hard wear and tear! He needs considerable help to relate the various aspects of his personality. He needs synthesising activities to gain mastery. All art forms creatively taught would help, movement particularly as this seems to be a natural means of expression for him, also painting, modelling, claywork and carving, for which he should show some originality and aptitude. Singing and music in general would also be useful if well and creatively taught—otherwise it could be frustrating for him. In both movement and singing, special attention should be paid to his breathing correctly in relation to his action. This would help his transitions, and his struggle to orientate inner and outer flow.

Socially, he has a certain poise and confidence, especially in speech. He relates himself to the world mainly through likes and dislikes. He is such an individualist that some group relationship work was difficult for him. Nevertheless, he reveals a desire for co-operative contact with others, but finds this difficult to work out in action. He can, and does, comply with rules, but finds it difficult to work with another child as an equal. He was quite content to follow another boy for a while, but soon ceased to co-operate. When acting as leader he was unaware of the other boy and therefore failed to hold him. His general tendency to be self-centred shows lack of awareness of the rights of others—but how can he develop this until his own conflicts are settled? His present assertiveness may later develop into leadership ability, though his general make-up seems to indicate rather a gifted individualist.

Although he exhibited some aggressive tendencies, they were too general and undirected (often even good-natured) to be personally vicious, and he positively enjoyed the momentary security of holding another boy's hand. His liking for and response to direct orders was an interesting contrast to his freedom, and showed his desire for outside security.

He has enterprise, vigour and sometimes a gaiety which is attractive. It is as yet undirected. If it is possible for him to have movement classes with a small group of boys and girls aged between eight and ten, perhaps the work could be based creatively on the above assessment.

This boy clearly needs outside help to gain control and direction—he is insecure and appears to lack a firm understanding of boundaries. His aggression turns in on himself.

Conclusions

Discussion with the parents of Derek was made after the assessment was completed. In this case (and in many others which have been undertaken) there was general agreement regarding the findings, and frequently an appreciation of the deeper understanding which resulted from the assessments. Different methods have been used in validating the assessments: questionnaires to teachers, directed discussions, comparison with other tests, etc. These will be more fully reported in Part Three.

Therapeutic work with children

Therapeutic work with children in a residential school for the maladjusted was undertaken over a period of time (and, of course, others are pursuing this work in many schools). It is impossible to calculate or measure exactly the influence of any one therapy, but the psychologists and teachers with whom I have worked have been convinced of its power and value to the children. The head of a residential home where I was given the opportunity for group movement classes once or twice a week over a considerable time gives some specific as well as general comments:

"The children come to us neurotic, worried and withdrawn, and it is for us to loosen them and gradually provide them with ways of expression and growth. So that, from our side, the movement class is ideal."

Then followed a list of improvements to individual children—a stutterer who began to move more freely and with confidence; a boy of eleven whose fantasy life was very fertile, and who had every reason to distrust the world, who found himself in the music and rhythmic side of movement; a timid girl who became more confident and exploring, and so on. No exaggerated claims are made here for the exclusive influence of movement, but those of us who have worked with children and adults are convinced of the positive contribution which it can make.

CHAPTER 6

ASSESSMENT OF DEAF CHILDREN

A senior psychologist for handicapped children invited me to work with a group of deaf children, and this chapter contains assessments taken from a series of reports on these children.

Practical problems

There is considerable difficulty in devising suitable tests for the deaf, as so many personality test situations depend upon language. The psychologist hoped that movement might provide a method of assessment which would be particularly useful, as little verbal communication is involved.

It was interesting when working with the children to observe general characteristics which might be due to their disability. In two groups with whom I worked (one aged twelve to fourteen; one aged eight to nine), neither of which had experienced this kind of movement session before, I found that their spatial sense was well developed (*i.e.* in relation to their age range); they manoeuvred their bodies with accuracy, and in general, with sensitivity to others, provided it was still personal movement (as distinct from couple or group work) which was required. This could, I suppose, well be a direct compensatory development.

Two major difficulties arose: the first was in finding ways of stimulating the children to work on their own, without continually looking for guidance; and the second, particularly with the younger children, was to enable them to appreciate sequences of action, or to make a choice of one action from a range of possibilities. With children who can hear, it is possible to withdraw and leave them to get on for some minutes, having told them they should continue working on a given action sequence. With these children, until their confidence in themselves, in the movement they were doing, and in me, became established, one try was enough, and repetition came only gradually by "again" and "again." The time taken for this independence to grow was much longer than for hearing children.

Inability to make choices turned out to be a result of failure of communication rather than their lack of understanding, and it gradually became possible for them to do so. The stimuli had to be much more through movement than from words, and it was soon clear that my active demonstrations had to be varied and rich, otherwise a mere stereotyped copying would result. They responded with great enthusiasm to moving with drums and other percussion instruments which they played as they moved; the vibrations were clearly felt, and surprising degrees of variation in sounds were achieved through changing the quality of their movements. Partner and group work seemed little different from that of hearing children, except that everything took longer to organise.

Assessment procedure

The following reports are on four boys of nine and one older boy. A similar procedure was followed as with hearing children (*see* also p. 123):

 (*a*) a movement assessment was completed;

 (*b*) the class teacher completed a special questionnaire;

 (*c*) Scale B test results were obtained from the class teacher;

 (*d*) in place of the Children's Apperception Tests (in which children make up stories about the pictures they are shown), the psychologist made her own tests by using miniature toys in certain situations, and her reports are given in full. (More detail about these tests is given on page 55.)

It is clear that each approach will give quite different areas of knowledge about the child. The movement assessment gives a picture of his present situation, his abilities to cope, his attitudes in various settings. It also gives clear indications for future development, by showing the capacities which are active or latent and those which are lacking, and any difficulties in the use of capacities (because of, *e.g.*, personal inabilities to relate one aspect with another, etc.).

This gives an indication of the lines that future educational or therapeutic work could take in order to help the child towards greater self-mastery and knowledge.

The psychologist's report gives knowledge of the child's family, his place in the family, and some indication of his attitudes there. In one case (Charles) a very interesting example of immaturity and insecurity was revealed in his reactions to a situation of danger. There is also the possibility for the psychologist to make some personal assessment of the boy's interest, absorption, concentration, imagination during the test period.

Comparison of findings is shown in tabular form, correlating extracts from the movement assessments with the class teacher's report and Scale B test results, followed by the psychologist's report and a final summary. (This is the method followed with the assessments of hearing children given in Part Three.)

Assessment II

Nick (West Indian): aged 9 years 2 months; I.Q.: not known; Scale B score: 27

GENERAL COMMENTS (THROUGH MOVEMENT)

Nick shows a very complicated mixture of movement patterns, but is not secure or mature enough to relate one to the other. Frequently conflicting patterns are occurring in different parts of the body at the same time, revealing conflict and lack of integration—*e.g.*:

(*a*) Upper part of body is held in bound flow stiffness (neck and upper spine) while lower part (hips and legs) is free and often uncontrolled.

(*b*) Centre of body is used symmetrically while limbs move asymmetrically.

(*c*) Complicated mixture of rhythmical alternations and changes (which could develop into positive adaptability and directed liveliness). At present there is a great deal of muddled, unfocused mobility.

(*d*) Reactions are unpredictable—frequently excessively sudden (almost vibrating) and aimless—sometimes surprisingly concentrated and purposeful. This latter response often fades away without carry through, but it gives an indication of a capacity which might be built upon.

(*c*) Often has flow inwards and outwards at same time in different parts of the body—*i.e.* continuous insecurity.

From assessment through movement	Class teacher's report	Comments from B Scale
RELATIONSHIPS Can be co-operative for limited period—can also be obstructive. Generally gregarious and a mixture of dominating and submissive at different times. No clear balance of the two. He avoids being dominated by others—insecure in general.	Co-operative when in a good mood. Gregarious. Tries to lead by domineering methods but not really accepted as a leader. Usually ends by following his classmates.	Q.5. Frequently fights. Q.6. Not much liked by others.

From assessment through movement	Class teacher's report	Comments from B Scale
Aggressive actions of slashing out usually fade fairly easily—not often purposefully developed. Cannot really lead others—his latent sensitivity is occasionally seen in his relationship with one other (could be developed further, but he is not consistent enough to be really able to develop good contacts).	Insecure in his relationships. At best he is tolerated by the other children. Not popular—he works hard for popularity by clowning, but the others become bored by his antics.	**Q.15.** Is often disobedient. **Q.26.** Bullies other children.
General agreement.		
ADAPTABILITY His ability to change and relate to external circumstances is very limited—rigid and conventional. Yet he has a mental mobility which is in conflict with this, and probably causes a good deal of anxiety in him. He clings to a rigid situation for security. When secure in an accepted situation he can show good positive rhythmical ability—when the situation changes he shows small movements of anxiety (tapping fingers, feet, etc.) and can lose control altogether momentarily, or become fixed and rigid. Unstable generally.	Outlook is very rigid—emotionally unstable.	**Q.1.** Very restless: hardly ever still. **Q.3.** Squirmy, fidgety child. **Q.7.** Sometimes worries—worries over many things.
General agreement.		
WILL-POWER AND DRIVE Has plenty of strength, but: (a) it frequently disperses after momentary appearance—*i.e.* giving way easily;	Gives the impression of a strong will but crumples suddenly.	

From assessment through movement	Class teacher's report	Comments from B Scale
(*b*) it is weak in body centre and pelvic area, showing lack of confidence and general weakness; (*c*) can be related to practical actions for limited time (usually with suddenness and urgency). Drive is not carried through.		

Agreement.

| ALERTNESS AND PRACTICALITY
 Has lively attention—sometimes over-exaggerated vibration (*i.e.* repeated suddennesses). Can retain direct concentration for limited period but excitement often overpowers thought, and he loses focus. Attention is easily diverted, but occasionally can retain over a longer period. Very alert—generally practical and actions adequate, though can be inappropriate when he uses strength wastefully. I doubt his ability with continuous or long-developed actions. | Very alert. Practical and quick in rather an impulsive way. Rarely finishes any piece of work of a practical nature. | |

General agreement.

| DREAMY ATTITUDE
 Not really a "dreamy" child, though momentary appearances of weight/flow show that there is a range of latent ability for creative work there. This would need great encouragement, and seems contrary to his extreme rigidity in other aspects of his life. These conflicts will account for a good | Practical and quick—not dreamy. | **Q.7.**
 Worries somewhat.
 Q.10.
 Appears miserable, unhappy, fearful or distressed sometimes. |

From assessment through movement	Class teacher's report	Comments from B Scale
deal of his insecurity, but also give indications of where he might be helped. Much of what might be expressed creatively is drawn inwards and appears as doubt and apprehension (inward flow and heavy giving up). Already has some original rhythmical ability (as shown in movement class).		**Q.19.** Tells lies. **Q.20.** Has stolen things on one or more occasions.

General agreement, though movement assessment shows quite rich store of latent ability for creative work, contrasted with external (? cultural) rigidity. Quite impossible to develop in present stage of development and situation.

REACTIONS Reactions can be: (a) quick and lively; (b) over-quick and unfocused; or (c) resistant and stubborn; according to situation.	Very quick, but quite often reckless and stupid.	

Agreement (*see* also later comments on attitude to authority).

THINKING AND REASONING ABILITY Probably a bit above average ability. It is here where his rigid and routine attitudes show. As this is the more conscious side of his nature, it could be that this is much more a learned pattern, whereas his rhythmical spontaneity is very fundamental to him, and the conflict of the two causes him a good deal of insecurity and unhappiness. Although he con-	Very pinpointed in thinking.	

From assessment through movement	Class teacher's report	Comments from B Scale
forms, he will not be absorbed (directness appears in shadow movements frequently: flexibility often in body attitudes).		

General agreement.

From assessment through movement	Class teacher's report	Comments from B Scale
ABILITY TO INVENT, CREATE OR MAKE ORIGINAL CONTRIBUTIONS Not at all developed at present, though he showed some good originality in movement. Could be developed (*see* comments under "Dreamy Attitude").	Not creative in practical or artistic sense.	

Agreement—though it is fair to say that there does not appear to be a great deal of opportunity or encouragement towards creative work in the class.

From assessment through movement	Class teacher's report	Comments from B Scale
TOLERANCE Mostly actively intolerant. Very fussy, very agile, very aware of what is going on—but lacks security to understand others.	Very intolerant—complains loudly of other children.	**Q.4.** Sometimes destroys own or others' property. **Q.5.** Frequently fights. **Q.9.** Irritable. Quick to "fly off the handle."

Agreement.

From assessment through movement	Class teacher's report	Comments from B Scale
ENTHUSIASM AND CONTINUITY OF ATTENTION Impulsively enthusiastic, quick dying away of interest. Short attention span. Nevertheless he has ability for sustain-	Very short span of attention.	**Q.16.** Poor concentration or short attention span.

From assessment through movement	Class teacher's report	Comments from B Scale
ment (with directness, with lightness) which could be developed.		
Agreement.		
ATTITUDE TO AUTHORITY, DIRECTION, ORDERS AND ORGANISATION He reacts as though he has learned a "craftiness" or "slippery" attitude (*i.e.* flexibility and over-mobile in body attitude with inward flow). Such a reaction would be either: (*a*) his natural make-up of buoyant resilient rhythmicality resisting over domination, or (*b*) reactions to lack of consistency in treatment (or both of course!). Previously mentioned obstinacy can be relevant here—though sometimes he is responsive and willing, if interest is caught. Unpredictable. His best response is to enthusiastic leadership which catches his rhythmic sense.	Most uneven attitude. Some days he resents *all* direction. A very obstructive child when he is moody. Sometimes responds willingly to direct orders—sometimes not.	**Q.15.** Is often disobedient.

Psychologist's report: Nick

Note: This test was given by presenting four situations to the boys:

1. To set up family group, identifying dolls with members of his own family.
2. Television room.
3. Dining-room.
4. Picnic.

Details are given under each heading.

1. *Family*. Understood quite quickly. Chose self—Dad—Mum and demanded a baby and found the miniature doll to complete family.
2. *Television*. Arranged chairs almost in line opposite TV in order—Mum—Dad—Nick—baby.
3. *Dining*. Placed Dad and Mum together with baby next to Mum and Nick at fourth side of table. Insisted that baby had sugar bowl because it had two handles.
4. *Picnic*. Arranged in line—Dad—Mum—Nick—baby. Later rearranged to Mum—Dad—Nick—baby, still in line.
   Action. Bull comes—didn't find it easy to pretend, but with help he showed that when bull comes, Dad gets up and edges away bull by pushing. Little pig comes, Nick takes it and puts it on his lap and then puts it back in the pigsty. Three sweets were offered by me: first he gave to Mum, then Nick, then Dad, and then demanded another for the baby.

SUMMARY

Much less inclined than Roland (*see* p. 57) to go in for fantasy with little things. My impression was that of a child in rigid family structure—the baby was important but had to take his place in the hierarchy below Nick. It seemed to me that he showed quite a bit of rigidity.

N.B. I met Nick's family when they came to discuss the problem of Nick with Mr. B. and myself. Father appeared to me to be a very dominant man who saw himself very much as head of family and expected immediate obedience from Nick. Although Mother seemed to go along with Father, I had the impression that when he was not around, her own management of Nick would be rather more easy-going and vacillating. I also had the impression that because of his colour, the father is in a job of lower status than his qualifications would warrant, and feels this very much. There was emphasis on the fact that Nick was not allowed out to play with local "rough children." I suspect part of the reason is to avoid rejection.

General conclusions

There is considerable agreement between the movement assessment and the teacher's report. The psychologist's report confirms rigidity of outlook, and a supporting comment on the handling of Nick by his parents (*see* movement assessment "Attitude to Authority")—*i.e.* over-rigid by father, vacillating by mother.

There is a great deal which movement experience could give Nick. He is a natural mover/dancer, having excellent rhythmic sense, and gaining great satisfaction from absorption in this activity. Other creative work would also help him to co-ordinate his dispersed and scattered abilities. As far as I could see, little creative work of any kind is taken in this class. The Scale B report indicates a very maladjusted child, and this is confirmed in the movement report. The head of the school and the class teacher both said that he is a great nuisance and that they are worried about him (hence the parents' visit to the psychologist).

Aspects of movement which indicate possible ways of therapeutic help:

(*a*) Integration of upper and lower parts of body.

(*b*) Insecure in leaving known ground—help in elevation through whole body.

(*c*) Integration between extremes of action styles—*i.e.* transitions between rhythms.

(*d*) Increase ability to hold on to strength of intention—particularly working on body centre grip.

(*e*) Development of spatial awareness. This will help muddled shapes, and lead to increased clarity of thought.

(*f*) Increase extention awareness beyond immediate sphere.

(*g*) Development of weight/flow combinations in positive drive outwards—*i.e.* increasing creative activity and participation. If necessary, within a limited framework at first.

(*h*) Increasing sensitivity and fine touch in relationships.

In general: away from extremes, towards more sensitivity and awareness, without losing the spontaneous rhythmic ability ... this could well be used as a starting-point. One of his basic problems is reconciling the imposed rigidity with his natural mobility.

Assessment III

Roland: aged 9 years 6 months; I.Q.: not known; Scale B score: 9

GENERAL COMMENTS (THROUGH MOVEMENT)

Roland seems to be a simple, relatively uncomplicated boy, but he is fairly solitary, shows little initiative, and a general passivity towards life—he easily slips into day-dreaming. He lacks rhythmical awareness, and resiliency, and presents a fairly even, placid attitude, unless provoked by external forces to react. He has a charming slow smile when at ease, and is very agreeable.

From assessment through movement	Class teacher's report	Comments from B Scale
RELATIONSHIPS Not positive enough to make real contacts—mainly withdraws, but given the stimulus to work on a definite project with another child, he worked conscientiously and well ... most co-operative, and even appeared to have a few ideas to contribute. If they were not accepted, he became static, a bit heavy and passive again. Needs a great deal of encouragement to further endeavour. Could be provoked by an aggressor to resist and fight back. Likely to be picked on by others.	Co-operative enough most of the time. He tends to "tag along." No real initiative. Tends to be odd man out. No leadership ability—a born follower. Does not make easy contacts—no real friends. Not popular. Very shy and timid. Occasional bursts of aggression—usually on being teased.	**Q.6.** Not much liked by other children. **Q.6.** Occasionally fights with others, or **Q.26.** Bullies other children.
General agreement.		
ADAPTABILITY Not very actively so—rarely uses flow/time combinations. Tends towards rigidity, but can be led to further mobility. Has a strong stubborn streak of immovability when not co-operating. Needs to work slowly and routinely most of the time—is down to earth and stolid.	Rather rigid, but amiable enough when he understands that there has been a change in the situation. Very obstinate if his teacher tries to "push" him in his work.	
Agreement.		
WILL-POWER AND DRIVE Usually uses reduced strength but occasionally has a full sense of strength in the body—he lacks resiliency, and therefore the drive fades away easily. He learns through repetition, easily gives up and needs reassurance.	Can be obstinate. Drive and enthusiasm die quickly away.	
General agreement.		

From assessment through movement	*Class teacher's report*	*Comments from B Scale*
ALERTNESS AND PRACTICALITY Not alert—rather he is "present." Often dreamy when attention wanders, and becomes withdrawn. Quite practical in everyday sense, but has not yet developed a great number of externalised drives (combinations of three elements). Lives mainly in his inner world.	Dreamy — though practical about everyday happenings and situations and about objects and handling things. Withdrawn.	**Q.10.** Sometimes appears miserable, unhappy, fearful or distressed.
General agreement.		
DREAMY ATTITUDE Fairly wide range of weight/flow, mainly used passively—which means he tends to dream and live in an inner world (though he excludes the strong tense inward flow and is therefore not desperately inhibited in a nightmarish or fearful sense). Withdrawn and isolates himself.	Dreamy when action is required. Not dreamy in a positive way—imaginatively, creatively.	**Q.8.** Rather solitary.
Agreement.		
REACTIONS Mostly his reactions are delayed or slow—his cautious attitude is not balanced by sudden spontaneity, except occasionally in down-to-earth decisions. Reacts with reduced directness.	Delayed action most of the time.	
Agreement.		
THINKING AND REASONING ABILITY Probably below average (limited use of movement combinations, with frequent reduced	Very narrow range of understanding.	

From assessment through movement	Class teacher's report	Comments from B Scale
degrees and lack of alternations, also limited directional sense, and predominantly symmetric movement).		

General agreement.

| ABILITY TO INVENT, CREATE OR MAKE ORIGINAL CONTRIBUTIONS

A small degree of latent capacity which could be developed—especially through movement, as his body awareness became more acute. Mainly withdrawn in daydream rather than actively creative. | Not inventive or original in any sphere. | |

Agreement.

| TOLERANCE
Generally tolerant in passive amiable way. | Tolerant. | |

Agreement.

| ENTHUSIASMS AND CONTINUITY OF ATTENTION
Not enthusiastic—lacks forceful drive—even and passive. When enthusiasm is kindled, it quickly dies away. Short attention span, unless frequently urged. | Watches others rather than works with them. Wants a lot of help. Not often excited about anything . . . if enthusiastic, it quickly dies. Complacent in the extreme. | Q.16.
Has fairly poor concentration or short attention span. |

Agreement.

From assessment through movement	*Class teacher's report*	*Comments from B Scale*
ATTITUDE TO AUTHORITY, DIRECTION, ORDERS AND ORGANISATION Amenable. Accepts willingly organisation and directions.	Responds willingly to direct orders from teachers and most of his classmates.	**Q.15.** Is not often disobedient.

Agreement.

Agreement is fairly complete between assessment through movement and the teacher's report, from many indications—*i.e.* his time/weight, down-to-earth stress, his mainly downward focus; his evenness of rhythm, his amenable, unexcited attitude; his fairly neutral attitudes (I wonder if he will find his niche in life in working with animals . . . he has something of the isolated, passive attitude which might find contentment in such work).

Psychologist's report: Roland

1. *Family.* Mum—Dad—Susan—Janette—Roland. He understood very well and rearranged two dolls so as to get appropriate figures for mother and sister.
2. *Television.* Half circle around television. Roland opposite Mum and Dad—a little isolated.
3. *Dining.* Again, Roland opposite Mum and Dad on length of table. He put himself in last in a small chair.
4. *Picnic.* Roughly half-circular order. Roland again opposite Mum and Dad.
   Action. Quickly joined in fantasy of when the bull approached the picnic party—Dad got up to repulse him—Roland gets up to help Dad. Then spontaneously Roland brought out a little piglet—children quite happy with it—little pig got into picnic things—into the sugar bowl—Dad kicked the little pig! (All with a smile and good nature.) I gave him three "Smarties." He fed them to the animals. Then I gestured that they were for the children—he gave one to Roland first.

SUMMARY

Of the four boys tested, he was the most imaginative. He joined easily into the game and showed humour, *i.e.* piglet in picnic things, etc.

Seating arrangement seems to show a degree of independence from parents.

Of the four boys, he was the only one who helped his father to chase the bull—*i.e.* a sign of some grown-up awareness of masculine role.

General conclusions

Although the score on the Scale B is 9, Roland does not seem to be maladjusted in any serious sense. He is working at a pretty low level—fairly neutral in his amenability; there are some facets of his make-up which could be helped, and which would encourage a slightly greater development of drive and participation:

(*a*) The rhythmic development of alternations in all elements. The ability to alternate is a simple form of movement mastery—he could go further.

(*b*) Loosening of the stiffness and lack of movement in the spine (his limbs simply hang on to the body)—and the integration of whole body movement.

(*c*) Increased extension of body (at present it is held rather neutral—neither open nor closed) and development of awareness of space—both directional and shape.

(*d*) Generally sharpening up intensity of reduced elements.

The reports altogether give a similar picture of Roland; the psychologist's finding of some degree of entering into imaginative play at this simple level seems to me to relate to his capacity for day-dream and latent creative ability as noted earlier, but I do not see this developing very far.

Assessment IV

Charles: aged 9 years 8 months; I.Q.: not known; Scale B score: 16

From assessment through movement	Class teacher's report	Comments from B Scale
GENERAL COMMENTS Charles' movements are frequently unrelated to each other and to his body—abrupt changes of focus, abrupt rhythmical changes—without seeming logic. This abrupt change and short interest span contrast with his		**Q.1.** Very restless. Often running about or jumping up and down. Hardly ever still.

From assessment through movement	Class teacher's report	Comments from B Scale
intense and compulsive repetition of action—rather like a build-up of energy which needs discharge, rather than a purposeful repetition. Body awareness (body image) weak—also lacking much spatial awareness of his body in space. Opposite traits are typical of him—a streak of orderliness contrasted with agitated restlessness; intense concentration contrasted with weak giving in before the end; easy reactions to external influences contrasted with stubborn, rigid resistance. Mainly concave body attitude, or completely dispersed for short period. All these contrasts and attitudes give a picture of a child much younger than nine and a half; he responds to adult or 1–1 relationship very well, takes advantage if in a group.		**Q.3.** Squirmy, fidgety child. **Q.9.** Irritable. Is quick to fly off the handle.
RELATIONSHIPS Dominating, and lacking fine touch sensitivity in dealing with others (sensitivity does appear as balance or recovery in practical action). Boisterous and lively, easily outgoing, and will make contacts fairly easily and generally gregarious. "Edgy" and aggressive, and no doubt continually fighting. This, however, is in a relatively friendly spirit much of the time—he just wants his own way. He has a sense of fun and is comical in his rather clown-like way. Quite original but ideas	Very co-operative with other children. Occasionally defies authority. Very gregarious. Takes the lead with children of own age—he is domineering. Not really content to follow lead of other children. Friendly boy and has many friends. Generally popular. Not shy.	**Q.5.** Frequently fights with other children. **Q.6.** Is liked by others. **Q.15.** Is often disobedient. **Q.26.** Sometimes bullies other children.

From assessment through movement	Class teacher's report	Comments from B Scale
seem not to get carried through—as soon as others are inspired, he shoots off on some other scheme. Not easily led—stubborn if pushed—can resent organisation. In a large space, he loses his orientation easily. In a confined space he is much more amenable.		

General agreement.

ADAPTABILITY		
Often shows agitation rather than purposeful adaptability—has flow/time combination, but sometimes used in extremes and with inward flow. His frequent changeability is more from inner urges than adapting to external world. Not rigid or static, and is well able to take normal change of activity in his stride.	Adaptable.	

Movement assessment differentiates between different kinds of adaptability and adjustability.

WILL-POWER AND DRIVE		
Strong-willed (mainly in the middle of phrases), lacks resiliency and therefore tends towards dogmatic and harsh—particularly as he combines strength frequently with bound flow suddenness in repetition. This contrasts with a weak giving in at the ends of many phrases, and breaks his attention span. Almost over-alert to everything, so that he is diverted and drive winds down.	Very strong-willed.	**Q.16.** Has poor concentration or short attention span.

General agreement: movement assessment gives greater detail.

From assessment through movement	Class teacher's report	Comments from B Scale
ALERTNESS AND PRACTICALITY Alert and awake (*see* above)—almost extremely so. Very practical with external objects (more aware of things than his own body).	Practical and well balanced.	
Agreement.		
DREAMY ATTITUDE Not a dreamer—he uses weight/flow in recoveries and in practical activity and has a good practical inventiveness.	Not dreamy attitude.	
Agreed.		
REACTIONS Very bright and quick—alert to practical happenings—can be impulsive or resistant.	Very quick and alert.	
Agreed.		
THINKING AND REASONING ABILITY Probably average I.Q. or (?) higher. Difficult to assess because of his conflicting states. Not fully utilising his capacities as they are unconnected and dispersed. Not very flexible—rather a direct, straightforward approach.	Rather rigid.	
General agreement.		
ABILITY TO INVENT, CREATE OR MAKE ORIGINAL CONTRIBUTIONS Has originality in practical way—probably likes working	Very good original drawings and prac-	**Q.16.** Has poor con-

From assessment through movement	Class teacher's report	Comments from B Scale
alone on visual arts or modelling—where he can use his strength and practical ability.	tical hand-work. He applies himself to these things. His span of attention is better here than anywhere else.	centration or short attention span.
Agreement.		
TOLERANCE Probably ignores a good deal of what he observes around him. Not intolerant.	Tolerant.	
General agreement.		
ENTHUSIASMS AND CONTINUITY OF ATTENTION Enthusiasms burst out, but also change or fade after short time. Does not concentrate long. (*See* general comments.)	Has enthusiasms which die away quickly.	
Agreement.		
ATTITUDE TO AUTHORITY, DIRECTION, ORDERS AND ORGANISATION Wants his own way, but changes between agreement and disagreement ... size of space seems to affect him greatly, and he loses concentration away from small confined classroom —a certain wildness creeps in, which can be seen in uncoordinated body movement— sudden changes and compulsive repetitive movement.	Accepts organisation in class. Often disobedient in the playground. Responds willingly to direct orders.	Q.15. Often disobedient.
General agreement.		

This strange mixture of lack of body image—unco-ordinated and dispersed movement, interspersed with times of orderliness and clarity, sums up this attractive but somewhat disturbed boy.

Psychologist's report: Charles

1. *Family.* I made the schoolboy doll into Charles, but when he realised that there wasn't a bigger boy (toy) for his big brother, he made himself into the toddler and made the schoolboy brother Michael— also in family, Mum, Dad and sister Carol. He wrote the names himself (on a card).
2. *Television.* Arrangement of family in semicircle round TV—Dad— Charles—Carol—Mum—Michael.
3. *Dining.* Michael at head of table with Mum and Carol one side, Dad and Charles the other.
4. *Picnic.* Circular arrangement—Charles between Mum and Dad, opposite Michael and Carol.
   Action. When the bull came, Charles didn't quite know what to do about it. Then made Charles jump into Mum's lap and the other two sit up close to Dad. I produced a rake and suggested it could be used as a stick. Offered it to family. He made Dad take it and chase bull away. When piglet came, he again made Charles jump into Mum's lap.

SUMMARY

From the beginning Charles took an active interest in the play. After Roland, showed much more imagination. The fact that he twice made the toddler Charles, which he had chosen for himself, jump into Mum's lap is, I think, quite a pointer to the fact that he still thinks of himself as the baby of the family.

General conclusions

The psychologist's report confirms two things: (1) his imaginative capacity, (2) his immaturity—as seen in the movement report.

Charles could be helped through movement to reconcile some of these contrasting aspects of his personality. It would be best to have him alone—or with one other—at first, in a smaller space than a large hall—and only gradually go out into larger areas. He would need help:

(*a*) to relate unco-ordinated extremes and contrasts;

(*b*) to develop concentration (sustainment with strength and flow) over longer periods;

(*c*) to change the disconnected focus into positive purpose;

(*d*) to enlarge and develop his weight/flow inventive capacity;

(*e*) to become much more self-aware—to develop stronger body awareness; and

(*f*) awareness of himself in space;

(*g*) extension in space gradually (a later stage);

(*h*) shaping in space (also at a later stage).

Assessment V

Paul (? Indian or mixed parentage): aged 10 years 0 months; I.Q.: not known; Scale B score: 4

GENERAL COMMENTS (THROUGH MOVEMENT)

Paul is placid, even in rhythm, agreeable and withdrawn (though I was delighted to see some occasions of independent "naughtiness" the last time I took the class (after eight weeks of trying to give them some independence of choice). Pauses of quite long duration are typical of him. He is symmetric in body use, and a hint of excitement appears (as a latent capacity therefore) in vibratory movements in centre of gravity and lower parts of body, legs and feet. Outbursts of activity seem to take him by surprise, and they fade away quickly, resulting in withdrawing and pausing again. Lacks body flow—an unnatural kind of "stoppingness" in his body. Uses arms and legs in isolation from body. Lacks rhythm—can just cope with a beat. Works at a very low and limited level.

From assessment through movement	Class teacher's report	Comments from B Scale

RELATIONSHIPS
    Limited—withdraws and isolates himself (though this could be helped through movement, as was seen in his ability to work with a partner quite easily after a few weeks).
    Not a leader—willing to co-operate, but possibly not an
	Timid and shy. Paul is always amiable and co-operative. Isolated not gregarious. He is a follower not a leader —yes, he will fall in with any activity. He is pleasant and agree-	**Q.8.**
		Tends to do things on his own—rather solitary.

From assessment through movement	*Class teacher's report*	*Comments from B Scale*
active member. Happy and content to follow—though there is always a kind of detachment in his body attitude.	able but never seems really in contact with anyone. No real friends. Neither popular nor unpopular—does not impinge.	

General agreement.

ADAPTABILITY Adaptable in a passive way. Gets carried along.	Adaptable.	
WILL-POWER AND DRIVE Lacks firmness in upper part of body—uses pausing to give balance and stability which he lacks in movement. Will-power weak—drive mechanical—just sufficient to get along. (Could be developed through movement.)	Shows no evidence of will-power.	

Agreement.

ALERTNESS AND PRACTICALITY Manual dexterity poor but could be developed somewhat. Not a practical person basically —tends to lose interest . . . goes rather into a pause—a kind of neutral blankness. Turns into himself, away from the demands of the world.	He dreams in class. Very withdrawn.	**Q.8.** Solitary.

Agreement.

DREAMY ATTITUDE This inner attitude is most frequently used of all—a wide range. This means that he is often escaping from reality (lack	Very withdrawn but not anxious.	

From assessment through movement	*Class teacher's report*	*Comments from B Scale*
of space/time) and living a life inside himself. Such latent capacities are the main source through which he might be helped towards a more active participation in life.		
General agreement: latent capacities here.		
REACTIONS Delayed but amiable. (Quantitative use of time rather than quality.)	Very delayed in most situations.	
Agreement.		
THINKING AND REASONING ABILITY Limited (lacks spatial alternations, shaping, etc.). Probably below average.	Not very able.	
Agreement.		
ABILITY TO INVENT, CREATE OR MAKE ORIGINAL CONTRIBUTIONS Too passive, too much inward flow and stops to be creative or inventive—but there could be some impact on his general attitudes and participation by a stimulation of some creative activities—movement, painting, modelling.	No.	
Latent capacities.		
TOLERANCE Completely tolerant.	Very tolerant—nothing worries him.	
Agreement.		

From assessment through movement	Class teacher's report	Comments from B Scale
ENTHUSIASMS AND CONTINUITY OF ATTENTION Shows only occasional spark which quickly fades—generally even and consistent. Movement seemed to enliven him, so that a richer range of movement was seen in his facial expressions. Attention either not there—or held in a static, rather detached manner.	Complacent in the extreme. Life just "happens" to him.	**Q.16.** Not applicable (*i.e.* question asks "has poor concentration or short attention span").

There is some disagreement here—I do not see in movement how he can have a "good attention span."

ATTITUDE TO AUTHORITY, DIRECTION, ORDERS AND ORGANISATION Passive and accepting—lacks dynamic drive to be positively active—though could react negatively if pushed too far, but still not in a positive driving way.	He accepts organisation cheerfully. Yes—he will do as he is told either by his teacher or his classmates.	**Q.15.** Is not disobedient.

Agreement.

Paul is a child who seems not to be really living his life—but is content to go through it. It seemed that movement was an opportunity to help him to turn into more active participation many of his more passive or neutral attributes—*see* above.

Psychologist's report: Paul

1. *Family.* Understood quickly. I asked for Mummy and he chose a figure and wrote the name. Then he chose Daddy and explained that that was all in the family.
2. *Television.* Three members of family grouped around TV set—Paul—Mum—Dad.
3. *Dining.* Paul and Dad on one side of table, Mum on other.
4. *Picnic.* Paul and Dad on one side, Mum opposite.
   Action. He couldn't really join in fantasy about the scene with the bull.

I picked up figures querying whether they ran away or not. He made Mum run away, then Dad, then Paul. At my suggestion, Dad then repulsed bull after I had more or less demonstrated. When pig came, Paul took it back to pen. Sweets given to Mum, Dad, Paul.

SUMMARY

Perfectly willing, but didn't show much imagination. On two out of three occasions he sat next to Father and opposite Mother.

General conclusions

The general picture from all sources is the same. Specific aspects which could be helped through movement would be:

(a) Increase in intensity of elements and opportunity for alternations and integration.

(b) Using the pause as recovery for next action, rather than detachment.

(c) Inward flow balanced by outward flow.

(d) Help to extend bodily range and awareness.

(e) Shaping and spatial awareness.

(f) Balance should be improved and therefore give confidence for more mobile action.

These four assessments are really the end of this study, but the school for the deaf were having considerable trouble with an older boy, and asked if I would make an evaluation of his capacities for them. The assessment of Keith is the result of this. I saw Keith for one thirty-minute period only. It also gave me an opportunity to teach a group of older deaf children, and this was very valuable. The class teacher's comments on the assessment follow my report.

Assessment VI

Keith: aged twelve

Keith had a wide range of both inner attitudes (combinations of two movement elements) and externalised drives (combinations of three elements). Many of his gifts cannot be fully used because of the excessive degree of "fighting" which is typical of his present behaviour. He has the capacity for intelligent actions and attitudes, more in practical, down-to-earth situations than in abstractions. He does not show any marked degree of manual dexterity, so that real craftsmanship is probably not within his powers.

He is alert and quick to respond, often too quick, so that he becomes jerky and agitated. Together with excess suddenness, he sometimes uses free flow heaviness which gives rise to, or reflects, uncontrolled slashing out against things or people. Contrasted with this reaction, he can be sustained (even excessively so) and careful—and a certain unpredictability is seen in his alternations between these alternatives.

He has a strong degree of intention and will-power, which in excess can become stubborn and rigid. This alternates with a wilder, free explosion of exuberance or aggression, which needs channelling into constructive paths. He has many of the qualities of a leader, firmness, ideas, presence and originality, but will be frustrated in exercising these powers because of a present lack of subtlety. He is heavy-handed when sensitivity is needed, dominating rather than leading, and this will be resented by all except possibly weaker colleagues. It will be difficult for him to achieve this sensitivity to others until his own insecurity is relieved, but he does have the capacity for it (as seen in his extremity shadow movements). His own insecurity is revealed in his withdrawal when unsure, his wringing shoulder movements, his tentative reactions in some circumstances, and his lack of movement co-ordination between lower and upper body. His withdrawal, however, is not a cowardly turning away but a kind of attacking defence, which would become quite desperate if provoked too far. He has a surprisingly good sense of fairness and give and take, considering his lack of inner security. He faces problems and fights back with over-tension, which means that his fighting is not always the most effective or discerning.

He responds to direct leadership, though he is not subservient. He is anxious to be successful, though the anxiety can hinder his progress.

He has a well-developed sense of direction and space, and has a fine awareness of himself in relation to others and situations. He is essentially friendly and outgoing and enjoys people, but is not always able to adjust throughout his whole body, which shows a lack of integration.

In some ways, he shows many of the extremes and alternations of attitudes of early adolescence, though his exaggerated degrees of some movement elements give rise to anxiety about his future ability to cope with both inner and outer stresses. In a good stable environment, he could learn to be more discerning and harmonious in behaviour: with a less secure background he will have great difficulties in coping. There is nothing inherently discordant or unrelated in his movement patterns. I could not see any patterns which seem to be specifically related to his deafness, except perhaps his well-developed sense of direction and space, which might be a compensatory development. He has good rhythmical potential which could be developed further. Perhaps the tensions and frustrations of being deaf are worse for a child who is quite well endowed than for those with a more limited ability.

Teacher's confidential report on movement assessment of Keith (six months later)

"I was a little cynical when Keith underwent the movement assessment, but, on reading the report, find it very much in keeping with my own more subjective assessment of him as his class teacher.

"As regards his alertness and quickness, the remarks are quite true, but they tie in very much with his intellectual attitude also. This can be seen in a lesson where he picks on an idea and instead of waiting for it to be developed through the lesson, goes off at a pace in a direction of his own. For example, in a recent lesson on the Arab–Israeli conflict, mention was made of the increased cost of food brought from East of Suez. Instead of following this thought as the rest of the class, he wanted to discuss the rearing of sheep in Australia and New Zealand. The answer is not simply to follow his dictate as there is the rest of the class to consider, and also one is never sure when he will be off at another tangent with his usual rapidity! His attempt to dominate is resented by the other children. He regards this resentment as dislike from other children, but whenever he gets their attention he is quite animated again and friendship is re-established. Friendship for Keith is the other children gathered around watching him and paying attention to him!

"It is felt most strongly, as pinpointed in the assessment, that Keith needs stability. This is much easier said than done, as he is like quicksilver himself. There is no doubt, however, that in school, he is settling down and the extremes of behaviour noted six months or so ago are no longer so obvious. He has also settled down to learning, perhaps, for the first time in his life. This necessitates special work being prepared for him as his language attainment is so far behind the others. In fact, now that he is more adjusted in himself, one can now see how big the problem of his educational retardation is—a retardation which is out of all proportion to his obvious innate intelligence.

"Unfortunately, the improvement at school is not mirrored outside, where he is proving most difficult to his foster parents. He has run away twice recently and also stolen and done damage. This month he ran away to his old school at Yarmouth—which incidentally he had also run away from on a number of occasions.

"His future is once again in the balance as his foster parents cannot really cope any longer and it is not likely that any others will be able to do so either. We hope that he will be able to stay with us at H—— as he certainly seems to be responding, both socially and educationally. Incidentally, we took him away with us for a week and he behaved quite well and really enjoyed himself and learnt a lot.

"There's so much more that can be said, but it does fit in along the lines of the assessment, which is the point one wants to make in this report.

Deputy Headteacher,
School for the Deaf"

CHAPTER 7

VOCATIONAL GUIDANCE FOR YOUNG PEOPLE

Introduction

For many years, the value of using movement assessment techniques for vocational guidance has been recognised and used. Vocational guidance for the young is concerned with assessing the personality and gifts (both active and latent) of a young person and making specific suggestions for career or occupation. Requests for such help usually come from parents, or adolescents who cannot make up their minds, either because they have too many ideas, or too few. As with children, it is preferable to have the person involved in a movement session, where we can be sure that all aspects of his or her make-up are stimulated. This is not always possible, and movements can be recorded through an interview only. Assessment VII is of a boy of nearly fifteen, ready to leave school from a low stream in a comprehensive school, and the assessment was sent to the school. Assessment VIII is of a seventeen-year-old grammar school boy, which was sent to the parents and boy. In both cases I attempted to write the report in a way suitable for parents and teachers to read. In the first case, the teachers were very interested in the movement basis of the report and so this is more detailed in that respect.

Assessment VII

Vocational guidance and advice based on observations of movement:

Geoff: aged 14¾

From the movement observations which were made of Geoff, it appears that he is still at a stage of development where numerous vaguenesses and contradictory tendencies are unresolved. This is shown in some unco-ordinated bodily movements; the stress of action in the limbs unsupported by an appropriate body stance and adjustment; the lack sometimes of related movement action between the upper and lower part of the body; and the repeated dying away of energy and focus, towards the end of a movement phrase. Because he is at this stage of transition and change, his experiences during the next year, or possibly two years, will be likely to influence him and his future considerably.

It seems that the exact job which he takes is less vital than that he finds an environment which will support and foster his positive qualities. This is, of course, not unusual at fifteen, though some boys do show more clearly defined leanings towards a particular vocation or occupation by this age.

He is a friendly boy, and at the interview he quickly lost his initial shyness and reticence. He showed little self-consciousness, and was able to take in his stride the questions and tasks which were given to him. He is responsive to a straightforward approach, but lacks as yet the poise and confidence which are, however, latent in his make-up. Bodily he is reasonably agile and adaptable, and mentally he was able to cope with a variety of changing situations without much concern.

A typical feature revealed in his movements is his tendency to lose focus and concentration, even after a good initial attempt at a task. This will be echoed in his present approach to most of his activities, even to some degree to those in which he is interested. This trait, though typical of adolescence, is in his case rarely relieved, and it will require good leadership gradually to encourage the development of persistence and purpose. The exceptions to this general fading away of effort and focus are on the occasions when his imagination is captured, and when a short-term achievement is possible. Perhaps this gives an indication for an ideal future situation for him—one in which reasonable and short-term *challenges* are given to him—and which are likely to be overcome.

Emotionally, he swings between casualness, friendliness, anxiety and intense feeling. He is fundamentally upright and straightforward, and the intensity referred to can be seen positively as a degree of daring or audaciousness. If properly channelled, this is a valuable asset. If no legitimate outlet is available (and he will find it difficult to provide this for himself), this strong feeling may become negative and even destructive as it sweeps him along. He needs physical activity to take up his energies, and should not be debarred from participating in normal activities because of an earlier accident. Contrasting with this energy and emotional drive is his seemingly lethargic "giving up" attitude. The wrong environment could increase this casualness, and with it would decrease his ability for developing and using constructively his drive and energy.

Geoff showed an ability to learn and repeat actions, which will be an advantage in practical work. He is more able to reproduce known and learned actions than to initiate and originate them for himself. This means that he will be happiest at a job which he can learn and repeat, and not one which needs constant original ideas. He shows no ability for real craftsmanship (because of a basic weakness in space and shape awareness), and because of a lack of really sensitive manual dexterity. He can, however, handle materials, but he should be engaged on general rather than detailed concentrated activities requiring fine and exact alignment. With interest in a job, the decreased efficiency because of fading interest should be overcome gradually, and with better-sustained concentration he could become a reliable worker. Repetitive and routine work would not distress him, but this should not be unrelieved for long periods. (*See* reference on p. 26 about short-term aims.) It would be better for him not to be sitting down all the time.

He showed a surprising awareness of himself and his own achievements and failures. He can be stimulated to develop a reasonable argument and he could be helped to recognise degrees of efficiency and achievement. He can definitely learn and improve when kindly challenged. It is unlikely that he would respond to domineering or bullying. Mental gifts are practical rather than abstract or theoretical; a kind of shrewdness is detected, but needs stimulating to be useful.

Geoff revealed a liking and ability for time repetition and rhythm. This sometimes appears with a gift for numbers and figures (though there is no indication here of specialised mathematical ability). It may be reasonable to expect either a present or latent ability to cope with figures and numbers as a minor part of his job. It should not, however, be thought of as a main vocational basis.

Geoff responds to individual attention and treatment. He is basically friendly, and shows no signs of being fundamentally over-aggressive or unreasonably antagonistic; he is essentially communicative in spite of his stage of shyness. (*See* reference on p. 76 above about emotional intensity.) He will be happiest working with other people and shows no gift for solitary work. He should not, therefore, take a job where he will be left entirely alone for long periods. He is agreeable to follow a good lead, and will be stimulated by exchange and participation with another person's activity. He shows neither the inclination nor the gift for leadership at present. His main motivating force seems to be through likes and dislikes, and not considered judgment.

As mentioned previously, Geoff reveals a basic enjoyment of, and a gift for, rhythmical activities—this will no doubt be developed through dancing later on. He has an appreciation of colour rather than form, as shown through his ability to use effort rather than spatial aspects of movement. His familiarity with dramatic expression gives him the beginning of a pleasurable mastery of himself. All of these activities—painting, dancing, drama and music, could be developed further to his greater benefit even though there is no indication of their becoming careers for him. His present need for excitement and adventure is real, and if this could be caught up and focused, it would be of particular importance; perhaps he could be encouraged to join a group climbing, sailing or camping.

SUMMARY

Help could be given directly to the boy through:

(*a*) movement

(*i*) to co-ordinate the upper and lower parts of the body (the legs are much less active and frequently do not support the actions of the top of the body);

(*ii*) to co-ordinate the body adjustment with the actions of the limbs;

(*b*) painting to develop his colour and pattern awareness;

(*c*) drama and dance to help his rhythmical and social development;

(*d*) clubs to focus interest in practical activities, perhaps even semi-mechanical ones, and some strenuous activities.

This would be in addition to his general school work.

Details of vocational openings

Some suggested openings for which Geoff is suited are outlined below. A few of the suggestions may be rejected by him on the grounds of lack of interest, and this of course is important, even though we may consider that he is able to do the job.

1. PRINTING TRADE

The only vocational interest which Geoff expressed was in this trade, but he did not seem to know much about the openings. It seems that his gifts might qualify him for such a post, and the details of employment were made available to him.

2. CATERING INDUSTRY

Employment in the first instance *as a waiter*. The advantage of such a post for Geoff, apart from the contact with people and the variety of occupations, is the later opportunities for travel which present themselves, for employment abroad, on foreign-going passenger liners, railways and so on.

3. ELECTRICITY BOARD

To be employed as a trainee electrician or electrician's mate. This work would involve a variety of occupations and travelling (from one job to another with a qualified man).

4. NORTH THAMES GAS BOARD

Similarly there are openings as trainees in the Gas Industry.

5. PAPER—and similar industries, where general and varied work is available as cutting, punching machine operator, etc.

6. MOTOR MECHANIC OR ASSISTANT—involving work in garages—either as an apprentice or as an assistant.

7. HORTICULTURE AND AGRICULTURE—through apprenticeship schemes or by direct employment. (This may not appeal to him with his strong town environment.)

Assessment VIII

Harry: aged seventeen

Harry has reached a stage of development where he is resting on his abilities, which are considerable, and he needs wider and broader stimuli to extend his capacities to anything like full usage. If he does not, for any reason, utilise the gifts he has, there is a considerable danger that later in life he will be frustrated and despondent in whatever job he takes. Such reaction will not be evident at present but there is a need now to take the jump from the accepting, passive stage, to the more active, seeking stage. This would not be so important for a boy with more limited gifts, who has already fully extended to reach his present level. In his particular case, such development as is suggested will not be achieved by discussion or mental pressure from others: it will happen of itself by his own personal reactions to circumstances. Perhaps he can be helped best by providing opportunities or encouragement to participate much more in a wider, fuller range of activities.

He is mentally mobile and active, able to grasp and deal with a variety of ideas; his next stage is to relate the ideas, to follow through and draw conclusions from them, to have a personal reaction to them, to have an opinion which he can substantiate and to look beyond the learned facts to the underlying logic. This is a mature attitude for which he has the capacity, but which needs training, as well as opportunity and stimulus. Without this way of thinking, he will never be secure with others of equal intellect and status (thinking ahead to some executive positions in a company or with colleagues in business). He is clear and precise when sure of his ground, and he is sure of facts, of learned material and precise practical applications, but becomes vague and lacks focus in spheres outside his immediate experience, such as relating ideas, or applying his knowledge to a wide or comprehensive vision. This is not surprising, since, at seventeen, few boys have both the exact view as well as the larger vision and he probably will always work mainly from the small to the large; that is to say, he will accumulate details which, added together, will make the whole picture or view. If he never learns to see the whole, he will always be at the mercy of others and will always be the assistant, and this would not ultimately satisfy him.

The inevitable teenage inconsistencies tend to show as extremes which can gradually develop into positive attributes. The hasty, jerky reactions, which can become lively, quick-witted mental adaptations, contrast with the slow evenness, which, in extreme, can be ineffectual loitering about, but which carries with it the gift for sustained concentration and persistency.

Practical outlook dominates—creative tendencies take a passive rather than active form, such as day-dreaming. Abilities for active, creative work seem to be undeveloped but not lacking. There is a whole world of artistic experience to be investigated before his attitudes become too rigid and eventually dead; theatres, painting, music and poetry (though this is less likely to be of great interest to him); architecture and design, particularly as these could be linked with people's practical needs.

He is generous and friendly and essentially reasonable in relationships. It would be a pity if this were not used actively in his future career. His kind of leadership will be by his own example rather than by his inspiring others to act. His firmness and ability to insist will be used more discriminately when his personal assurance is developed. He has a sensitivity of mind as well as a sensitive handling of objects, and his strong emotional feelings are hidden beneath a casual exterior. This should not be the reason for assuming that he lacks feeling or that he is not influenced by the emotional reactions of others. In his self-contained way, he is relatively mature and stable.

The foregoing comments relate to his personal development and needs, and they give some indication towards his choice of a future career. The next two years will be important and he will probably be much clearer in his personal choice after his wider sixth-form work. Although any choice of career depends mainly on his own preference, he has a good range from which to choose as his abilities happen to be in demand in our contemporary society. Spheres for which he does not appear to be suitable include the Armed Forces or the Police, banking, salesmanship, journalism and office organisation.

He may develop interest and ability in a medical or semi-medical sphere, as a doctor of medicine, a dentist, an optician or a pharmacist, the last being a choice which he would do well to consider, either with a view to joining a large company in research (like Boots) or working privately, where he would be in contact with the general public more directly.

His technical abilities could be used in a variety of spheres in industry, according to his choice and the possible openings. He could consider lecturing in technical subjects, either as a full-time job or as a subsidiary to his practical work.

Conclusion

It has not been possible to follow up the first boy, Geoff, as he has moved from the area, but Harry (who is now twenty-six) left school at nineteen, with two "A" levels in Physics and Chemistry—worked in a chemical firm for four years as a laboratory assistant, and during that time took "A" level Maths, as well as Ordinary Certificate. He has now gained a B.Sc. II (1) in Chemistry.

CHAPTER 8

WORK STUDY

Movement education for factory workers

For a period of nearly three years I worked in a factory which manufactured plastic goods. The owner of the factory and I formed a partnership for the development of social and artistic work with the factory workers and their families. There were opportunities for taking part in large movement choirs (both Christmases, we had a half-hour movement production) for the men, women and children together, for individual movement therapy, drama, music, pottery and painting. In addition, remedial training, work study, vocational guidance and personnel selection were undertaken, all in an integrated pattern of activity.

There were many reorganisations undertaken because of the movement study made in the factory such as job-switching and simplifying of job-sequences.

The following assessments are of three women supervisors in the factory. All three had been in the factory for some years, were familiar with the work and its difficulties, and indeed had helped to build up the size and reputation of the business by their loyalty and hard work. The reason for making the assessments was primarily to help the individuals and secondly to make the factory more efficient. The form of assessment was evolved to meet the requirements of the factory authorities who wanted answers to specific job requirements.

It should be noted when reading the recommendations for help which are given at the end of each assessment that the opportunities for classes were available to all the factory members and their families as mentioned above.

Each supervisor, apart from being seen in the work situation, was given a personal interview of twenty minutes or so, during which time a record was taken of her movement patterns and rhythms revealed in gesture and posture. (It is not necessary to give a movement class to adults, as sufficient information can be recorded during a well-conducted interview.) Each report was the result of analysing these observations, and an attempt was made to word the recommendations so that the supervisors themselves (and their husbands, who by request were included in the discussions following the assessments) should be able to understand and benefit from it.

Assessment IX

Woman supervisor: aged thirty; married with one child aged eight

Areas of responsibility

MORALE OF PEOPLE IN HER TEAM AND OTHER ASSOCIATES

Ability is present—but not used fully. She must often weaken morale by showing her own depressions, anxieties and lack of confidence.

DEVISING MEANS OF PRODUCTION

Ability is present—but lessened in effectiveness because of personal despondency in face of difficulties. She herself still needs help to maintain the inner drive necessary to face an unexpected situation without being overwhelmed by it. This could be done by a deliberate stepping away from the situation, and an attempt being made to isolate the problem. There is always some way to achieve the object, and she should try to solve a problem before seeking help despondently. This should give a definite satisfaction to herself as well as build up the confidence of her team of workers in her leadership. (*See above.*)

TRAINING OF PEOPLE TO DO SPECIFIC JOB

Ability active. This is a clear gift which she uses, and can communicate easily and freely. More attention should be paid to physical help in positioning and arranging equipment. Acuteness in anticipating these needs before complaints are made could be sharpened. In the first instance, if in doubt, request for help should be made to the factory manager, until she feels confident to decide for herself. Preferably, go for advice with a selection of ideas of her own, and try to decide various alternatives first. It will take time to do this.

CO-ORDINATING ACTIVITIES AND ALLOCATING PEOPLE TO MACHINES

Ability active. This should be possible without assistance, based on the production schedules. Co-ordination will of course depend on keeping a steady and alert view of all the workers, and this is in danger when she becomes disturbed by a situation.

CHECKING STANDARDS (against sample given)

Ability active.

CHECKING OUTPUT (against schedule)

Ability active.

SUGGESTIONS FOR IMPROVEMENTS

Ability present—but surely not fully used except in a negative manner. As in the case of training, she could and should make active suggestions, and offer alternative solutions.

ANTICIPATING SUPPLIES OF MATERIALS AND ENSURING THAT THEY ARE READY WHEN NEEDED

Ability could be developed. It is necessary to have foresight and a clear view of future output; then to contact various other supervisors or the factory manager. Lack of foresight is the result of becoming overwhelmed by activities; as her foresight improves, she should be freer to work properly.

General aptitude and abilities

Worry and anxiety is a negative reaction to a problem; tackling and facing the situation is a positive reaction. This passive inturning is characteristic of many of her reactions (revealed in a somewhat over-relaxed posture, together with a tense expression). A positive action is seen where she is sure of her ideas, or opinions. Sometimes this assurance leads to forcefulness or dogmatic assertions. Her ability to lead would be enriched if she could consider the person receiving her comments and adapt to that person's particular needs. As her own confidence increases, this should follow.

She likes to feel responsible and influential and has the leadership potential for this. However, abrupt defeats by circumstances will lessen the confidence which others have in her leadership.

She has a definite ability to focus her attention clearly and firmly, and, if she can avoid stubbornness, has a great sensitivity to the views and ideas of others.

Hastiness dominates her decisions, and the resulting lack of patience may often lead to avoidable bad feelings. Frequently there is a need for urgency, rather than hastiness, but this has to be more regulated, and less impulsive.

She could be energetic and vital, and future development should help to disperse the lethargy of heaviness which has been the natural compensation for excess tension and worry. An active sustaining of interest and drive would be aided by rhythmic buoyancy—and this she could get through some experience of dancing and movement activities, under guidance.

She is happiest in a clearly defined setting and is disturbed by the absence of a clear routine, when one seems necessary.

Mentally capable and lively, she has a tendency towards variability and changeability. She has a latent gift of sensitive awareness to other people, just as her ability to handle materials is exact. She enjoys good standards and likes a job to be done well. The ability to relate the degree of exactness necessary to the occasion needs further development.

It seems that she should not deal with too many activities at the same time, so that although she needs change and balance, the area of work should be collected and not dispersed.

LATENT ARTISTIC CAPACITIES seem to be:

(*a*) a definite gift for movement and dance;

(*b*) an ability to develop observation capacities particularly of a kind relating human needs to handling material (this is her work situation);

(*c*) a visual sense and use of words; a sense of drama and action could be developed;

(*d*) a craftsmanlike ability with materials.

ANY DEVELOPMENT depends upon:

(*a*) overcoming the tendency to give in after brief periods, which necessitates increasing sustaining of purposes;

(*b*) sustaining and developing the desire to contribute to the community group.

Assessment X

Woman supervisor: aged thirty-eight; married with two children aged fourteen and ten

Summary of present stage of development and potential

The assessment reveals a person of average abilities. Her natural gaiety and responses to form and pattern have been curbed by a desire to conform to conventional standards.

LEADERSHIP

She can lead by her ability to inspire affection and respect rather than by a strong personality. She would find it difficult to lead a group larger in number than she could contact personally; and she would not be able to lead along a path which had not been clearly pointed by a superior in whom she trusted.

RELIABILITY

With leadership in which she can trust, she could be relied upon to follow to the end any clear task given to her. She would find it easier than many people to work at repetitive operations for long periods.

PRACTICAL ABILITY

She has the ability to handle materials and could do a good job well for a long time. She would not find new handling problems very easy to master, but would have the persistence to continue trying. The design of new products or the design of new methods of production would be outside her capacities.

SENSITIVITY TO PEOPLE

Aware and sensitive to moods in other people, she can help where necessary in a quick, human and emotional way. But she would find it more difficult to help if a more intellectual response were needed; and her ability to help even at an emotional level can be lessened by the rigid acceptance of the conventional standards referred to above.

Spheres in which immediate remedial work would be valuable

(a) She lacks inner security: there are continuous movements of doubting and inner tension, and anxiety sweeps over her and causes inner freezing.

(b) A release of this tension would make her need to fall back on rigid conventional standards unnecessary and would give the natural gaiety referred to above a greater chance to heighten her general level of living.

Possible methods of helping her development

(a) Movement and dance is the most obvious way through which this person could achieve greater awareness of form and pattern. Her very quick and vital response to rhythm (except when she consciously tries to control it) shows again and again in the movement observation.

(b) Participation in a choir would be another way of developing her rhythmical awareness.

(c) She could react quickly to the feeling of materials and this could be used through clay to develop her sense of form. A gradual building up of her self-confidence in this art form would be necessary.

(d) Painting could be used because she has a latent gift for colour appreciation. The method to follow would be through colour, texture and free design, gradually leading to exact form and style.

Assessment XI

Woman supervisor: aged forty; married with three sons aged twenty, seventeen and nine

Summary of present stage of development and potential

The assessment reveals capacities for vigorous living, combining action and feeling; but the considerable potential richness of her life has been prevented from developing by the constant waves of inward-turning emotions; this is revealed in the movement observations by strong freely flowing action which degenerates into cramping rigidity.

LEADERSHIP

She will be able to lead by force of example, rather than by a dominating personality. This capacity for inspiration by personal example could be developed a great deal. Here her innate physical energy, spontaneity and natural exuberance will be tremendous assets, once they are no longer affected by the rigidity mentioned above.

RELIABILITY

She can be relied upon to work to specific instructions. The maintenance of a standard of work would be more easily achieved if she had fairly constant contact with other people. Work involving variety of action or contacts would be particularly suitable.

PERSONAL RELATIONSHIPS

She has a quick intuitive response to others and can make contacts easily. This capacity is, however, at this time, impaired by the waves of inward-turning emotions mentioned above. These emotions would be likely to give rise to forthright, ill-considered utterances, which perhaps give scant consideration to the feelings of others. Her very evident energy, buoyancy and resilience when allowed free play would be a great source of cheer to those around her. Her innate resilience has probably been the greatest counter-influence to the destructive effects of the inward-turning emotions already mentioned. She has not lost the capacity to understand her own emotional difficulties.

ARTISTIC ABILITIES

Her whole assessment reveals strong rhythmic and visual senses.

Her appreciation of form and pattern, though less marked than the rhythmic sense, is a positive attribute, and could be encouraged fairly easily.

Methods of helping

The basic need is to relax the cramping physical rigidity which is inhibiting so much of her emotional and physical energies.

This will be achieved by:

(a) remedial movement;

(b) movement and dance;

(c) individual and group painting;

(d) assisting through conversation, her ability to understand—and work on her personal development.

Remedial work was undertaken with all three supervisors, and definite improvements were seen. This was, of course, in the general context of interest and activity in the factory and recreational activities as a whole.

Other movement practitioners have worked for many years in the industrial field, both as assessors (for selection and appointment) and as trainers, to help develop latent capacities suited for a particular occupation.

Assessment XII

An illustration

A detailed assessment is included finally to show the kind of observations made in a particular case. These observations and comments were made by Laban himself, and given to me as an example of an early assessment made when he was working with Mr. F. C. Lawrence in industry. Later on he refined his technique:

"The differentiation between the visible movement effort and the actual working action is a fundamental discovery on which all the new procedures are based. It will be evident to all who have to struggle with these problems, how important and valuable it is to get an insight into the technical capacities of a person and at the same time, be able to assess the upper and lower limits of his personal ability to adapt himself to the demands of any particular task."*

Personal effort assessment from interview (mainly shadow movements)

This gives an example of the kind of observations which would be made at an interview (in this case for suitability for Job Study Technician Course). At the end of this, some indication of the interim stage between notated movement observations and the conclusions drawn from them are given.

Movements		*Remarks*
Enters		
Sits down		

Actions		*Remarks*
Takes cigarette		Arm only
Holds and strikes match		
Places matchbox in pocket		Simultaneously with shadow move of head
Puffs cigarette		

* "Effort and Work. Movement culture as a basis for personal development." Translated from an article by Rudolf Laban in *Deutsche Zeitung und Wirtschafts Zeitung* of 15th June, 1957.

Movements		Remarks
Demonstrates size of object		
Deposits ash		Arm leads body
Puffs cigarette		
Deposits ash		Arm and body
Puffs cigarette		Simultaneously with shadow move
Stubs cigarette		

Shadow moves		Remarks
Fingers eye		
Licks lips		
Fingers nose		

	Shadow moves	*Remarks*
Fingers chin		
Head reaction "Well . . ."		Sideways, upwards
Fingers nose		Several times repeated
Shoulders		Explaining facts hesitantly
Sucks finger		
Head reaction		Backwards—when asked interest in time and motion course
Fingers cheek		
Adjusts position		
Smiles		
Forehead		While being praised
Eyes		

Shadow moves	*Remarks*
Upper part of body	While stating mathematics distinction gained
Doodles with cigarette	
Thumbs chin	Subsequently often repeated
Head	Sideways, upwards— backwards. Talks about getting on with people
Purses mouth	Before action of puffing cigarette
Adjusts position	
Hand gesture	Talks about scope for advancement
Head	
Purses mouth	
Nose movement	

Movements		*Remarks*

Gets up

Exits

	Body attitudes	

General

Head

Eyes

Mouth

Shoulders

Arms

Hands

Trunk

Mental attitudes

Attention

Intention

Decision

Precision

Results of analysis

Personal effort graph:

```
                              ┌── 29%
                              │── 24%
                    35% ──────┤
                              │
                             32%
```

Basic efforts comprise:

> 42% of actions
> 25% of shadow moves
> 75% of body attitudes
> 37% of total

Strength predominates in actions; lightness in shadow moves.

Directness predominates in actions; flexibility in shadow moves.

Suddenness is very poorly developed (only 15%); none in body attitudes.

Lightness associated with directness in movements of the hands. Fine touch well developed.

Bound flow overcomes free flow. Bound flow is used as stopping quality. There is little co-ordination of flow qualities.

Degrees of effort hardly used at all in shadow moves.

Becomes more free flow and strong towards end of interview.

Rhythms include only fine resilient and gradual transitions.

Complicated rhythms used for simple, insignificant actions.

Shadow moves of contrasting efforts occur simultaneously with actions.

Movements are not extended in space, neither clearly towards nor away from centre.

The body is held and movement occurs mainly in extremities.

Mental attitudes show especially strong intention.

Aptitudes

Almost too well-developed active drive. Uses effort capacity purposefully but unconstructively.

He has considerable technical ability within a fairly narrow field, and is particularly useful with his hands. Lack of suddenness might be a hindrance in time and motion work, but would be developed with practical experience.

In study and practice he is painstaking. As a student he might appear to progress but he would be difficult really to teach, *i.e.* change his established convictions.*

He is naturally curious about situations which affect him personally but is uninterested in other people. His ambition would incline him to be ruthless in dealing with people, but there is the possibility of such ruthlessness being used beneficially.

He learns slowly from experience and lacks good judgment. He nevertheless judges spontaneously and makes decisions unhesitatingly, which he tends to carry out in an unstraightforward manner.

---

* This remark relates to a short course of training. He could more easily be developed over a long period of training allied with practical experience "on the job," but it is doubtful whether he would respond to a short intensive course.

CHAPTER 9

ASSESSMENT OF OFFICE STAFF

There are two sets of assessments given in this chapter. The first three are straightforward examples of movement assessments made (seven years ago) to find out the stage of development of three bank clerks and their fitness for promotion. They were requested, for experimental purposes, by the bank manager, whose comments are given later.

Two other assessments relate to other kinds of office staff in a hearing-aid company. They were actually used for employment selection purposes, as distinct from the experimental use of movement observation in the assessment of the bank staff.

Bank staff

Assessments were made after one personal interview of twenty to thirty minutes, during which time movements were recorded for subsequent analysis, in a similar way to those made for the factory workers. No previous information was obtained about the men, either personally or with regard to their ability at the job. The bank manager has now, after this seven-year interval, kindly sent a report on the three men's present positions, which is given after their assessments.

Assessment XIII

First cashier; man: aged thirty-four

This man is probably conscientious and hardworking within a limited sphere of activity. His gifts include a capacity to carry through a task and a desire to complete his work at an acceptable standard. He is essentially practical and down to earth, not given to flights of fancy or wild schemes. While ambitious in the practical sense of "getting on," he will not seek adventurous or unorthodox means but will rather work on in the hope of just reward. If, in his opinion, a just reward is not forthcoming, he may well become resentful.

His way of work is simple and straightforward. This may be an excellent gift in a well-regulated situation. However, in a situation requiring shrewdness, assessment of all factors and a "flair" for understanding people and the relative importance of one fact against another, he may take an oversimple view. He lacks the breadth of vision and originality of outlook to cope with complex situations. He does have a quick adaptability in practical matters, while not being able to explore new possibilities or devise new methods. He would tend to take the conventional and traditional approach without question. If, however, he is working within a smaller sphere of activity, and one where he is confident and familiar, he can work to a precise programme and could devise suitable programmes for others—even spontaneous planning within this range would be possible.

He has a degree of sensitive awareness of other people when at ease himself, when, for instance, he is working on familiar ground. His inhibited powers of leadership in such a situation could gradually develop, but if presented with opposition when he is outside his restricted range, he could become dogmatic rather than diplomatic or determined. This springs from his lack of poise and lack of ability to present himself clearly and to view the situation with detachment. His lack of self-confidence leads to an aggressive attitude when challenged and makes for difficulty in his relationships. It might make him reluctant to accept advice and could be a progressively developing trait if not consciously controlled. Nevertheless, he basically wants to co-operate with others and could be encouraged to do this. He seems to be more suited to work as a member of a team than entirely on his own initiative, preferably where the unusual is not a frequent problem.

His greatest deficiency is probably in abstract thinking; his greatest gift is rhythmical buoyancy, though this is curiously inhibited in him. A certain earnestness and flatness dampens what could be a much more lively and buoyant attitude.

He has difficulty in projecting his personality and therefore cannot at present command any special respect from others, except in the routine practical activities. Lack of vision, driving force and creative or daring imagination will limit his potential as a leader.

Assessment XIV

Second cashier; man: aged thirty-eight

He is a man of practical action and views, self-disciplined and with a capacity for hard work. He has a robust forthrightness which has become subdued and restrained, and he would be happiest in a simple routine where everything and everybody is accepted without much discrimination. He can handle objects and situations efficiently, provided they do not become too refined. Subtleties are discerned more intuitively than sensitively, and there is a kind of naturalness in the man which can appreciate in others those gifts and capacities which he himself lacks, as well as those with which he is familiar. His lack of fine touch might make him clumsy, but he avoids an aggressive use of his strength.

Mentally he is methodical and systematic and anxiety of mental concentration is relieved through routine. A high degree of concentration and generosity of time and energy will be typical of his way of work. He is open-minded, willing to learn and to adapt himself as required. He can make independent decisions, based on previous knowledge, can justify these decisions and is not easily shaken from his view. A reasonable suggestion will make him reconsider. He is, in fact, a reasonable man and does not take offence easily.

He lacks imagination and vision, and therefore will find difficulty in selecting accurately the important from the unimportant. If kept within his known range of knowledge, he will be reliable, but he should not be asked to make balanced judgments relating many aspects of situations and people.

He has an innate sense of balance, and could have developed a kind of audacity if circumstances permitted; as it is, any such drive seems to be caught back into the routine of security.

He is co-operative and willing and in a secure situation would deal freely with people. Perhaps the atmosphere of a bank is a little too refined for him. He is sincere and obliging, kind and pleasant.

He is ambitious in a practical way and will endeavour to progress methodically. It is possible that his intuition will recognise his weaknesses without his being able to analyse them or do much about them. His restraint and inhibitions of speech reveal his lack of confidence. His inability to project his personality will preclude him from real leadership but he will be a well-liked member of a team and a valuable worker.

Assessment XV

Fourth cashier; man: aged twenty-seven

Restraint covers richness and variety of gifts, many potential rather than developed, and which could develop one way or the other, depending upon circumstances.

This man is worth a considerable amount of training and guidance and he will need this to develop fully the inhibited traits.

He is mentally versatile and quick: in regular and routine jobs he has a staying power through conserving his energies, but he wastes energy in circumstances which are less regular and obvious. His inhibition and lack of ease is, however, likely to be overcome if he is given responsibilities and encouragement in progressive situations. His present stage is a mixture of self-protective restraint and confident awareness of his abilities.

Potentially, there appear all the signs of ability as a supervisor of others; sensitivity to other people, quick mental awareness, aspiration, and ability to plan and devise schemes of work. His independent attitude and his self-discipline will develop under appropriate guidance. It seems likely that this kind of leadership will be through example and ability, rather than through authoritative or inspiring stimuli.

His present weaknesses are in presenting himself and his ideas confidently and clearly. He tends to work towards intensity of interest and absorption, rather than attacking a problem with initial intensity and vigour. This pattern will presumably remain with him, and has its positive value in any long-term activities. It is possible, however, to encourage a greater gathering of intensity to tackle each job and no doubt having personal responsibility will assist this.

Regularity and evenness of some of his movement rhythms contrast with lively spontaneous variations. Usually such regularity will indicate a gift with figures and a liking for accounts, according to mental capacity which in this case is apparently above average.

Adaptability to completely new situations needs time, and caution is shown in his approach to a problem. When confident, this hesitation disappears and he has a kind of restrained daring.

His vision is lively and, in a practical sense, imaginative. His work within a restricted range and to a precise programme can be efficient and clear-cut. The connecting of these two aspects, clear-cut precision and his long-range vision, is still insecure, so he swings from one to the other. He could be helped to see the implications of his ideas in terms of practical working-out by having specific practical problems to cope with. The development of stronger self-discipline would both help and be helped by this. The inner confusion which this lack of relatedness is causing could be diminished by success at a rate which is reasonable and consistent with his personal effort.

He is innately friendly and co-operative, and is able to maintain his own point of view without dogmatism. He has a straightforward approach which is fair and down to earth: his own "cleanness" of outlook might be a danger in dealing with a variety of people if he does not take into account the complexity of human beings. By nature he will expect the best and may jump to conclusions without regard to all the evidence and circumstances. The mastering of this attitude, that is, a conscious development of deliberate consideration of less obvious facts, is well within his own abilities, but he can be both stimulated and helped to face this problem.

He is ambitious without being ruthless. He may at present be swayed too easily by impressions and environment, but responsibility and mistakes will teach him to make a firm stand. A delicate balance of firmness without rigidity and aggression should be possible for him to achieve.

He works more from conscious awareness and down-to-earth consideration than from emotional feeling though his feelings frequently inhibit him. He is not particularly creative in the artistic sense, but could bring his originality into practical spheres with success. His appreciation of material values does not cloud his awareness of human considerations. It seems as though his future development depends upon his own self-discipline and the right environment and opportunity, in that order. He will respond to personal help.

Bank manager's comments on the reports

"At the time these assessments were made, an opportunity was taken to put them in front of two officers from Staff Department at Head Office. The men assessed were well known to the Assistant Staff Managers concerned, who had read many assessments on them made by managers and inspectors. They were both impressed by the accuracy of the information.

"Personally, I knew the men well, and was surprised at the amount of detailed information which emerged. If the assessments had any fault, it was that they were too detailed for any purpose within banking, but I found them astonishingly accurate.

"Progress in a bank is not predictable on any one count, since availability of appointments and the amount of competition for those available can mean that at one time a less suitable man obtains an appointment whilst at another time an extremely good man is held back. Nevertheless, in general, people seem to receive the promotion they mèrit, and in these three cases the present position of the men concerned seems consistent with the assessment given.

"Assessment XIII: then First Cashier, is now a Chief Clerk in charge of the staff of a medium-sized branch.

"Assessment XIV: at that time Second Cashier, is now a First Cashier, and unlikely to progress further.

"Assessment XV: then Fourth Cashier, is now a Chief Clerk of a medium-sized branch with every possibility of making substantial further progress."

Other office staff

The following assessments were written during my period of work as Personnel Manager for a hearing-aid company.

Assessment XVI

This assessment was made after an interview which the man attended in applying for a post as salesman of hearing aids. Contrary to the non-recommendation of the assessment, he was appointed, but failed to complete the initial training. The brevity of the report is due to the fact that a large number of assessments were being made at that time, and the company required only an outline report.

Mr. X: aged twenty-eight

A contained personality, but he lacks an awareness of his own limitations, in spite of admitting a lack of achievement.

He has a limited sensitivity, and therefore others do not make much impact on him. (This could be encouraged over a long period, but would need special help.) Although his forcefulness is lively and enthusiastic, he lacks discernment.

His relationships are fairly spontaneous, but lack "follow-through" as though he cuts off after the initial contact. He neither develops a relationship cautiously, nor does he become involved in it uninhibitedly. A certain negative detachment is evident, and a lack of protective warmth.

He is mentally agile and attentive, and has the ability to see practical applications. He is not sufficiently discerning to be aware of deeper motivations, although he is intelligent enough to understand specific problems.

His strong emotional feelings probably carry along imaginative paths, but he seems to block off his ideas without fulfilment. His intuitive awareness is inhibited by emotional feeling and lack of sensitivity.

There is a strong streak of almost vicious aggression not very far beneath the surface.

He is honest and reliable within his own scope, though restless. His firmness of intention needs support to be effective. His views and ideas are short-term and narrow, rather than long-term and broad. His intensity lacks focus and an ease of flow which would harness it into effective action.

He is not recommended as suitable for training.

Assessment XVII

This candidate applied for the post of assistant to the training officer in a medium-sized business. She had come straight from college, having taken a second-class degree in French and German, and had just completed a secretarial course. The post was to be a new opening, and the kind of position it ultimately became depended upon the person appointed. In an attempt to clarify at least some job requirements, the questions answered at the end of the assessment were posed by the training officer himself.

Miss Y: aged twenty-two

(Based on movement observations made during her interview with Mr. N.)

GENERAL COMMENTS

Her immaturity is revealed in her somewhat dogmatic attitude and in the one-sided development of her abilities. At present she uses fully her mental agility and versatility, her reasoning and purposeful awareness of practical considerations, but they are untempered by real tolerance or understanding of people. These latter qualities are latent, and so far little touched. There is at present a split between her feelings and intuitive grasp of a situation, and her ability to apply this awareness in her actions and reactions. This would preclude her from efficiently working in a situation primarily concerned with adaptability to people, or the leading or training of them. It appears unlikely that she will be able sufficiently to develop these inhibited traits ever to become primarily interested, or efficient, in a career such as salesmanship, personnel, teaching or welfare.

In the sphere of mental activity and play of ideas, she is self-contained and poised in her own knowledge. She would honestly attempt to understand, and will achieve a good standard of work. She is mentally active, willing (indeed anxious) to prove her ideas, to the point of stubbornness, but this has also its positive aspect of tenacity and doggedness.

With the development of greater sensitivity and fine touch, she will become more adaptable and cling less to a conventional or learned attitude (which may, however, be quite "modern").

Her views and outlook are restricted in breadth, but are not superficial. Although she may intellectually understand broad principles, she will work best when relatively restricted by clear practical objectives and tasks. Her need for achievement will best be catered for in short- rather than long-term projects which she will tackle with intensity and enthusiasm, and for which she can utilise a surprising amount of sustained determination.

She shows only minor traits of imaginative and really creative vision and this aspect of her development is far behind her mental agility. She appears to be more a "technician" in ideas, than one who enjoys ideas for their own sake and implications.

She is trainable within the limits mentioned. She would benefit greatly from working with those of broad vision and compassionate human views.

SPECIFIC QUESTIONS RELATING TO THE JOB

Q. Will she be able to obtain a sound and comprehensive knowledge of audiology?

A. Yes—this is well within her range.

Q. As an application of this knowledge, will she be able to:

(*a*) read incoming magazines and channel the information to the relevant people?

A. Yes—this is exactly the kind of detailed and specific activity referred to above which she will work at with intensity.

(*b*) produce literature on such subjects as hearing re-education?

A. From information and acquired knowledge, yes: from direct experience and working with people, certainly not at present. This might be somewhat developed, but will never be her main way of approach.

(*c*) do routine jobs such as running a small library for audiologists?

A. Yes.

Q. Will she be able to formulate and write a magazine for users, bearing in mind that several issues need to be produced before one goes into print to ensure continuity and impetus, and that I expect her to contribute considerably to the "ideas" and maintain a guiding hand?

A. Yes, with the proviso that her supervisor has the overall vision and direction. She will be able to contribute a great deal, and to offer specific ideas as well as work on given topics.

Q. Will she be able to work on her own for reasonable periods of time once given an objective?

A. Yes—the objective should not be too broad or distant.

Q. Will she be able to contribute suggestions that will be constructive to the workings of the "image" we are trying to create?

A. At present, her conventional attitude limits the free flow of original ideas, but these could gradually be encouraged.

Miss Y was appointed to the post, where she stayed until reorganisation of the company a year later. She was quite successful within the limits specified above.

Conclusion

These last two assessments were used as the only means of selection, and the conventional methods of testing and personal interview (other than during the observations) were discarded.

CHAPTER 10

A CASE HISTORY OF MOVEMENT THERAPY

Introduction

I am attempting in this chapter to give some indication of one aspect of the therapeutic use of movement, as given to one patient who was deeply disturbed and whose reactions are quoted below. Extracts are made from the records of the treatment, and the particular selections which are given were chosen because of their relatively simple nature. The more complicated movement experiences and discussions can best be transmitted by demonstration or orally—in so far as they can be transmitted at all. An additional assessment from a well person seeking self-knowledge is given for comparison at the end of the chapter.

The patient was a woman teacher, aged thirty-four, married with three children.

The patient is now well, has a fourth child, and all unpleasant symptoms of her seven-year illness have gone. She started treatment with me in July 1960, and finished in 1963, by which time she felt more able to cope with any remaining difficulties of a minor nature. This patient, although suffering greatly, was able to continue with a relatively normal life pattern, and this was due mainly to a helpful and sympathetic husband. Nevertheless, she was obviously not as disturbed as many patients who have to enter a hospital or clinic. Other movement practitioners have greater experience than I have of working with patients in hospitals and residential clinics, and the work there has been described in other publications.

The patient's own account

How the patient felt at this time is described in her own words:

"How it all began, how it felt

"February 1954: a feeling of deadness, no positive emotion.

"May 1954: one afternoon I suddenly became aware of the strange feeling—a remoteness—a feeling of being outside the world around and inside myself.

"This resulted in an overwhelming sense of fear. I went to church—was overcome by a feeling of panic—I was going to faint—something dreadful was about to happen—had to leave the church.

"From this time on the dreaded feeling of unreality persisted. I taught as before, but I felt I had no contact with the things I was doing and the people I contacted. Life went on but I was stuck 'inside-out' as it were.

"Emotions were non-existent apart from fear—it persisted day and night—I was in a constant state of being afraid, afraid of being afraid always. The overwhelming sense of 'not being here'—this feeling was always at war with what I know to be fact—I was alive—I was here—I taught—got married—had children—ran a home and yet never felt I was doing it all. This resulted in tremendous tension—a trying to 'be here'—a striving to get back. Eventually, after much help in explanation as to what had happened and why, I found I was understanding more, yet still trying and striving—striving now not to mind the condition—striving not to strive! The physical symptoms were, I learned, simply the working of the automatic nervous system—a feeling of sheer panic—feeling of going hot and cold all over—feeling of inability to balance—a tightness inside—a tight band round my head—a tightness in the pit of the stomach which sometimes resulted in being very sick—a tightness up the back of the neck—a feeling of sinking through the bed in the mornings! The result of this was a constant feeling of dual concentration—within and without. This resulted in constant tiredness—always more than half of my energy seemed to be going into dealing with this awful feeling! The effort involved in fixing my attention on anything else was tremendous, whether anything complicated like making a dress or merely writing the grocery order, thinking of meals or peeling the potatoes. The 'panic' manifested itself in an inability to pursue one job of work.

"This wasn't manifested so much outwardly as inwardly—I was always agitating about everything that needed to be done—I never stopped working, I couldn't seem to ever sit down and rest. The house seemed huge (it isn't!). The jobs endless and everything dirty and needing my attention. The garden seemed to me a wilderness and I felt I ought to do it. All the panic and tension seemed to get worked into and out on the things I had to do. I simply never stopped. I daren't go to bed at night with things left undone, as it were, because of the terrible feeling of the fact that I have more to do tomorrow and would still feel the same.

"After the children were born, I was physically exhausted too—I just felt I couldn't do more, but always this sense of tremendous drive forwards urged me on, to carry on with this fantastic amount of work. Something was started but immediately something else seemed to need doing and so it went on. The only way to get through the day seemed to be to grit my teeth and get through!

"With all this came a horror of being alone—a horror of travelling anywhere which involved working out where to go, etc., a fear of people and shopping—in fact life was just one big fear. I felt as if I had 'got stuck' somewhere and couldn't move backwards or forwards, inwards or outwards.

"To read (to go inside) was impossible as it was so frightening, and to visit people (to go out) was sometimes even worse!

"The only relief seemed to be to escape in sleep or to cry it out which was a temporary relief but afterwards the tension seemed to build up with even increasing speed.

"Things I tried to 'get out'

"1. To not mind 'being in' [*i.e.* inside herself—Author]—very difficult to be relaxed in it [*i.e.* to accept her state—Author].

"2. Dressmaking. I did it but the effort in concentration was almost too exhausting.

"3. Learning poetry—a terrible experience as it was formerly so easy. I did manage it but yet felt I couldn't go on doing it; I got 'tighter,' tighter round the head in concentration.

"4. Arithmetic—tried it for a while but the thing itself was too dull.

"5. Modified pelmanism (very modified!!). I made a list of things to watch for when I went out (yellow coat, black dog, etc.) and recorded them when I returned. Very difficult to do and at the same time look after three children!!

"6. Making up stories for the children—it took a great deal of thinking out but was a tremendous strain—one day I just got so 'drawn' I was sick. I just couldn't go on doing it.

"Added to these were numerous things such as taking a small class, entertaining people to meals, etc., trying to become really interested in other people's lives—writing letters and visiting. All these were worth doing, and I believe helped and prevented it getting worse, but nothing seemed to really break the 'inside out' habit."

The therapist's view

This patient is intelligent, was desperately keen to be well and was willing to co-operate actively with her therapy. Because of this, as well as travelling difficulties, visits were made once a week, but with most patients, especially those who are less able to co-operate so fully, more frequent sessions would be necessary. Inability to co-operate can arise from many inner reluctances; from a lack of understanding of the necessity for continuous practice of the right sort, from a lack of feeling for movement, and a lack of awareness of the accuracy of what is being practised (when it differs or deviates from the movement required at a particular stage of treatment). This awareness gradually grows with experience, but in the early stages a patient can often only be helped by a knowledgeable outside observer. Persistency in practising was in this case a reflection of the deep-rooted desire to get well, together with a natural personal tenacity and a belief in the particular medium of treatment which she had chosen. There were also frequent and lengthy telephone calls.

She was one of a group who attended group movement sessions which I was taking for a doctor and her patients, both men and women. The work in group movement is mainly related to developing awareness and relationships with others, while at the same time giving an opportunity for individual expression and development. After attending a few sessions, this patient asked if it would be possible to have individual movement help, and this was arranged on a weekly basis with the full co-operation of the doctor.

The method and pattern of this particular treatment was unique to this patient and some parts of it are given in detail as an illustration—*not* as a guidance for the treatment of others.

The patient's characteristic movement behaviour

The initial observation of the patient (who looked quite normal to the casual observer) showed her characteristic movement behaviour, overlaid with some exaggerations and distortions.

She was bodily active and physically mobile and poised, and had no obvious restrictions or deformities. The centre of the body, while physically mobile, did not carry through or link movements of the upper and lower parts. The shoulder girdle and top of the spine were tensed, though there was still no real loss of physical mobility in the joints. (In many more-severely sick patients, this tension is far more obvious.) Her hips were narrowly held, and lacked tension; balance was therefore shaky as she moved away from a symmetric alignment. Her hands were agile but tended to be kept closed.

Her basic movement rhythm was characterised by energetic buoyancy, and strong determined action, balanced by a sensitive, outgoing, protective warmth. Quick intuitive impulsiveness and a generous vision would normally have made her a sociable and friendly person. By the time I first saw her there appeared an overlaying of these patterns with a binding of the flow movement, involving countertensions in the body, and a recoil after an initial outgoing movement, as she was thrown back into herself.

She was not so severely disturbed that her fundamental rhythms and bodily health and functions could not still be discerned. The "recoil" action, within a normally harmonious pattern, could be a valuable and simple self-protective action, but it had already become too pronounced, used indiscriminately, and with excess strength—in fact, a repetitive escape mechanism on all occasions. This was seen to inhibit an outgoing opening action before it could be fully developed.

She worked very frequently on the axis of space and time (practical) and its opposite, weight and flow (dreamy). Practical action had become less efficient by exaggerated tension (determination to do a job) together with a lack of ability to retain a focus towards it (directness wavering and dissolving into bound flow). There was no clear follow-through of a decision. The resulting frustration and muddle, causing increased fear and bewilderment, led to even greater tension and determination, greater inhibition of the flow of movement, lack of focus and so on. The reported periodic outbursts of weeping and exhaustion would be a natural release from this mental and physical bound flow tension.

The use of weight and flow, which is basic in her make-up, had come to be used only in its negative aspects, strong tension and bound flow, inwardly orientated (the negative of creative outgoing activity, in thought and idea). This nightmarish struggle had contributed in forming a pattern of response and behaviour to all situations, which was becoming, or had become, habitual. Even with the clearing away of the causes of the fears and the cause of the forming of the pattern (and this of course was being worked upon by the doctor) it seemed that the habit itself had still to be broken at some place or places. The relief from fear, appreciation of the causes for the escape pattern and all the associated mental and emotional refocusing were, I believe, supported by the movement therapy. Its particular role in this patient's rehabilitation was by breaking into the habitual response pattern revealed in her movement, and helping to release the tensions.

The movement sessions

The first concern over the initial sessions was to give the patient confidence in the person with whom she was working; in the movement taken; and in her own ability to "feel" the movement and its subsequent improvement. A strict pattern was therefore chosen, one which gave room both for some immediate achievement, and some obvious failure. Also the movement was chosen to relate in an obvious way with the main problem of "being inside." It was taken in a simple physical sense in the first instance.

Gathering-in—a grasping, closing movement, contrasted with a scattering opening movement. This was taken in the hands, the upper part of the body and finally with the whole body, including a shift of weight. The initial session produced mainly a feeling of frustration and inability, but also a challenge to master the movement. (With this particular patient, I was able to ignore the usual necessity for entertaining and provoking a pleasant and easy sensaticn of achievement in order to gain co-operation.)

More exact details of the actual working together cannot easily be given. Each session demands acute observation of the subtle differences and developments, and quick adjustment to the constantly changing situation: a mixture of encouragement at the right time and place, comments on aspects unachieved, and illustrating new implications and tasks. It is a co-operative effort, guided by patient or therapist at different times.

A remark of this patient was illustrative of one of the values of individual movement therapy (as distinct from group therapy). After this first movement sequence had been practised for some days, she said: "I ought to try very hard to be 'out' [*i.e.* she concentrated on the scattering, outward movement] and not enjoy the inward movement." It was explained that this was not the object of the movement —but that all of us are "inside" at some time and that it is a normal and, indeed, desirable attribute, but what we wanted her to find was her way or route between the natural inward and outward experience.

The route between, *i.e.* the movement itself, as distinct from a static state, was at this time the most important. This understanding helped the patient not to concentrate exclusively on the opposite state to the one she was experiencing: this would have been unhelpful and would probably cause an even stronger rebound into her own inward escape.

It is not possible to give the patient's feelings and comments at all stages of the treatment, as verbalising is valuable only in certain situations (similar to that described above).

That movement can act as a clear explanatory guide, an illustration of mental and emotional patterns, proved to be a means of focusing attention, without focusing on the feeling. To perform the movement, whole-hearted concentration is required, and the close relationship between the movement and the inner feelings and attitudes works in a very direct way on the personality.

A further series of sessions was concerned with a different aspect of movement. This was the achievement of expressive positions, to be held securely in space and in sequence. After the mastery of the positions, the pathway or routes into them (the transitions between one and the next one) were worked on. This sequence took a long time to master, and meanwhile the original movement sequence, extended by new phrasing and rhythm, was retained and practised.

The sequence included:

(*a*) a rising, lifting movement to high;

(*b*) an advancing, extending movement forward;

(*c*) a closing, covering movement backward and down; and

(*d*) an opening, spreading sideways.

An outstanding moment of achievement for this patient came in the rising movement; the movement travelled through the body, instead of breaking at the insensitive centre of the body. The first time that this happened, it was a new sensation which caused great satisfaction.

Another sensation commented upon by the patient was the first awareness of "feeling the ground" with the feet.

The stabilising effect of this whole sequence was subsequently used by her as a means of achieving security in moments of panic.

Movement sequences can be so used, can become tools, *only* when mastered sufficiently to be familiar.

There was an attempt to interest the patient in creating her own sequences of movement, but apart from the contribution of a hesitant phrase, there was obviously no confidence or desire for this at this stage.

Efforts were made to relax: the tension of face, neck and upper spine had gradually been worked on, but, after three months, was still obvious, particularly in moments of strain, when striving to achieve an objective, and when consciously trying to relax. Special exercises (particularly including breathing) were given, as well as placing emphasis on correct breathing at each part of a movement sequence.

After a considerable build-up of security of movement in space, the patient was ready to tackle more precisely the rhythmical and accent aspects of her movement. Again, this was introduced through a simple spatial pattern of movement. The introduction of specific accented rhythms into this pattern caused resistance, frustration and depression. The first rhythm, lightness changing to sudden strength (impact), without exaggerated tension or the inclusion of excessive bound flow, took a few sessions to master. The second sequence, of smooth, light gliding, was simpler for her, and the transition to light, flexible free flow sustainment was another hurdle to be overcome. This light, flexible, free sustained movement was isolated from the sequence, and practised to music. There was an emotional struggle and great concentration by her on this part—but ultimately she learned to "give way," to "enjoy" the swimming sensation, and then she could afterwards recapture this sensation when in a tensed state.

This practice was utilised as a freeing of the strong bound flow, and the releasing of the imaginative indulgence in light (or, at first, heavy) free flow. In isolation, this was gradually accomplished. Now came the difficulty of alternating this "inward-flowing mood of release" with practical efficient choice of action, as here:

Intermediate stages of more gradual change helped this transition but the immediate change from one to the other took considerable time to be mastered.

Gradually, she could only manage to come to London every other week, and the telephone calls between sessions became fewer and fewer. Both she and I are sure that she received great help from the movement, both in understanding and in direct action on helping her to release tensions, and reform and regain her natural responses.

Movement assessment as an aid to self-development

The final assessment is of a woman in her mid-thirties, who wanted to know what help we could give her for her future self-development, based on self-knowledge. There was no vocational need, and she wanted to understand her present make-up more clearly. Many movement terms are used as she had an interest in the method of assessment.

Assessment XVIII

The effort disposition is well spread over each element, with an obvious stress in time and weight. In each case of time and weight the indulging and fighting qualities are well balanced. Less stressed is space awareness—with only half as much used as time and weight—and flow is even less stressed (also notice a preponderance of neutral flow).

The combination of elements, and the inner attitude balance, is seen here:

Predominantly time and weight (29 times)
Predominantly time and space (16 times)
Predominantly time and flow (14 times)
Predominantly weight and space (9 times)
Predominantly weight and flow (4 times)
Predominantly flow and space (4 times)

In the combinations of three elements, action drives (flowless) predominate (spaceless, weightless and timeless combinations are in equal balance).

Functional actions tend towards strong actions. Fine touch appears more readily in mental movement.

The most obviously mental outstanding stress is the care and interest in human relationships and contacts. Abstract intellectual considerations play a very minor role and do not greatly influence the behaviour. There is an ease of contact in dealing with other people—not so much as a member where her own personality is sunk into the whole—but rather as an independent individual, conscious of the needs and feelings of others. She is generous and warm-hearted without reluctance. Sometimes there is a hesitation and withholding from contact, but this is usually based on doubts of herself rather than an unwillingness to make a contact. Her services to others, whether a group or an individual, would be practical rather than theoretical, and there is no hint of subservience or weakness through domination. She has the power to inspire others, and is aware of the influence of others on herself. Such power makes her a quiet but persistent leader, able to stand firmly to her principles and impose her will on others. Such command over other people originates in the desire for the achieved action itself, and not for the personal experience of power. The impactive force of her will could lead to stubborn resistance if unreasonably crossed. Equally, she can follow through a course of action with strong persistence if she believes in its value. Her strength of determination to finish a course of action usually grows after a decision is made. Co-operative with colleagues, she enjoys affectionate relationships without excess sentimentality. (*See* later.) She has a skill and ability with handling objects, and a pleasure in movement and rhythm. Efficiency, ease and rhythmicality are innate, but sometimes hindered and cramped by intellect, thought and concentration. She avoids mechanical repetition and routine, but the creative, artistic imagination is never allowed to breathe properly before being squashed out of existence! She lacks the ability actively to carry out inner ideas when they occur: there is also a lack of confidence in her own abilities in this direction, as well as a distrust of her quick intuitive reactions. Such reactions are immediately justified by thought, and when they are given the impetus of free flow, become quickly anchored in stability, which rarely gives rise to inspirations, and her conscious thought intrudes to destroy them. Confidence appears more in practical action, where the flow is allowed to run unimpeded—so often in other situations the rhythmical flow is interrupted or stopped by held pauses with fine touch or space consciousness.

Surprisingly little use of heaviness in mental attitude is revealed; when it is, it comes at the end as a natural relaxation after absorption. Adjustments to situations of the moment are mainly stable, sometimes with a certain heaviness and look of inertia which gives a false impression of lack of interest, or lack of determination; she is stimulated by interchange with other individuals, and is probably most fully active when working with other people.

She likes to make her own decisions and does not lean on others for guidance, though she is willing to consider with care any problem which interests her, looking at all its aspects; she may sometimes lose the focus of attention, though she strives to recapture it immediately. She has an alertness of mental attitude when her interest is aroused, but she can indulge happily in heavy self-indulgence of slackness and lazy-mindedness. She is able to carry out her own decisions into persistent future action. Sometimes her decisions are slow, leading to firm but sufficiently flexible action to avoid over-dogmatic and narrow action which is not too rigid to be influenced by new ideas. She is sound in judgment, and is unlikely to be carried away by excess enthusiasm; she keeps a pretty firm hold and balance on her inner feelings.

Any inner turbulences are kept in hand, and rarely allowed to influence her relationships with others. Sympathetic consideration and help and genuine interest in other points of view are clear assets as well as an ability to keep to her own ideas when necessary. She explains with clarity and straightforwardness—and is able to grasp new ideas quickly when the fundamentals are clear. There is a lack of pretension and of interest in creating impressions; dramatic play situations do not appear (perhaps she feels embarrassed). She would give whole-hearted and loyal support to any enterprise if once committed to it. Steadfastness and reliability, sensitivity, which helps observation, and straightforward clarity are characteristics of hers. She has movement characteristics of a certain passivity in flow, space and weight which give sometimes a "suspended" and unrelated attitude. She probably distrusts a good deal of philosophic or abstract thinking which has no basis in outer reality, or at any rate, she ignores it. She has a useful natural body resiliency and balance by fine touch in inner life, contrasting with relaxed body attitude. Her legs limit body mobility by being anchored in stability; she is relatively inexpressive in the lower part of her body, except in stability and rhythm. There is an inner buoyancy and resiliency, seen also in the light and quick adjustments to a situation. She may be reluctant to express inner feelings (as in avoiding dramatic situations)—and she considers material adjustment only in terms of human values. This may lead to doubting her own abilities. She can see further than the immediate outcome, but does not always rely on her own vision, which then becomes purposeless. She acknowledges the good things in life and has a capacity for enjoying them.

CHAPTER 11

GROUP THERAPY

Movement practitioners consider that one of the special advantages of movement as a therapeutic means (or educational and recreational for that matter) is that people can work out in a positive way their experiences of human contacts and relationships. As relationship problems are usually associated with any kind of malfunction, this kind of movement therapy can contribute a great deal to treatment, by helping the patient to cope with new or difficult situations in a semi-protected atmosphere.

Structured and non-structured movement sessions

The therapy can be fully structured, as when composed sequences, dances or dramas are presented, when direction is given, and the people are moving at the service of the composition. This is a parallel situation to their participation in a choir or an orchestra. Sometimes such compositions are called "movement choirs." The situation can also be non-structured, or at least have a minimum structure, such as a time and place of meeting only. Here no preconceived pattern or response in movement is expected or required, and the patient may go off alone, work with another individual or join a small group as and when he desires.

These two extremes of fully structured or non-structured sessions are rarely used in isolation by a therapist, although the first may give, for selected groups and at special times, an experience for the patients beyond their normal range and offer an opportunity to participate in a creative enterprise greater than themselves. Similarly, a therapist may decide on some occasion that the non-structured form has a particular value as an opportunity for "self-expression." It may be conducted in silence or with self-made sounds, where the discipline comes from the personal requirements, or the requirements of others in the group. The obvious danger of releasing, without channelling, drives and emotions necessitates that such a course is not lightly undertaken. If some outside stimulus is given—a rhythm, music, an idea or a story—some kind of structuring occurs, and some bounds and limits are set.

Personally, I prefer to work with a mixture of the two approaches, when, as in everyday life, some things are prescribed, and others left to our own decisions.

In this case, a guided framework might be given, and sometimes even exact set parts, with opportunities for individuals to contribute or for a group spontaneously to compose certain parts. There is no limit to the choice of theme, and either the therapist or the group or one member can initiate this.

This work demands great skill from the therapist. Apart from the human understanding and knowledge of the patients' sicknesses he must be able to weld together into a satisfactory artistic whole the contributions from his group. This demands an initial creative effort and knowledge of the effect of the composition and the incorporated movement sequences on his patients. Also he needs a knowledge of ways to stimulate a required response, and the effect of such stimuli, or a given starting situation and so on. All this requires a dynamic adaptability.

For the patient, there is the value of spontaneous experience, the participating in living activity and the opportunity of mastering and composing with a spontaneously experienced movement sequence, either alone, or with the help of the therapist. It is, therefore, essential for the therapist also to be able to help the patient to develop his own work, without imposing a preconceived pattern or form on to what may be only a vague and hesitant original movement idea.

The actual planning of a session must take into account that new patients are not likely to have had any similar movement experiences in their education or recreational activities, though some have. It may be necessary therefore to use the first sessions to build up the patients' confidence in the therapist and the medium, by starting with prescribed, individual exercise, though it has not been found to be necessary in all situations. Care must be exercised in the allocation or encouragement of individuals to take special roles or to become members of groups with special qualities, such as the strong, aggressive group, or the devious, avoiding flexible group. The therapist must gradually build up his knowledge of the patients as individuals, and of the group as an entity by his acute observations. An assessment of a patient might recommend his participating in group movement, or might specify that individual movement therapy would be more appropriate at first. Equally, a patient taking part in a movement session would give an assessor an ideal opportunity for making observations which could be helpful in the whole therapeutic situation.

Group relationships

There is a continuous building-up and breaking-down of group situations and relationships, either arising spontaneously or used deliberately (in a structured group action). These situations and relationships are exactly the same as those occurring in everyday life, but are highlighted, clarified and enlarged. Physical touch arises spontaneously on some occasions, but may have to be avoided for a considerable time with some patients.

Some basic group relationships which arise are the following:

(a) The group acts as a whole; there is no obvious leader and the activity seems to arise from a "group feeling." This does not often last very long before a disruptive force from inside the group causes a change, perhaps into smaller units or when individuals break away.

(b) The group acts as a whole, but throws up a leader, either by choice, where one person is pushed forward, or by the dominance of one individual. The leader may be either accepted or rejected.

(c) Two or more leaders and their followers develop action either as self-contained groups or in opposition to, sometimes in co-operation with, each other.

(d) Couples pair off and become self-contained and are relatively unaffected by others.

(e) The group rejects and throws out one or more members and becomes united against him, or them, surrounding, attacking, crushing, and, in response to these, avoiding or resisting.

(f) From scattered individuals, couples or groups, there is movement towards reforming and regrouping into small or large groups, through approaching, appealing and moving in unison with, either to re-establish the same situation which was left, or towards a new relationship.

(g) If the leader or therapist is actively involved, there can be clear opposition or clear following by the group or its parts. Occasionally, and in certain situations, the therapist becomes accepted just as one of the group.

The endings of such sessions can be spontaneous when absorption stops, or the therapist can interpose and bring it to an end if necessary—for either inner reasons such as the needs of the group, or outer reasons such as limited time and use of the room.

The changing effort content, which is a reflection of the moods and attitudes of the participants, can be contained either within a relatively small range, or the whole range, of possibilities. A highly provocative stimulus can be picked up or rejected, such as peaceful, calm music, or a repetitive dynamic rhythm, or the effort content and its accompanying emotional states develop through the group situations. All kinds of antagonism, aggression, viciousness, as well as cooperation, dreaminess and practicality are possible.

As Bion says:*

"All groups stimulate and at the same time frustrate the individuals composing them; for the individual is impelled to seek the satisfaction of his needs in his group and is, at the same time, inhibited in this aim by the primitive fears that the group arouses."

Value of group movement

The values of such group movement as described might be as follows:

(a) There is an actual working-out of a personal situation in relation to a group; this requires spontaneous responses and may help in releasing and focusing an individual's inhibited responses.

(b) Attention is drawn to the group problems, and to the individual's problems within the group, and discussion material may be provided for the doctor to use.

(c) The movement encourages some patients to be in a moving dynamic situation, where they are not alone and exclusive; some feel a security in this situation, where the first contribution need only be to "go along with the others."

(d) The actual physical movement is related to and unified with feelings and mental life (as discussed in the first part of this book), so that at moments of absorption a real unifying process is taking place.

To summarise, Bion's three formulations of group aims are clearly seen—(a) dependence, (b) pairing, (c) fighting or fleeing—and the participation in movement situations supports his view.

* *Experiences in Groups*, W. R. Bion (Tavistock Publications).

CONCLUSION TO PART TWO

It will be clear to the reader that so far the form of written assessment has been adapted freely to each situation. Sometimes special movement vocabulary is used; at other times, little reference is made to the way in which the results are obtained. This is partly due to circumstances, and partly due to my experimental approach using this technique. It seems that the time has arrived to make some selection from the range of approaches, and to begin to formulate a more standard procedure. The students who are now learning to use this technique might evolve this themselves; this is an area of research which they can investigate to advantage.

As hinted through the book further validation needs to be undertaken—this will be possible as soon as there is a group of observers ready to be independent. Comparisons of results from different observers must be undertaken; the comparison between movement assessments and other forms of personality tests; experiments excluding all verbal communications; assessing different groups of handicapped children; the comparison of the "normal" with the specially gifted child; studies of babies and longitudinal studies of their development over years; the use of movement as a therapeutic tool for both children and adults, with many patients, carefully recorded; these and many more research projects appear to be urgently needed.*

The most frequent criticisms which are made about assessing personality through observing movement are:

1. that it is only or "merely" subjective; and
2. that this method does not show the specific cause of the state of the person observed.

1. In answering the first criticism, I quote R. D. Laing once more:

"It is unfortunate that 'personal' and 'subjective' are words so abused as to have no power to convey any genuine act of seeing the other as a person (if we mean this we have to revert to 'objective'), but imply immediately that one is merging one's own

---

* Two major research projects have been started since this was written and results will be published in due course.

feelings and attitudes into one's study of the other in such a way as to distort our perception of him. In contrast to the reputable 'objective' or 'scientific,' we have the disreputable 'subjective,' 'intuitive,' or, worst of all, 'mystical.' It is interesting, for example, that one frequently encounters 'merely' before subjective, whereas it is almost inconceivable to speak of anyone being 'merely' objective." *

The observations which are made are in fact recognised by the whole body and mind of the observer—not only by his intellect. That is, he observes with his bodily senses, tuned and refined through experience and practice. The "objectivity" of the observations can be, and has been, validated by the agreement of a team of observers.

As for the interpretations, at the level of movement understanding there is common agreement and "objectivity," though it is true to say that when these observations are translated into words, there has not been an exact common terminology. After all, words mean to each one of us what our experience of them has given; although it is easy to achieve agreement of interpretation of observations in principle, the exact form of expression has not been systematised.

2. There is no claim that this form of assessment will reveal the exact background causes leading to the personal movement patterns as revealed at any given time. It can give a picture of the present configuration of a person's movement rhythms, and holds within such a diagnosis hints for therapeutic guidance. As previously stated, I regard this system as a tool to be used in co-operation and co-ordination with other diagnostic and therapeutic techniques. There is no doubt that experience of movement can affect and help an individual to relate conflicting aspects of his personality—not necessarily to adapt him to some outer social requirement but for his greater inner consciousness. Better social integration may follow this.

If this book stimulates some interest in the future developments of this work, it will have served its purpose.

---

* *The Divided Self*, R. D. Laing (Pelican Books).

Part Three: Validation of Assessment through Movement

CHAPTER 12

BASIS OF STUDY

Reasons for making the study and description of the problems involved

The study which follows has been undertaken with the specific purpose of validating the system of personality assessment through movement. The problem is that this method of observation and assessment, having been initiated by Rudolf Laban, has been utilised by the few people to whom he taught the fundamental principles, and over the years, no one has systematically organised, clarified and published information about it in a form which others can use. This I have now undertaken to do.

To validate the system, only a small area of application could be taken at one time, and I chose to work with children aged between eight and nine years. The difficulty has been to find tests already acknowledged which cover the same or similar areas of personality assessment. The comparison of results is also a problem, as I am sure that there is no common method of quantitative evaluation or scoring which can properly be applied with any degree of accuracy. The scoring and measuring which can be made of movement observations is relevant only within that framework; for instance, the fact that a certain rhythmical phrase is used repeatedly by one child, and another phrase only half as many times by the same child, reveals something about his movement make-up, but those figures are not relevant to other scorings from a different test situation.

Choice of children and method of procedure

I chose a class of children who were working with a sympathetic teacher who knew them individually very well. This was important, as I wished to make use of her reports for comparison with my results. Of the class of twenty-six children, twelve were taken at random, six boys and six girls—and, with the exception of two extremely disturbed boys whom the teacher asked if I would include, no special selection was made. The school is in a very deprived area, and the children are mainly underprivileged, to be in this small class, although a few of them are fairly average, buoyant children of this age group.

The order of procedure was as follows:

(*a*) The children were observed, and reports made about each child from the observations of his or her movement only. (These reports form Chapter 13. Other tests used for comparison as mentioned below are explained in Chapter 14.)

(*b*) The class teacher and the head teacher completed specially planned questionnaires. (This was done before showing them the movement assessment reports so that there could be no influence from those reports.) It was seen from the head teacher's answers, and frequent omissions, that she did not know the children well enough for her comments to be useful, so only those of the class teacher are included. (The questionnaire is shown on p. 146.)

(*c*) The twelve assessment reports (excluding any indication of name or sex) were given to

(*i*) the class teacher and

(*ii*) another interested teacher who knew the children well,

and they were asked to name the child described. Both teachers made correct namings on first choice. They were given each assessment separately, and were not able to compare one assessment with another. This naming was from the complete list of twelve children, not the whole class, because the teacher knew with which children I had been working.

(*d*) Individual Children's Apperception Tests (C.A.T.; *see* p. 150) were given by me to the twelve children, and the results analysed.

(*e*) A Stanford–Binet intelligence test was given to each child (*see* p. 150).

(*f*) All the material for each child was compared.

(*g*) Assessments were compared with the educational psychologist's reports, and the class teacher's report form. (*See* Chapter 14.)

(*h*) For all twelve children, the Child Scale B (test for maladjustment, Maudsley Hospital) was completed and results are shown (*see* p. 151).

CHAPTER 13

THE PERSONALITY ASSESSMENTS THROUGH MOVEMENT

Procedure

The children were seen for half an hour, in a specially arranged movement class. Normally, a movement teacher would take a small group, or the whole class, through a pre-arranged sequence of activities. The observer would then observe and notate each child's movement responses. According to the skill of the observer between one and four children can be observed in, say, a twenty- to thirty-minute session. However, in this situation, I did not have a movement teacher with me, and so had to teach the children and try to observe one of them in detail at the same time. This was very difficult, and very slow, as I had to be as concerned with the whole class or group as with this one child. However, this was achieved over two terms' work. If I had had a teacher to work with me, I could easily have assessed the whole class during my weekly visits over two terms. As the class teacher was also very interested in the work, it happened that I was also helping her in her general teaching of movement, and this was also time-consuming.

The twelve assessments

Examples of movement report sheets which I have devised for use in transferring the initial observations to an intermediate stage for analysis are seen in Chapter 15.

The first three reports are written in a form which explains the movement reason for each statement; the final report is usually written for parents or teachers who are not familiar with movement. The last nine reports are in the final form, mainly excluding movement references. As described in Part Two (Chapter 5), initial observations were made and notated during a movement class with the children. The next draft involves the recognition of characteristic movement patterns for each child. The final interpretations are based on these characteristic patterns of movement.

Assessments 1–3. These are written in a form somewhat like the intermediate stage (*cf.* Chapter 15) before the final report (as in Assessments 4–12). Assessment 1 is tabulated in a rather rigid form which has since been discarded.

1. Cheryl: aged 8 years 3 months

A. RELATIONSHIPS

(*a*) Cheryl is an emotionally insecure child, as shown in her *use of flow.*

(*i*) Bound flow tension in shoulders, and occasional releases into heaviness with free flow.

(*ii*) Flow used neutrally in relation to heaviness, which relates to an indulgence in feeling and sensation.

(*iii*) Frequent inward flowing of movement into narrow body posi tions.

(*b*) She lacks sensitivity as shown in the *use of weight.*

(*i*) Stress on heavy indulgence of her considerable body weight.

(*ii*) Lack of fine touch.

(*iii*) Forceful strength in beginnings of phrases which then weaken and fade away.

(*c*) Lacks intuitive perception as shown in her ˙lack of *rhythmical awareness* and adaptability (also lacks flow and time elements in combinations).

Among other factors, these show that Cheryl would not have the confidence, sensitivity or awareness to make easy relationships. Given the opportunity, she might well develop a strong emotional attachment to someone who showed her affection. Her lack of initiative makes her unable to lead or even actively co-operate with others, except in the sense of obeying orders —particularly if they are quite routine. She lacks a sense of appropriateness of action to situation. She is quite submissive, but has a stubborn, rigid streak which is revealed occasionally in postural actions of strong bound flow. The inhibitions already mentioned in her inwardly oriented flow will make her need for affection less able to be expressed, and could lead to some emotional explosion; if, for instance, she were led by a stronger character, her lack of discernment and tight inhibition, when released, could well lead to anti-social activities. Her mental ability is probably average or above, but her assessment of a situation is poor. At this age she is probably still getting some satisfaction from repetitive routine conformity.

B. ADAPTABILITY

(*a*) She lacks the combination of flow and time which indicates change and mental adaptability.

(*b*) Her body attitude is stolid and somewhat static (can be stubborn) in weight and space combinations.

(*c*) She is very symmetric in the use of the body, which indicates a lack of mobility.

(*d*) She lacks rhythmical changes; her time quality is not really sustained and is rather quantitatively slow.

(*e*) There is heaviness going into pauses and held positions.

(*f*) Flexibility is only in occasional body adjustments, and is not shown as active in shadow movements.

All of these factors make her unable to adjust easily to people or situations. The known and familiar is secure and can be coped with.

C. WILL-POWER AND DRIVE

(*a*) Weakness rather than strength is shown in her use of weight; even when strong (in pressing and thrusting actions) it easily fades away; it is, perhaps, tense rather than strong.

(*b*) Strength does appear occasionally in body attitudes with spatial tension, and in this situation it indicates stubbornness as previously noted.

D. ALERTNESS AND PRACTICALITY

(*a*) She lacks alertness, and shows only neutral time with space, and frequent slowness rather than sustained quality; she can be reasonably alert in everyday situations. She has a certain persistency in her slowness but effort dies away and needs recharging.

(*b*) Her actions frequently lack follow through as they die away.

(*c*) Spatial awareness is limited; often actions are undirected and futile, though routine, practical action can be efficiently performed.

E. DREAMY ATTITUDE

(*a*) Neutral weight and neutral flow together often appear in body attitudes and movement phrases. When there is a more positive flow with weight, it swings her into some kind of activity. This negative, passive dreaminess rarely influences her life actively, and can interfere with practical living.

(*b*) Anxiety, fear and insecurity show in her inner "nightmarish" dreaminess of inwardly flowing bound tension with strength.

It is unlikely that this dreamy side will develop to any high degree of creativity, as there is too little active drive, but she could be encouraged to express some of this inner tension through creative work—words, sounds and colour.

F. REACTIONS

(*a*) Her use of time is neutral, with very little quality, and lacks much rhythmical alternation. She is slow.

(*b*) She lacks spontaneous reactions as she shows very infrequently the active time and space combinations which would indicate alert or considered reactions.

(c) She is moved from heavy lethargy by external stimuli to slow responses. She is fairly consistent in differing circumstances. Occasional more lively responses are temporary and fade easily.

G. THINKING AND REASONING ABILITY

(a) "Practical" thinking is shown in her fairly average space awareness in shadow movements: she can use some directness and clear focusing in mental activity. This is, however, clouded by heavy slowness.

(b) Her shaping awareness is fair: she can be vague and lacking in definition when dreaminess takes over.

(c) Her body attitude positions show some consciousness of position in space, sufficient to control and relate to her surroundings.

Abstract thinking is not very likely: she is practical, of probably average ability or above. Probably her attainment is below her ability.

H. ABILITY TO INVENT, CREATE OR MAKE ORIGINAL CONTRIBUTIONS

(a) Few of her movement phrases are developed to a full conclusion; that is, rarely more than two elements combine.

(b) Frequent use of negative or neutral flow and weight gives inhibition rather than creative or inventive flow.

(c) There is inward rather than outward flow.

Given sufficient outside incentive, Cheryl could be greatly helped by creative activity and expression to become more positive and active; there is some latent ability which is not being utilised. She lacks confidence on her own.

I. TOLERANCE

She is tolerant in a passive kind of way and hardly influenced by others, except when she is hurt emotionally; she is relaxed and lacks a great deal of externalised drives and narrow pinpointed attention.

J. ENTHUSIASMS AND CONTINUITY OF ATTENTION

She is usually routine and repetitive, especially if she is given frequent stimuli; her passivity implies a kind of routine working, so does evenness in rhythms. Her dying away towards the ends of phrases indicates a loss of attention, although if emotionally involved she could be interested over a period. She lacks any rhythm of sudden bursts, and therefore is unlikely to be highly enthusiastic.

K. ATTITUDE TO AUTHORITY, DIRECTION, ORDERS AND ORGANISATION

She is most secure when under direct guidance and routine activity; she is unlikely to resent reasonable and kindly orders. Stubbornness (as seen earlier) might be shown if she resents someone.

GENERAL COMMENTS

Physically, she is very overweight, and movement is limited in range and variety; there is a heavy, even attitude. She lacks elevation and stresses down-to-earth movement. Shape awareness is less defined than she is capable of; there is narrow inturned movement, except when stimulated from outside. There are very few developed drives (consisting of three elements). She lives in an inner world, with just sufficient adaptation to the outer world to enable her to manage. Insecurity and anxiety are inhibiting what development is possible. Without special help, this could become progressively worse.

MAIN ATTRIBUTES

(a) Inward flow and either tension or heaviness.
(b) A fairly limited range of movement combinations.
(c) Shape awareness which is vague and undiscerning.

2. Lenny: aged 8 years 2 months

A complete contrast in movement with Cheryl, he is lively, jerky, changeable, rhythmical and outgoing and lacking in stability. He is frequently overwhelmed by uncontrolled giggling and a "don't care" attitude.

Jerky transitions between movements, and an over-hasty use of time, give him his characteristic restless and fidgety attitude. He has good alternations of movement, but cannot utilise them adequately because of a lack of linking or transitional flow. Bound flow appears in small movements of inner apprehension or insecurity.

Free flow with liveliness is extreme, revealing changeability and also restlessness. Each phrase is retained for a very short duration only.

Excessive suddenness with lightness makes for tentativeness, but balances his stronger, impactive action beginnings. These two extremes are not yet brought into relationship (except in opposition).

Frequent repetitions of movements give indications of extreme restlessness, again contrasted with weak giving way at ends of phrases.

There are outward-flowing movements with lightness, and sometimes quickness; his relationships are superficial, but perhaps gay and lively or amusing. (Many of these attributes are those of the acquired patterns of a kind of clown—when comedy is the result of the unexpected, and the extreme opposites of movement!)

He will not stimulate anyone to follow his lead, as he lacks completely any follow-through action, as well as an awareness of others. He is attracted by everything within his reach for a short period: he is very aware of himself and plays for the attention of others.

His lack of balance is seen in his body changeability of position; he has to bend down and move near the floor to gain balance, as he lacks it within himself. He does not use the body centre of gravity to give stability. He is easily knocked over but soon recovers (like a very young child).

The tensions of bound flow which appear in small facial expressions reveal that he is by no means as confident as he might seem.

Quick and jerky changes of movement show adaptability, but not of a harmonious or purposeful kind.

Nevertheless, flow and time combinations show a latent possibility for harmonious adjustability which could be developed.

Lack of holding on to space and weight combinations reveals a lack of stability, but latent ability is present and could be developed. He changes too easily according to his moods and circumstances, which shows a lack of self-discipline. He could be easily led by a stronger personality.

Will-power is weak and not consistent; there are quick changes, concentration is short-lived, but he has a masculine impactive force which could form the basis for development: at present it fades away uselessly, or switches to something else.

Every indication of alertness and awareness of practical things (which are combinations of space and time, and are minimal) carry through into practical action (combination of three—space and weight and time).

Few indications of weight and flow—the time element dominates his movement too frequently to allow dreaminess; there is no positive outflowing to indicate creative or imaginative attitudes. (This could be developed, as the presence of neutral weight and flow indicates latent possibilities.) Light bound flow in this case indicates tentative apprehension.

There are jerky reactions preceding space awareness and therefore before thinking. He could be highly intuitive if a general personal integration could be achieved. As it is, he is simply thoughtless and "scattered."

There is a relatively good development of body awareness; he uses space neutrally in body attitudes.

His ability for directed attention is weakened by (a) losing focus, or (b) changing focus without transitions. At some moments he can show clear, pinpointed ideas in descriptive gestures. He lacks flexibility in shadow movements and does not see many sides of a problem. Perhaps he has below average I.Q., but he is by no means unable to learn.

Little of his fairly rich movement vocabulary is brought to any external drive; it is dissipated without purpose.

Latent powers of imagination are crushed beneath his restless, unstable "flitting about."

He is tolerant of others because he is not very aware of them except in relation to himself, as an audience, and he will tend to ignore anything which does not impinge on his own activities.

Sudden enthusiasms are shown in quite strong drive with suddenness, but quickly disperse. Occasionally he shows an impacted, directed enthusiasm which should be fostered and recharged to help him concentrate; this is mainly in response to outer direct stimuli.

He is amenable to direct authority; a fleeting light attitude makes for an unresentful lack of discernment.

SUMMARY

The fairly rich variety and range of attitudes cannot be fully utilised by this boy, as few are brought to externalised actions and drives. Quick-changing, lively, jerky, lacking space awareness and concentration, an absence of bodily control from the centre of gravity or body centre, all of these add up to a dispersed, weak and disorganised make-up, which needs help.

3. Josie: aged 8 years 2 months

Her body attitude is mainly high and forward, outgoing and co-operative, but also she has counter-tendencies to this, when excessive suddenness makes her impatient on occasions.

From security of stability (weight and space), she can make quick decisions, and together with her open (wide) and forward attitude, will often inspire others to follow her, especially when she uses her strong action phrases.

This strength and directness might lead to a dominating attitude at present, but she can learn to ease this as she has a natural buoyancy and fine touch. In using bound flow instead of strength she weakens her poise, and tends to be over-emotionally involved when a simple practical attitude of holding on to a position is required.

Endings of phrases are varied; when secure, she can be stable (space and weight adequately used); when she loses interest, or is insecure, she either flops (use of heaviness) or becomes bound and agitated (inward tension here). This would indicate that she would follow through a situation to a satisfactory end in most cases, but in some will give up and withdraw.

Also, as she is direct rather than flexible, except in manipulative actions, it will mean that any deviation from her own ideas might be difficult for her to accept when once started on a project with others. This is also supported by tension in the neck area which appears sometimes in conjunction with sudden bound flow.

Good rhythmical and down-to-earth ability (weight and time) indicates generally good human contacts, though hastiness sometimes interferes. She needs help to develop sustainment further, especially with lightness (sensitivity).

She has ability over a good range of practical actions, which is shown in flexibility, in weight/time/space combinations, and in body attitudes.

Shadow movements are more frequently direct, therefore limiting ideas to a fairly narrow range once they are decided upon (at present stage of development).

A variety of states of mobility (flow and time) indicates good mental adaptability to new situations and ideas. This means that although adaptable to general ideas, she is less so in carrying them out. She will enjoy new situations, although there is tension and bound flow in the neck area, which inhibits complete participation on occasions, or is the reflection of inhibition.

A well-developed strength quality is used both practically and in shadow movements, and indicates her ability to exert her own will-power and drive. (This is a good example of a contrasting personality attribute to the first two children assessed; Cheryl lacked much will-power (heavy floppiness) and Lenny could not exert what strength he had.)

The combination of outward flow and strength can lead to stability and pause at the end of a phrase, which indicates an ability to hold on to an idea. This is not excessive, however, and not always used (she sometimes withdraws at the ends, as previously noted).

Sudden direct reactions are typical of her alert and bright attitude—sometimes over-quick, while at other times a well-considered response is made; she needs some further encouragement.

The pauses between a mental idea and practical action are very short.

She has a wide range of practical actions and good transitions which carried through to externalised drives (weight and space and time) reveals her basic practicality. Her main lack is light sustainment; her sensitive mental attitude needs further help to develop—it is still latent at present.

There is a very rare appearance of weight and flow which reveals a slight dreamy side to her nature. When it appears, it is mainly strong and bound, more fearful and inturned than practical and outgoing. This shows that Josie is not entirely secure; there is anxiety which relates to the observed sudden withdrawals from a situation (suddenness with inturned flow and backward direction).

She is not an abstract thinker, and rarely, if ever, uses the space and flow combination. She is a practical thinker and is very efficient (weight and time and space). She uses directness more than flexibility in thought (shadow movements) and is therefore pinpointed and accurate rather than contemplative and thoughtful. Accuracy can be spoilt by over-hastiness.

Supporting this practicality is her fairly good shaping ability together with a good awareness of herself in space. These attributes, and her rhythmicality, indicate good active thinking ability. She is probably above average intelligence, though not outstanding. (Note limitations as above.)

She is inventive, mainly practical and not very creative, which is shown in the variety and range of her inner attitudes, but there is very little weight and flow. Inventiveness will take a practical line—in words, materials and movement. She has a well-developed rhythmic sense which reveals a wide range of openness to aural, visual and touch sense impressions.

There is a rather direct narrowness (together with hastiness) which shows her somewhat intolerant. There is a latent capacity of sustainment. Lightness would help her if developed.

Sudden strong bursts of energy (weight and time), repeatedly recharged, show her typical way of working; sustained and regular evenness is not present. Attention is direct and retained for the period of strength, then it changes. There is sufficient long-term stability for her to return and rework on an idea.

Her quite wide range of movement content will ensure that she is interested in almost everything new, with the exception previously mentioned of abstract thought—figures, numbers and so on.

Her independent and self-contained attitude, usually good body balance and quick decisions indicate that she is neither subservient nor resentful of being organised, provided she can see the purpose of it, and respects the authority.

SUMMARY

She is bodily compact and small—well controlled, with an ability for mobility and stability. She uses the centre of levity easily and frequently, but lacks elevation in jumping (a down-to-earth attitude). There is good body awareness, which is practical, rhythmical and usually wide rather than narrow body-shape. Usually there are good transitions. Generally, there is a reasonably integrated development, needing some help gradually in the areas noted above.

Assessments 4–12. These are set out in their final form and headings are dispensed with.

4. Brigit: aged 8 years 4 months

The main movement patterns which Brigit uses are coloured by bound flow, inward and narrow movement (reserved) and rather isolated body actions. She has a good range of inner attitudes and drives, which probably implies a good intellectual ability and range of gifts, but they might not be useful or used by her, as she is so reserved and contained. She has probably well above the average I.Q.

Relationships are sure to be something of a problem, as she withdraws frequently—probably she is happier with her own small circle of contacts, for she is sensitive and gentle. Her lack of outward flow will make it unlikely that she will take the initiative in contacts. Obviously she is not the leader, and is likely to be actively happy following the lead of others. Her timidity and shyness is excessive; aggression is completely outside her revealed movement range, and instead of a natural strength of resistance or aggression she becomes tight and rigid; *i.e.* aggression is turned inwards.

Her lightness will make her sensitive to others, and unobtrusive. She seems even and lacking in physical and mental buoyancy, and probably consistently so. She has considerable potential for adaptability, but is unlikely to be able to utilise this. Even a small degree of release of her bound flow, her narrowness and inward-flowing movement would allow her gifts to develop; they might otherwise atrophy.

She is bright and alert in her attention, particularly in practical situations. She has good manual dexterity and persistency. Her evenness of rhythm has the effect of rather dull routine persistence; the only spark of vitality comes from her reaction to very exuberant stimuli and she shows a small lively sparkle in facial expressions and smiles are quick, light, free and direct. She has little chance to develop her inventive capacities; there is only a small hint of the possibility, and there is so much against any creative development, such as an evenness of rhythm, a withdrawn timidity and a narrow rather than a broad view. Such capacities are present but latent.

I should judge from her movement that she is not intolerant—as distinct from actively tolerant—and although aware of others she is probably not very affected by them except if in direct contact with her. There is a definite attitude of repressed, inhibited and timid narrowness, indicating strong neurotic tendencies. She is far too obedient and lacks enthusiastic rebellion. She must have been considerably repressed over a long period.

MAIN ATTRIBUTES

(a) Wide range of inner attitudes and richness of movement potential. Intellectually able.

(b) Intense inhibition and restraint, shown in rhythms, body attitudes and spatial restrictions.

(c) Evenness of rhythms, showing lack of enthusiasm and drive.

(d) Relationship problems with children and adults.

5. Patrick: aged 7 years 9 months

Patrick uses exaggerated movement elements in all aspects except space. His droopy body attitude can alternate and contrast with his held positions; his sudden, jerky movements, with slow and exaggeratedly reluctant ones; and his excessive bound flow, with occasional outbursts of excessive free flow. All these extreme contrasts make for variability of mood, with changes of an immediate and extreme nature, sometimes violent. His body attitude is either (usually) inturned, concave and withdrawn, or (occasionally) over-extended, convex, with a tense, bound position of spine. When he is inturned, he is very aware of himself and his position in space, and frequently keeps a quite alert attention to outer happenings. It is as though he is under a spell from inside himself and unable to change from this withdrawn situation. Only when extremely confident of his relationship can he respond to outer stimuli at this time.

Clearly all these attitudes will mean that he has relatively little social contact—at any level. His unpredictability will cut him off from his peers. Even with an adult with whom he has a close contact he reacts unpredictably, though he often reaches a small degree of normal communication after coaxing. There were also some moments of good communication on a one-and-one basis between himself and another member of the class which did not last long, but seemed temporarily satisfying to him, but then he withdrew again.

His reactions also vary according to his mood and situation: sometimes he is excessively sustained, reluctant, slow and restrained; at others, there is a normal, quick, direct response. Sometimes his response is completely blank, holding a position where he is and apparently unable to respond (though he shows signs of an awareness of the approach). He is at the mercy of these varied responses and extremes, and lacks transitions between them. This means that he cannot master these over-strong emotional surges which sweep over and bind him. They are mainly directed inwards, on and at himself (as shown in his over-bound, tense attitudes), but when directed outwards can also be violent, aggressive and uncontrolled—probably both to other children and adults. He quickly swings back into a tense inward boundness, so that there is in fact little release from these outbursts.*

He is not aware of himself in space, in relation to his environment; often he observes quite statically the activities around him. He lacks stability and adjustment to a changing situation, and his habitual pattern of response is to withdraw and isolate himself, both physically and emotionally. He can handle material quite adequately, having a certain manual dexterity when focused on an activity. His undeveloped shaping awareness, however, would preclude him at present from being really efficient in practical manipulation of materials—equally in manipulating ideas and thoughts. He has a fairly clear directional sense which saves him from completely submerging himself in feeling.

His movement patterns show a richness of variety, revealing a potentially gifted boy in many spheres. Very few of these gifts can be used positively or purposefully, and he is certainly very backward. This, of course, will add to his frustrations. How far he can be helped to cope with his difficulties (which are also revealed in a lack of clarity of speech) is not clear, for he is a very disturbed child. His movement patterns show many of the extremes of early childhood, as well as extremes of inhibition or lack of control, subsequently acquired. Any therapy will be slow, because it will be entirely dependent upon the relationship between him and the therapist; with a good relationship, he could greatly benefit from all kinds of practical, including movement, therapies. He appears to be in great need of help, probably beyond what can be and is being supplied as one of a larger group in school.

MAIN ATTRIBUTES

(a) Extremes of all elements except space.
(b) Lack of transitions.

* He did not receive any special help. His adolescence is now stormy and violent. His school achievements are minimal.

(c) Excessive inward flow and pauses, contrasting explosive out-pouring.

(d) Extremes in body shapes.

(e) Repression of rhythmical flow.

(f) Downward directional stress—also backward.

(g) Weakness of shaping, though clear directional sense (*i.e.* can see where he wants to go often, but cannot shape his world to achieve his goals).

6. Arnold: aged 7 years 11 months

Arnold is a pathetic, cowed child, both weak and small. His most out-standing characteristic is his split or divided attitudes; in attention he looks with his eyes, but his body actions are avoiding and have a different rhythm; in body movement he has contrasting rhythm in different parts of the body; in effort he has disconnected and often irrelevant phrases, contrasted with occasional spells of consistent and focused action. When his attention is caught there is an almost pathetic desire to conform and please, but atten-tion wanders in spite of himself and changes easily into vagueness and weak spacelessness.

There is a distinct lack of body co-ordination, and no awareness in the body of related actions; he lacks a "body centre" to which he can refer his movements, and therefore seems completely lost in space. Transitions be-tween movements are vague and meandering or abrupt and lacking effi-ciency. Together with all this lack of relatedness, the quality of his move-ment patterns is consistently reduced (except in his bound flow tensions); weakness instead of strength, reduced sustainment and free flow, and reduced directness are typical, and neutral states are frequently used in weight and flow. This shows a lack of positive drive of any sort. Any therapy would need to aim at a heightening of awareness, and encourage-ment of a positive response and drive. He is not aggressive, and is subdued far beyond the range of normality. His bound flow tensions show his inner aggression.

This response to his environmental influences is depressing, and indicates a complete lack of understanding from his home. No doubt he was not strongly endowed in range or strength of personality characteristics but now he appears to be crushed beyond reach of a normal school situation. He has withdrawn himself. Obviously his real social contacts are nil, and he can only truly react to direct orders. It does not seem to matter who gives the order—just a crisp direct command results in his immediate unthinking response.

This automatic, mechanical attitude is also seen in his metric sense of time; a real rhythmical awareness is lacking. Given a repetitive rhythm, he can usually react to the beat or the stress of action, although always just behind the rhythm. He has no ability to anticipate or prepare for the next activity.

He makes few gestures; his changing body attitudes are his movement way of adapting to situations as far as he can. He flops on to the floor or chair for stability, for he has no inner control. Excessive bound flow, revealing emotional inhibition and restraint, appears as inward flow, and the very frequent use of flow and weight, inwardly experienced, is a passive vacancy or "passive tenseness" rather than a creative active drive.

There is just sufficient outer drive to cope with practical minimal requirements. His persistency over a limited period was undiscerning and mechanical. The very limited range of inner attitudes and drives—and their infrequent use—reveals a restricted and limited intellectual capacity. He appears to be slightly more aware of the situations around him now than when I first saw him six months ago. (He is a very sick boy, whose parents refuse to allow any treatment for him.)

MAIN ATTRIBUTES

(*a*) Split and divided attitudes in body—attention.

(*b*) Predominantly body attitude movements—little gesture.

(*c*) Inward flow—often exaggeratedly bound—rarely free.

(*d*) Lacks rhythm.

(*e*) Lacks body centre and co-ordination in body.

(*f*) Little space awareness.

(*g*) Downward directions predominate.

(*h*) Reduced degrees of effort qualities mainly used.

7. Richard: aged 8 years 4 months

Richard presents the picture of a child who possesses gifts and cannot quite dare to use them. But occasionally (especially this was seen in the supportive situation of a dynamically taken movement class) he showed some daring and audacity, almost to his own surprise! He has a good range of "semi-latent" abilities, which come and go according to his confidence. His emotional feelings are clearly inhibiting his development, rather than any lack of ability.

In an established situation, he has a certain confidence, but he lacks the ability to adjust to a changing situation, unless it is a purely practical situation. Nevertheless he has a wide range of movement combinations showing time and flow, and therefore all these subtle adjustments are possible for him, but they need a firmness of intention (strength). In practical actions (of which he has a wide range) he can be strong and rhythmical. His shadow movements and often his body attitudes either are too weak to be effective, or, after a promising beginning, fade away.

He has, as his primary way of working, a practical attitude to situations, and has a certain sense of himself in space. It is likely that he has an I.Q. above average, although whether his performance is equal to his ability is questionable. He is probably inventive and able to manipulate ideas and objects. His weakness of determination makes him vague and irritatingly passive.

His relationships will be undeveloped because of his tentativeness, and his insecurity (shown in reduced and inturned flow) will mean that he finds it difficult to take the initiative. He is sensitive and aware of others, however, so that the lack of relationships is not due to incapacity, but is a result of personal insecurity. With increased security, a strengthening of his own will-power and a development of some independence, he will make relationships more easily. He will not be a leader, but could grow up to be a good colleague and worker with equals. The first stage is to help him to be involved—probably by following actively. Obviously, he is quite tolerant of others—even friendly, in a timid way. Authority seems overwhelming to him, but this again is only a stage through which he is at present passing. He seems to have very immature movement reactions to situations—I would say that he is a slow developer, or one whose circumstances have not encouraged him to be independent.

Although he seems more withdrawn than is necessary, more timid and even fearful than seems reasonable, there does not appear to be any fundamental disturbance or maladjustment at this stage. His movement phrases and his body and space awareness show that he has good mastery of alternations and transitions, and a wide enough range of capacities to be potentially able to cope with life in many aspects.

His main requirement is to strengthen his weakness of determination and intention, and to help him to grow up. Movement, within the group, or in a smaller group, could contribute a great deal to this need, especially if taken by someone who was aware of this need. All kinds of creative activity and situations demanding independence and choice will help. This is becoming an urgent need, for if Richard does not overcome these hurdles now, he will not be able to cope with later ones.

MAIN ATTRIBUTES

(a) Immature development, shown in frequent latent or semi-latent capacities.

(b) Good range of inner attitudes.

(c) Practical abilities.

(d) Weakness of determination—vague and passive (shown in reduced strength, reduced and inward-turned flow).

8. Katie: aged 7 years 10 months

Katie is well co-ordinated, bodily and mentally. She has a strong practical streak and should be gifted in manipulating materials, words and colour. She has a wide range of practical action sequences, with good transitions and periods of rhythmic and natural recovery. Her shaping ability is average, and therefore she is likely to be quite able in her thinking and reasoning ability, though less in her abstract ideas than in concrete situations; however, this side may be latent in her. Generally she can be described as eager, lively and efficient. She has, nevertheless, insecurities which appear in her movement rhythms from time to time. They do not seem to overwhelm her, but she may well be much more anxious than it generally appears from her lively appearance.

Her relationships are likely to be good; she has a spontaneous and natural use of flow (both bound and free) appropriate to the situation, and a natural resiliency. Her awareness of herself in space (weight and space combination) is in a healthy balance with her adaptability and changeability (flow and time combination), making her able either to appreciate others or to stand up for what she wants. She is well able to take the lead, at present in a rather domineering way, but not excessively so, and this is balanced by her genuine sensitivity, which as she grows older could well result in her developing into a really aware leader. She is independent and self-reliant, and it does not seem likely that she will develop too aggressively, as she lacks the vicious-ness of attack. Slash goes into free flow not strength. Her aggressiveness at present tends to be more an irritation or annoyance with things being done incorrectly, rather than a personal emotional antagonism. When it comes to matching her strength with an equally strong personality, she is well able to hold her own, perhaps she even enjoys the rivalry. There is, nevertheless, a need for her to develop a greater range of awareness in relation to people— at present she has a limited "feeling" range, of hitting out or cramping up if she is challenged. This could look like resentment or resistance. This wider range is certainly latent. She is fairly content to follow the lead of adults— but only of children if she can see the purpose and reasonableness of it. Her sensitivity is often directed inward; perhaps she needs help to project this to others. No doubt she suffers somewhat herself, and is sometimes "over-sensitive."

She is adaptable and able to see more than one side of a problem (flexibility as well as directness is developed); her ability to adjust herself to situations is quite harmoniously developed (flow and time) and she is suffi-ciently stable (weight and space) to keep a balance and not be too easily influenced. Transitions from one action to another are good, making an ease of adaptation possible.

She is strong-willed, but not excessively so; she should develop into an adult who knows her own mind, but she is not so rigid that she cannot see other points of view and adapt to them; she is a little young for one to expect such maturity at present.

The flow element of movement is used more as bound than free flow, and this, combined with strength or heaviness, is her only use of the weight and flow combination. This means that she does not rely on inner creative motivation for her inventiveness, so much as outer stimuli, and her "dreamy" moods tend to be tight and apprehensive rather than wild or free. She shows an advanced, almost mature, ability for controlling herself in relation to her environment; this breaks down occasionally and she withdraws, almost resentfully, but this over-control does not appear to have any serious inhibiting effect as yet, though, as noted previously, she is probably more anxious than she generally reveals. I think her natural resiliency and rhythmical recoveries help to mitigate too much self-control of inward boundness, but positive help could also be given to her through movement.

Her reactions are lively, thoughtful and appropriate. She appears to absorb impressions easily, and to react spontaneously (she has good rhythmical ability), which could develop into real intuitive perception. When she is tolerant, this is a genuine conscious attitude, not caused through a lack of awareness and interest. She shows no sign of active intolerance, though it may sometimes appear so, as she likes her own way, and then her control slips a little!

She is enthusiastic and has the ability to sustain an interest over a considerable period. She does not need constant "recharging," and prefers to follow an activity through to its conclusion. Her imagination can be fairly easily caught and held, and she is consistent in her attitudes.

She may resent other dominating children, but should respond to reasonable leadership from adults or older children, and be co-operative. She has a good ability to work alone, as well as with a group; indeed, she gets positive satisfaction from personal achievement. She has a sufficient balance of gifts, combinations of movements, and good poise in space, as well as mental powers, to enjoy being stretched and stimulated to work hard.

She is above average for this class, and is mostly well co-ordinated and adjusted; she seems almost too mature in some ways, but maybe she has had to fight for herself already. She needs creative activities for development and outlet, particularly to integrate her feelings into actions, rather than isolating them; if too hard pressed, she could become negative and strongly anti-social.

MAIN ATTRIBUTES

(a) Well co-ordinated.

(b) Practical.

(c) Good range of inner attitude (richness).

(d) Good relationships generally.

(e) Anxiety as shown in inturned flow with tension.

9. Tom: aged 8 years 5 months

Tom's movement is typified by his lack of central control; his body (and mind) is not always co-ordinated, so that there are frequent occasions when he sprawls and shoots out his arms, legs and body, without any idea of direction or form. This contrasts with his frequent heavy giving-in, particularly at the ends of phrases. He is physically well built and has a good body structure. Movements relating to practical action tend to be more co-ordinated, and he responds with initial enthusiasm to a vital, dynamic stimulus. His interest quickly fades, unless carried by outside influence. Contrasts of movement patterns show that his behaviour will often be typified by extremes.

Because of his relatively little-used fine touch, and frequent lack of control, he will find relationships difficult; he is to some degree too unpredictable for other children to find easy. (His use of fine touch appears mainly as a natural preparation for practical strong action, and rarely as a positive action itself, though this could be developed.) He will tend to work alone more than with a group, though a strong leader-type of child may find him a ready companion. He is a masculine boy, with exuberant bursts of energy, but these quickly fade into apathy. He is not a leader.

He is a mixture of confidence in some aspects (mainly practical) and great insecurity in others. He has a certain physical daring which has not been sufficiently channelled and developed to be a positive attribute, and at frequent moments of insecurity he becomes stiff and tense (coming down from a height). He parallels this physical pattern with mental and emotional tightness and apprehension, though often masking this to the outside world.

The hint of aggression in his movement quickly dies away. He could be provoked to antagonism, though any attacks he makes are not very vicious. His personal resilience is hindered by neutral weight and flow, and it seems that often he will withdraw from a situation rather than see it through. This seeming apathy probably hides a fear of failure.

His stability (strength with good space awareness) comes from reactions to outside stimuli (and quickly fades if the stimulus is withdrawn) or from deep, low movement near the floor. This shows a lack of inner confidence (see also first statement above of his lack of central control). He is easily diverted, and easily knocked off balance when depending on his own strength of purpose. His strength is his main movement element, and he shows good attention and strong intention, but weakens on the follow-through of his decisions. He can be stubborn—either in a passive, heavy way, or in a tense, active way, though this does not last long. He is mainly a practical person, though when he withdraws, his action is impaired obviously. There is a small hint of weight and flow, particularly strong and free flow which could indicate a latent capacity for imaginative work, though this would not be manifest in his present alternations of attitudes and insecurity.

His facial expression (his eyes are direct and quick) is alert and bright, but simultaneously with this, his body is flexible, and even other parts of his face, such as the mouth, are flexible. He can and does react easily and spontaneously, giving thought to the problem in hand. His mental action is direct rather than flexible, but a fairly good alternation is achieved. He can consider a task or problem realistically, but the follow-through is weak.

He is too involved with his own inner conflicts to be very tolerant of others and also he lacks sensitivity which will inhibit tolerance.

His contrasts have not been brought into relationship with each other, and therefore he is rather at the mercy of his moods of enthusiasm and apathy.

MAIN ATTRIBUTES

(a) Lack of central control.

(b) Opposite attitudes not reconciled.

(c) Fading of interest.

10. Jane: aged 8 years 4 months

Jane lacks co-ordination in the upper and lower parts of her body; is unable to unite ideas and the "higher" aspects with her "earthy" characteristics. There is no obvious distortion of movement, but the link and connection is broken. She has an almost metric evenness in her actions, giving a pedestrian dullness to her responses and actions. The non-time movement combinations of three elements are very powerful in her make-up; a kind of timeless, spell-like or hypnotic state—sometimes as though inwardly spellbound, at other times as though reacting to an outer force. She does not exert influence in outward flow, however, but is the victim of it. One wonders what she is bound by.

She is rarely fully at ease, and is almost too anxious to please, or to do what is required. She responds to warmth by a surge of slow and free flow, and heavy feeling; she needs great reassurance—perhaps she has been deprived of such physical contact as cuddling, comforting and so on. She could attach herself to a friendly adult in an excessively passionate way. Perhaps too much is expected of her. Her tensions are despondent rather than agitated, though sometimes there is a hint of a "break-out" in her thrusting and pressing forcefulness (if only she dare), but this is immediately smothered down in bound flow.

Perhaps she will find contacts with children easier than with adults, though it is unlikely that she will be very popular; her anxiety to be accepted and involved may well make her an acceptable member of a group. Obviously she is not a leader: she is willing to follow others.

It appears that she is working as hard as she can, though her capacities are not very wide. She is probably not able to utilise them fully, as seen in her lack of rhythmical alternations in all elements, time rhythms, weight rhythms, space patterns and flow rhythms.

This lack of transitions and alternations will make her unable to cope with original, inventive or creative situations or activities; she needs to be "right" and accepted, and therefore she will tend to formal, stereotyped responses. She lacks real spontaneity and responses are delayed and careful.

She is tolerant because of her desire to conform rather than a genuine understanding. She enjoys best direct orders which she can easily follow. Outside stimuli can hold her attention for a long time; if left to her own drive, either this dies heavily away or she holds on rather rigidly; this should not be confused with enthusiastic absorption.

She is a child in some trouble, and under great pressures, who is struggling to reconcile inner conflicts but has not the inner make-up to do so alone. This could deteriorate. She is also overweight.

MAIN ATTRIBUTES

(a) Split of upper and lower body.
(b) Extreme evenness and lack of rhythmic alternations.
(c) Excessive caution—despondent.
(d) Routine and fairly practical—lacks resilience.

11. Sam: aged 8 years 5 months

Sam has good mental ability, probably well above average, but shows in his movement patterns evidence of considerable emotional conflict and tension. It is significant that he frequently shows conflicting movement phrases in different body parts at the same time. He appears all the time to be fighting—either inwardly or outwardly. This does not always imply aggression. There is sometimes a tense and strong grip, as though attempting to master himself. A practical boy, with a good range of latent abilities, such as manual dexterity, practical working-out of situations and appreciation of problems.

Relationships generally will be difficult, as can be seen in his tension and withdrawn attitude, though when he is confident, he can be more co-operative. He is intelligent enough to cover his own insecurity with "fooling about," but underneath this is his desire to participate. His weak endings to phrasings (bound flow with lessened lightness), and his inability to hold a really stable position, show his lack of a stable centre; he is easily disturbed, but he covers up by an aggressive action, rather than by giving-in. This would basically mean that there is the latent capacity to master himself, given the right sort of help, to establish confidence in himself. It is unlikely that he will be either very tolerant or co-operative with other children of his own age; he may well find older children more congenial, and has enough strength of mind to hold his own. No doubt he will challenge authority frequently, and may therefore appear to be difficult in class. He desperately needs to be able to establish himself as a person; he shows very little awareness of himself in space. His usual reaction to an approach is flexible avoidance, but this can change to strong bound flow or light, reduced free flow if the approach is maintained, and he becomes more amenable, though this is not necessarily carried through! On the whole he works best alone, and gets satisfaction from personal achievements. He needs help towards group work. He would be stimulated by an equally intelligent partner. He has exuberance which could well be infectious. Sensitivity is not very well developed, and this could gradually be encouraged as a contrast to strength.

He lacks resilience, so that he probably suffers a great deal more than he shows to others.

Although Sam has a latent capacity for adaptability, he does not always achieve this now (his time rhythms are even and restricted) and he is usually slightly behind a rhythm. His ability for intuitive perception is inhibited by his emotional feelings which are tense and inward-flowing. Transitions between actions are very poor, sometimes non-existent, sometimes jerky and crude, and this will make for an inability (at the present time) to adapt to a changing situation easily.

He is very strong-willed, particularly in his presentation to the outer world, but it is interesting that the strong movement is often associated with bound flow, or fades into weakness. This strength of will is probably his main way of coping with his problems, but sometimes it seems almost to be desperation.

Sam takes refuge in practical and down-to-earth facts and information. Probably too tied up in himself to be very inventive, he certainly shows little sign of real creative ability though there is sufficient latent capacity (weight and flow) to make it appear that some development here could be possible, if his anxiety could be resolved; perhaps this would help the release.

A bright, alert attitude (he has a cheeky, rather attractive face) typifies his reactions; he is rarely dreamy or distant, and is aware of most of what is taking place around him. His spontaneous avoidance of challenges often changes after consideration to acquiescence. He is not tolerant, and would tend to intolerance in situations where he feels secure; this could be difficult to cope with, but is a symptom of his insecurity and intolerance of himself.

His powers of concentration are probably average when involved in a topic; enthusiasm seems to be focused and alert, but a real sustainment and enjoyment of solving a task seems lacking. Nevertheless he has a persistence in some chosen occupations which is shown in an even rhythm.

He probably leads weaker children and may even bully them, but he is not a real leader, as he lacks sufficient sensitivity and freedom to feel for his followers. His ideas may attract others. I think he would also follow others if the lead were stimulating, but see comments about resistance above.

He is an attractive child, who occasionally relaxes and smiles with some relief and release of tension.

MAIN ATTRIBUTES

(*a*) Transitions poor.
(*b*) Lack of integration of different parts.
(*c*) Poor rhythmical ability.
(*d*) Fighting elements.
(*e*) Good richness of range of abilities.

12. Edith: aged 7 years 11 months

Edith is small, angular and bright. She is absorbed in activity, has good powers of concentration, and within her limits appears to be working to capacity. Her gaiety is charming, and contained; she appears to be poised and fairly well balanced. She has an excellent awareness of herself in space, and is quite confident within her own sphere.

Although her movements are usually small and lack exuberant explosions into space, she is confident in a quiet way, and is able to go from her own established position to meet others, to work with them and to enjoy contact. Her facial expressions are more open than her body movements, revealing inner poise, though perhaps some timidity or shyness in strange situations. There appear to be no obvious extremes of movement patterns, so that she will be relatively consistent in her relationships. Not sufficiently strongly outgoing to be a real leader, she will no doubt contribute some good ideas to a group action. She happily accepts suggestions and leadership from teachers or others in authority.

She lacks real strength in the centre of her body, substituting for it bound flow, but has positive and active fine touch. She will therefore be sensitive to others, able to "feel" for them and probably sympathetic. If upset, which is no doubt rare, she will be tight and edgy, rather than aggressive. Equally, she is unlikely to be stubborn or very strong-willed over getting her own way. She will perhaps succeed in achieving a good deal of her intentions through a gentle, lively attractiveness; it is difficult not to smile at her in response. Her bound flow tendency reveals control, a certain caution and possibly some "light" anxiety in some situations, which appears to be no more than a healthy care and awareness.

She lacks dynamic resiliency, and an easy swinging action, and therefore is likely to proceed carefully (though with vitality and liveliness), rather than be caught up in a surge of enthusiasm or be swung off balance by others.

Her attention is direct, quick and light, and her ability to carry out activities will be practical, mostly conventional and precise. She has persistency, mainly through repeated, lively actions, but also by sustained action, particularly if it is light and bound. Her lack of swing, and tendency to bind her free flow into bound flow, when using weight and flow combinations, indicates only very limited creativity. However, she shows a latent capacity for more original work, and this perhaps could be gradually developed. Nevertheless, she is essentially a practical child, alert, precise and well organised. Probably a little above average in intelligence, she is not an abstract thinker. In a sympathetic easy environment, she will be able to develop gently: a tougher, rigid or harsh atmosphere would fairly easily send her into anxiety tensions and restrict her development more than it might a more robust character.

MAIN ATTRIBUTES

(a) Sensitivity and liveliness, lacking much strength.
(b) Lack of dynamic resiliency.
(c) Angularity of shapes, confident in space.
(d) Practical.

CHAPTER 14

TESTS AND MATERIAL OBTAINED OTHER THAN THROUGH MOVEMENT OBSERVATION

The questionnaire

The questionnaire which was given to the teachers is shown below. It was formulated in this particular way so that the answers which the teachers gave could be related easily to those personality traits which it is possible to discern through movement. The aspects of personality and behaviour which are covered are as follows:

Relationships.
Adaptability (*see* comment below).
Will-power and drive.
Alertness and practicality.
"Dreaminess."
Reactions.
Thinking and reasoning.
Ability to invent, create or make original contributions.
Tolerance.
Enthusiasms.
Continuity of attention.
Attitude to authority, direction, orders and organisation.

Clearly many of these areas overlap, and the sub-divisions make an attempt to clarify attitudes to different people and in different circumstances.

Text of the questionnaire

Child's name   *Age*   *I.Q. if known*

General statement or summary of his/her personality characteristics and attributes.

(Please add remarks to any answer to make it more accurate.)

1. Is he co-operative with:

   (*a*) other children of same age
        group,
   (*b*) younger children,
   (*c*) older children,
   (*d*) those in authority?

2. (*a*) Is he isolated or gregarious?
   (*b*) Does his general tendency vary in any particular circumstance?

3. (*a*) Does he take the lead in group situations:

   with children of same age,
   with younger children,
   with older children?

   (*b*) Does he lead by being:

   domineering,
   unobtrusive?

4. Is he content to follow the lead of others:

   (*a*) of children of same age,
   (*b*) of younger children,
   (*c*) of older children,
   (*d*) of those in authority?

5. Does he make easy contacts with:

   (*a*) children of same age,
   (*b*) children younger,
   (*c*) children older,
   (*d*) adults?

   Has he many friends, or a chosen few?

   Would you assess that he is popular generally?

6. Is he shy?
   In what circumstances?

7. Is he timid or confident?
   In what circumstances?

8. (*a*) Is he an aggressive child?
   (*b*) To whom is he particularly aggressive?
   (*c*) Under what circumstances?

9. Is he sensitive to others?
Over-sensitive?

10. Is he too easily hurt or upset:

(*a*) by remarks of others?

(*b*) by situations?

11. (*a*) Is he tough and resilient?

(*b*) If so, is he physically as well as mentally tough?

12. (*a*) Is he emotionally stable or easily upset?

(*b*) Is he changeable or consistent?

(*c*) Under what circumstances?

13. (*a*) Is he adaptable?

(*b*) Is his outlook rigid, and unadaptable?

14. Is he strong-willed?
Under what circumstances?

15. Is he alert and practical, or rather dreamy?

(*a*) Is he practical:

(*i*) about everyday happenings and situations,

(*ii*) about objects and handling things?

(*b*) Is he dreamy when he should be practical, or does he balance these two attitudes efficiently?

(*c*) Is he dreamy in a positive way—imaginatively, creatively?

(*d*) Is he withdrawn, anxious or fearful?

16. Are his reactions quick and alert, or delayed (perhaps considered):

(*a*) to situations,
(*b*) to people,
(*c*) to direct orders?

17. If intellectually fairly able, can he see more than one point of view, or is he rather pinpointed in thinking?

18. Is he inventive or original in his attitudes to:

   (*a*) practical things (materials of all kinds),
   (*b*) stories (words, poems, etc.),
   (*c*) sound (percussion instruments, songs, music),
   (*d*) drama,
   (*e*) paint, clay, etc.,
   (*f*) numbers?

   In each case, does he prefer to work alone or with others?

   Under guidance, or without help?

19. Is he generally tolerant and open-minded, or intolerant and narrow?

20. Does he have sudden bursts of energy and enthusiasm:

   (*a*) lasting over a long period; can he continue to pay attention over a long period,
   (*b*) dying quickly away,
   (*c*) recharged in short bursts?

   About what?

21. Does he gradually build up energy and enthusiasm?
   About what?

22. Is he fairly *even* in attitude to life?
Is he even complacent in accepting and responding to daily happenings?

23. Does he enjoy or resent direct organisation?
From whom?

24. Does he respond willingly to direct orders?
From whom?

It now appears that Question 14 should have defined "will-power" in more detail, as the teacher interpreted this in a mainly negative way as "strong-willed" against authority.

The Children's Apperception Test (C.A.T.)

This test was designed by Leopold Bellak and Sonya Sorel Bellak in 1966.*

The children are shown pictures and asked to tell stories about them. A small portable tape-recorder was used in order to obtain a full record of the children's responses and some of the transcripts are given in full in Appendix II.

I.Q. test

The test used was the Stanford–Binet Intelligence Scale—Third Revision Form L–M (Terman & Merrill).

Child Scale B

Reports from teachers (*see* illustration on page 151).
Over 9 points on this scale indicates possible maladjustment, and some hint is given whether the problem is one of anti-social behaviour or neurotic behaviour.

---

* Publishers: C.P.S. Inc., P.O. Box 83, Larchmont, N.Y.

FOR OFFICE USE ONLY

CHILD SCALE B

TO BE COMPLETED BY TEACHERS

Name of Child: .... **School:** ....

....

Boy/Girl **Date of Birth:** .... **Form:**..

Below are a series of descriptions of behaviour often shown by children. After each statement are three columns: "Doesn't Apply," "Applies Somewhat" and "Certainly Applies." If the child definitely shows the behaviour described by the statement place a cross in the box under "Certainly Applies." If the child shows the behaviour described by the statement but to a lesser degree or less often place a cross in the box under "Applies Somewhat." If, **as far as you are aware**, the child does not show the behaviour place a cross in the box under "Doesn't Apply."

1. Please put ONE cross against EACH statement. Thank you.

Statement	Doesn't Apply	Applies Somewhat	Certainly Applies	FOR OFFICE USE ONLY
1. Very restless. Often running about or jumping up and down. Hardly ever still	☐	☐	☐	☐
2. Truants from school	☐	☐	☐	☐
3. Squirmy, fidgety child	☐	☐	☐	☐
4. Often destroys own or others' belongings	☐	☐	☐	☐
5. Frequently fights with other children	☐	☐	☐	☐
6. Not much liked by other children	☐	☐	☐	☐
7. Often worried, worries about many things	☐	☐	☐	☐
8. Tends to do things on his own—rather solitary	☐	☐	☐	☐
9. Irritable. Is quick to "fly off the handle"	☐	☐	☐	☐
10. Often appears miserable, unhappy, tearful or distressed	☐	☐	☐	☐
11. Has twitches, mannerisms or tics of the face or body	☐	☐	☐	☐
12. Frequently sucks thumb or finger	☐	☐	☐	☐
13. Frequently bites nails or fingers	☐	☐	☐	☐
14. Tends to be absent from school for trivial reasons	☐	☐	☐	☐
15. Is often disobedient	☐	☐	☐	☐
16. Has poor concentration or short attention span	☐	☐	☐	☐
17. Tends to be fearful or afraid of new things or new situations	☐	☐	☐	☐
18. Fussy or over-particular child	☐	☐	☐	☐
19. Often tells lies	☐	☐	☐	☐
20. Has stolen things on one or more occasions	☐	☐	☐	☐
21. Has wet or soiled self at school this year	☐	☐	☐	☐
22. Often complains of pains or aches	☐	☐	☐	☐
23. Has had tears on arrival at school *or* has refused to come into the building this year	☐	☐	☐	☐
24. Has a stutter or stammer	☐	☐	☐	☐
25. Has other speech difficulty	☐	☐	☐	☐
26. Bullies other children	☐	☐	☐	☐

Are there any other problems of behaviour?

....

....

Signature: Mr./Mrs./Miss .... ☐

How well do you know this child?

Very well ☐   Moderately well ☐   Not very well ☐   ☐

THANK YOU VERY MUCH FOR YOUR HELP

	Score	Anti-social Score	Neurotic Score
Cheryl	15	–	6
Lenny	18	6	–
Josie	10	3	1
Brigit	7	–	5
Patrick	33	8	5
Arnold	15	–	4
Richard	17	–	6
Katie	10	6	2
Tom	23	6	4
Jane	18	–	6
Sam	14	5	2
Edith	1	–	–

This questionnaire is devised, I understand, to attempt mass screening of children for possible maladjustment. From my knowledge of the children, these results are accurate in some cases: Edith is a stable and happy child; Patrick is severely disturbed; Jane is anxious and neurotic; Brigit is, however, a quiet but extremely unhappy child, and I think probably very disturbed; and Arnold is also quiet and highly disturbed. The questionnaire highlights the outgoing, aggressive children more obviously than the retiring quiet ones, particularly those who are rather passive and withdrawn. Nevertheless, this test reflects some of the problems which are in this particular group.

CHAPTER 15

INDIVIDUAL REPORTS ON EACH CHILD AND COMPARISON OF MATERIAL

In order to obtain a full picture of the child, it would be better to re-read the full assessment (Chapter 13) before the extracts, which are headed for comparison with other reports. The extracts alone do not give the balanced picture of the child.

1. Cheryl: age: 8 years 3 months; I.Q.: S–B 114; Scale B score: 15 (with high (6/8) neurotic tendencies

It appears that Cheryl has a higher I.Q. than her class teacher suspected from her attainment and behaviour.

From assessment through movement	*Class teacher's report*	*Comments from B Scale*
RELATIONSHIPS Because of her lack of intuitive perception, her emotional insecurity and lack of rhythmical adaptability, she has no confidence, sensitivity or awareness to make easy relationships. Given the opportunity she might well develop a strong emotional attachment to someone who showed her affection. Lack of initiative and sensitivity makes her unable to lead or even actively co-operate with others, except in the sense of obeying orders, or falling in with routine suggestions. Usually submissive. Has great need for affection, which she is unable to express—will lead to emotional outbursts—could be led easily by stronger character—unable	Generally co-operative with other children of same age and with those in authority. She avoids older children. Not popular, but not particularly shy. Isolated, especially in playground. Does not make easy contacts with children or adults —has few friends. Never takes the lead with other children— content to follow lead of others and of the teacher. Presents a timid appearance, but is not in fact. Is not aggressive. Sensitive, but not over-much.	**Q.5.** Does not fight with other children. **Q.6.** Is not much liked by other children. **Q.8.** Does things alone—rather solitary. **Q.26.** Does not bully other children. **Q.4.** Does not destroy property of others.

From assessment through movement	Class teacher's report	Comments from B Scale
to direct her strong emotional drives. Lack of mental discernment inhibits her own assessment of situations.	Easily hurt or upset by remarks of others. Not tough or resilient. Emotionally stable or consistent in most circumstances.	

High degree of agreement on relationship questions—teacher agreed later that her "co-operative" statement really meant not obstructive—and she goes on to describe her as solitary and with few friends, not much liked. "Sensitive" was also used with a slightly different meaning—movement assessment in the sense of sensitivity or awareness of others—teacher's report, being sensitive about her appearance, habits, etc.

ADAPTABILITY		
Lacks both bodily and mental adaptability—shows a stolid, static and unchanging attitude. Lack of rhythmical changes even in small things makes her unable to adjust easily to people or situations.	Is not adaptable. Tends to be unadaptable or rigid.	**Q.1.** Is not restless or **Q.3.** Squirmy or fidgety.

General agreement.

WILL-POWER AND DRIVE		
She has a certain degree of energy which easily disperses into heaviness. Strength and purpose usually appears with tension and rigidity, rather than with positive outflowing. Could be stubborn on occasions.	Is not strong-willed.	**Q.15.** Is not often disobedient.

After reading the movement assessment, the teacher said that Cheryl is very obstinate with her mother. Agreement on other aspects.

ALERTNESS AND PRACTICALITY		
Lacks alertness, never really practical except in the crude sense of getting along with everyday situations. Effort quickly	Fussy more than practical.	**Q.18.** Not fussy or over-particular.

From assessment through movement	Class teacher's report	Comments from B Scale
dies away; therefore there is no follow-through. Action is often undirected and futile.		

Agreement on lack of practicality—disagreement in same teacher's statement about being "fussy" is due to the different circumstances—*i.e.* fussing about rather than practical—but not fussily over-particular.

From assessment through movement	Class teacher's report	Comments from B Scale
DREAMY ATTITUDE 　　A negative, passive kind of dreaminess, rarely influencing her active life—rather interfering with practical living. 　　Anxiety, fear and insecurity show in her "nightmarish" dreaminess. Not likely to develop this dreaminess in a creative way, as there is too little active drive—but she could be helped to express and form some of this inner striving through creative work—colour-movement and words particularly.	Dreamy—often so when she should be practical. Can be anxious sometimes.	**Q.7.** Often worried, worries about many things. **Q.10.** Often appears miserable, unhappy, fearful or distressed. **Q.17.** Tends to be fearful or afraid of new things or new situations. **Q.22.** Often complains of aches and pains.

Agreement on "passive" dreaminess and anxiety.

From assessment through movement	Class teacher's report	Comments from B Scale
REACTIONS 　　Reactions are slow and yet not considered. 　　Lacks intuitive and spontaneous reactions to a person or situation—enjoys strong, positive lead from, *e.g.*, teacher. This can stimulate some more positive and lively response temporarily.	Reactions are slow but not considered.	

Agreement.

From assessment through movement	Class teacher's report	Comments from B Scale

THINKING, REASONING ABILITY
    Practical reasoning—not much indication of potential abstract thinker. Emotional and sensual reactions cloud her clear thinking. Better probably in one-to-one situation, where attention is held.
    Subtleties are not recognised.
	Not intellectually able.	

(N.B.—S–B. I.Q. 114.) Seemingly does not use her above average intelligence.

From assessment through movement	Class teacher's report	Comments from B Scale

ABILITY TO INVENT, CREATE OR MAKE ORIGINAL CONTRIBUTIONS
    Very little active or latent powers for invention, though if sufficient stimulus could be given, she could find considerable outlet and satisfaction in manipulating materials—clay, paint, etc.—and in movement, and with words.
    Lacks confidence to try alone.
	Not inventive in practical things, in stories, sound, drama, paint or number. Tends to copy, needs help all the time.	

General agreement about her present lack of originality, etc.

From assessment through movement	Class teacher's report	Comments from B Scale
TOLERANCE Tolerant in a passive kind of way—not much affected by others, except when emotionally hurt.	Tolerant.	

Agreement.

From assessment through movement	Class teacher's report	Comments from B Scale
ENTHUSIASMS AND CONTINUITY OF ATTENTION Routine—can continue a task if given continuous stimulation —but own impetus soon dies away. Passive rather than enthusiastic, though there can be a	No sudden bursts of enthusiasm. Cannot continue to pay attention over a long period in class. Tends	**Q.16.** Has poor concentration or short attention span.

From assessment through movement	*Class teacher's report*	*Comments from B Scale*
short-term interest if emotionally caught. Attention wanders.	to be complacent in accepting daily happenings. Fairly even attitude.	
Agreement.		
ATTITUDE TO AUTHORITY, DIRECTION, ORDERS AND ORGANISATION Is secure under direct guidance and routine activity. Unlikely to resent reasonable and kindly orders. Stubbornness might be shown if resenting someone.	Accepts direct organisation from adults and responds willingly.	**Q.15.** Is not disobedient.
Agreement.		
GENERAL COMMENTS Physically overweight. Movement limited in range and variety. A heavy, even attitude, lacking elevation, and stressing down-to-earth movements. Fairly vague and undefined shape awareness, inturned and narrow except when stimulated from outside. Few developed drives—lives in an inner world, with just sufficient adaptation to outer things to get along. Insecurity is inhibiting what development is possible. Without special help, this will probably become progressively worse.	Size hinders development of personality. It inhibits her movement and activities and makes her feel separate from the other children. She is full of moans and groans about small knocks and cuts. Most of the time she is lethargic, but will try on the apparatus and in expressive movement classes. She very rarely runs voluntarily.	**Q.22.** Often complains of aches and pains.

There is overall agreement from the teacher with the assessment made from observing Cheryl's movement. I would question the final comment from the teacher that her size alone causes the feelings of separation from others and her inhibition, and wonder whether this gross over-eating resulting in her excess weight is not the result of her emotional instability. (Medical reports say that there is nothing organically wrong.)

The examples of her writing* (taken from a book) show the tendency to lose interest and not even finish a sentence. The painting shows quite a bold use of colour, but little form, whereas her two drawings—a man and woman—show quite an awareness of size and form in the human body.

C.A.T. findings

The illumination of personality traits which are obtained from this test is more related to the background reasons for attitudes, fears, etc., than can be obtained from an assessment through movement. In Cheryl's case, support is given to many of the statements made by the teacher and by the assessment, and some basis for her attitudes can be discerned.

Firstly, the stories showed how garrulous was her speech. (Transcripts of her stories and an analysis are given in Appendix II.) She had a kind of rambling speech, artificially dramatic, alternating with long, even use of the voice, which became worse as the pictures progressed. She certainly seemed to hang out the stories unnecessarily, perhaps to keep a hold of this unusual personal attention which she was receiving.

From the stories, we can see that Cheryl's anxieties are based on tension and conflict with her mother, and a general picture is painted of an unhappy child, feeling herself deprived of love (using food as a substitute), desiring her father's attention, but giving no indication of receiving satisfaction from either of her parents; alternating between slyness, playing safe and withdrawing, and occasional disobedience and punishment. Her fear of physical hurt is seen; her obsession with food, a feeling of being at the mercy of others, and the desire to help her father seem to be her main themes. Her fantasy of being a princess is an example of her day-dreaming, and her idea that when she is grown up there will be no more trouble. An unsympathetic environment is painted, particularly the dominating mother, but a dispersed, meandering wandering through this situation is her way of coming to terms with the problems.

---

* The teacher showed me various examples of the children's normal class work and the reports occasionally refer to this when it has any bearing on some aspect of the movement assessment.

General conclusions

All the questionnaires and tests, therefore, support the results obtained through the movement observation and analysis approach. The teacher's summaries are the nearest to the movement findings, because of the form of the questionnaire which directed her comments.

The C.A.T. covers an area of knowledge about the child which is different in some ways; specific causes of tension or anxiety can be seen, personal relationships (particularly at home) are revealed—and a general stage of emotional development can be assessed. This can pinpoint areas in which the family and the child need help, how, for instance, the environment could perhaps be influenced and how the child might be helped in psychotherapy or play therapy.

Movement assessment does not make this same kind of investigation. As previously stated it highlights the child's own way of responding to situations, his own personal rhythms and initiating actions (which reflect his mental and emotional states) and shows a picture of the child as he is now—his areas of developed awareness, his limitations, his inhibitions and his gifts. By this knowledge, seen in movement terms, therapeutic guidance can be indicated directly from the assessment. For instance, Cheryl needs help in many areas of her personality, and some suggestions are listed below. These suggestions are listed as isolated aims, but the method of giving the therapy would not be by directly working on each aspect independently. The method is artistic and integrated, and adapted sensitively to each child.

(*a*) Integration of shadow movements with bodily movement.

(*b*) Extension of range and variety of movement combinations.

(*c*) Overcoming of weightiness, particularly as it is shown at the end of phrases as a fading away of intention and loss of attention.

(*d*) Development of greater mobility and adaptability.

(*e*) Development of sensitive lightness and discernment.

(*f*) Development of shape awareness.

(*g*) Increasing rhythmical awareness.

(*h*) Development of true sustainment, instead of a static slowness.

(*i*) A balancing of the inward flow of movement with an outwardly orientated flow.

All of these are inter-related, and therefore as one aspect changes, the whole balance is different, and a new situation arises. The aim would be to develop what latent capacities are there, to help Cheryl to cope with herself and her situation more positively and to attempt to alter some of her unfortunate habits by a general increased awareness. For instance, Cheryl's energy and drive become vague and weak, and therefore in order to help her concentration and drive, it would be desirable for her to gain greater mastery over her strength, and to avoid the easy lapsing into weakness which is her habitual pattern. This could be learned, *to some degree*, and would influence her self-mastery of a situation. Also, by avoiding vagueness, and retaining attention (in movement, by keeping her space awareness) her discernment would be increased, which in its turn would affect her attitudes to life. Similarly, with all the aspects listed, some development would be possible. How effective this would be is dependent on many other factors.

Every person has his own limits, some inherited, some acquired; every person has his own latent or actual gifts and the extent of change lies, obviously, within these limits. External factors can be so inhibiting that the child needs to be taken right away from his environment and it is obvious that in the discussion of any therapeutic treatment, consideration has to be given to all factors. Nevertheless, in all cases, development of movement must be an enrichment and lead to a greater degree of positive mastery and therefore ability to cope with life. As has been stated many times, this is not an artificial changing of symptoms, or superficial "acting" of a new movement pattern, imposed from outside.

Obviously the greater the range of help which Cheryl would have, the greater the impact. Whether she needs play therapy and psychiatric help, and how much the family situation could be helped directly by this, is another question.

2. Lenny: age: 8 years 2 months; I.Q.: not known (left before I tested the children); Scale B score: 18 (with high (6) anti-social tendencies)

From assessment through movement	Class teacher's report	Comments from B Scale
RELATIONSHIPS Uses good alternations of bound and free flow, but with jerky transitions. This will make any relationship (apart from a superficial one) difficult for him	Is not popular. Is not shy. Not usually co-operative with others (except class teacher), children or adults.	**Q.6.** Not much liked by other children.

From assessment through movement	Class teacher's report	Comments from B Scale
to manage—*i.e.* unpredictable alternations. Bound flow appears mainly in small apprehensive movements, while free flow (together with time) makes for liveliness and adaptability—but this is excessive and becomes changeability, with a phrase being held for only a very short period of time. Not very co-operative over a period, because of lack of concentration.	Appears gregarious, but is in fact isolated. Never takes the lead with others. Content to follow the lead of other children. Does not make easy contacts with other children and has no real friends. He is not aggressive nor sensitive to others—neither tough nor resilient, but not easily hurt.	Q.3. Squirmy and fidgety. Q.1. Very restless—hardly still. Q.7. Does not do things on his own. Q.26. Does not bully other children.
His movement is excessively sudden and light—which reveals tentativeness. It acts as a balance to his stronger, impactive actions. But these extremes are not yet brought into relationship with each other. Could sometimes be in conflict with others.	He likes to clown for the other children to laugh. Outwardly he appears to have little reaction to people or events. Forgets easily if reprimanded and cannot concentrate.	Q.4. Does not destroy property of others. Q.5. Frequently fights with other children.
Frequent repetitions of movements give indication of restlessness, and this is contrasted with weak giving way at end of phrases—*i.e.* no carrying through or persistency. Easily led.	Not easily upset but not stable. Consistently "will o' the wisp."	Q.11. Has tics or twitches.
Outward-flowing movements predominate—particularly associated with lightness. This indicates that his relationships will be light (superficial) but probably lively—even amusing (because of his sudden and rhythmical time sense).	Timid with adults and not very sure of himself.	Q.13. Frequently bites nails or fingers.
Not likely to stimulate anyone to follow his lead, certainly not at present, as he lacks follow-through and consistency. No doubt he takes up with anything and anyone within his reach. Quite aware of himself and re-		

From assessment through movement	Class teacher's report	Comments from B Scale
actions to his own activities— basically outgoing extrovert at superficial level.		
Lack of balance is seen in his body changeability of position— he has to move near the floor to gain balance as he lacks it within himself. Centre of gravity not used to gain stability. Easily knocked over, and recovers quickly.		
Not as confident as he might, casually, appear to be.		

High degree of agreement on relationship questions. He is too dispersed to be able to relate easily—but he could be helped a great deal to develop more integrated phrases and longer concentration periods. (He has already improved in this stable class environment.)

ADAPTABILITY		
Quick and jerky changes— often appearing meaninglessly. He is not adaptable, but very changeable. His flow and time combinations show a real latent possibility for harmonious adaptability to be developed.	"All over the place." Sometimes presents almost spastic appearance.	**Q.1.** Very restless. **Q.3.** Squirmy, fidgety child.

General agreement—probably too easily adaptable to changing moods and circumstances, and lacks self-discipline to be positively adapting. Easily led. ("Adaptable" in the questionnaire is used as a positive attribute.)

WILL-POWER AND DRIVE		
He has at times a good and well-developed impactive force, but it is not used with efficiency as his phrases die away, and he gives up, switching to something else.	Not strong-willed.	**Q.15.** Is not often disobedient.

From assessment through movement	Class teacher's report	Comments from B Scale
His quick changes and short-lived concentration detract from application of will-power and drive.		

Latent ability could be developed (doesn't want to write as "Daddy can't").

From assessment through movement	Class teacher's report	Comments from B Scale
ALERTNESS AND PRACTICALITY He is quite alert to what is going on around him (uses time/space combinations easily), but not very practical (rarely uses time/weight/space combinations). Mainly not utilised practically as he is easily "alerted" to something else. Attention always switching.	Unable to concentrate and is not practical in everyday actions.	**Q.16.** Poor concentration. Short attention span.

Agreement on lack of practicality.

From assessment through movement	Class teacher's report	Comments from B Scale
DREAMY ATTITUDE Few indications of weight and flow combinations—the time element comes into his movement too frequently to allow dreaminess (no positive outflowing to indicate creative or imaginative attitude—though some potential development). Light-bound flow is more indicative of tentative apprehension than of active daydream state.	Not dreamy. Not imaginative. Not creative. He can be temporarily fearful—facially at least. Never anxious or withdrawn —extrovert.	**Q.10.** Does not appear miserable or unhappy. **Q.7.** Does not worry. **Q.17.** Is not fearful or afraid. **Q.19.** Tells lies. **Q.20.** Has stolen things. **Q.13** Frequently bites nails.

General agreement though I question the teacher's "never anxious or withdrawn," and this is also at variance with Q.13, "frequently bites nails." I think, from the movement picture, he covers up well his lack of security and his apprehensions, with a gay façade. (The teacher was not subsequently questioned.)

From assessment through movement	Class teacher's report	Comments from B Scale
REACTIONS Jerky suddenness shows over quick reactions—often before thinking. Could be intuitive if general personality were more harmonious.	Quick but unthinking in attitude to situations, people and orders.	
Agreement.		
THINKING, REASONING ABILITY Uses space neutrally in body attitudes, showing a certain awareness of himself and surroundings. Has ability for direct attention—but it is short-lived, and lacking transitions to new focus. In descriptive gestures, shows clear pinpointed ideas. Lacks flexibility in shadow movements and therefore does not see many sides of a problem. Certainly not an abstract thinker and may be below average, but has latent capacities which could be developed—his changeability will always be against his self-mastery.	Not intellectually able.	
General agreement.		
ABILITY TO INVENT, CREATE OR MAKE ORIGINAL CONTRIBUTIONS Very little of his fairly rich movement vocabulary is brought to any external drive—it is dis-	Not original or inventive in any way. Cannot work with others.	

From assessment through movement	Class teacher's report	Comments from B Scale
sipated without purpose. Latent powers of imagination have no chance with present instability.		

General agreement. Statement "Can't work with others" apparently contrasts with answer to Q.8, "Is not solitary—does not tend to do things alone"—but in fact, both are true—he neither works alone, nor is he really co-operative.

From assessment through movement	Class teacher's report	Comments from B Scale
TOLERANCE His movement shows such variation and inconsistency that he is likely to be unaware of others and therefore generally tolerant in a sense of not intolerant.	Generally tolerant.	**Q.8.** Is not solitary —does not tend to do things alone.

Agreement.

From assessment through movement	Class teacher's report	Comments from B Scale
ENTHUSIASMS AND CONTINUITY OF ATTENTION Sudden enthusiasms are shown in quite strong drive with suddenness—but it quickly disperses. Occasionally, he shows an impactive, directed enthusiasm which should be fostered and recharged to help him concentrate. Consistently variable!	Enthusiasms quickly die away—about everything. Is fairly complacent in accepting life.	**Q.16.** Has poor concentration or short attention span.

Agreement.

From assessment through movement	Class teacher's report	Comments from B Scale
ATTITUDE TO AUTHORITY, DIRECTION, ORDERS AND ORGANISATION His own drives and energy are so dispersed that direct orders probably give him some security. General "light" attitude would make him unresentful.	Accepts direct orders from almost anyone and responds willingly.	**Q.15.** Is not disobedient.

From assessment through movement	Class teacher's report	Comments from B Scale
GENERAL COMMENTS This boy's fairly rich variety and range of movement qualities should mean that he has a store of gifts to call up. But he uses them so inefficiently, has no transition from one to another, develops few external actions, and lacks space awareness and concentration, so that they are of little value to him. He lacks balance within himself, needing to revert to early childhood action of touching the floor to gain balance. Many of his gifts are therefore disturbances and negative, rather than positive, and he will need much help to gain any degree of integration.	Lenny is usually "all over the place," easily led, indulged in at home, he giggles at anything. Lenny is very spoilt by his father.	

Unfortunately Lenny left the school before I could make the C.A.T. and I.Q. tests. I include his report, as it was one of the first I did, and shows an interesting pattern from the movement point of view—*i.e.* not a limited range of movement (as Cheryl) but a fairly rich variety, with little chance for all the potential gifts to be effective. It would have been interesting to see how the C.A.T. would illuminate the background of his life, and indicate some of the causes of his disturbances.

The movement assessment gives some indications where Lenny would need help in developing his personal integration, in order to be able to use his capacities.

General conclusions

(*a*) His gift of outgoing flow could be developed into real relatedness by an improvement in concentration, *i.e.* longer phrases; purposeful development of attention (space effort); and holding on to a phrase at the end instead of weakly giving way.

(*b*) Transitions need transforming from jerky and disconnected to connected and smoother subtleties.

(*c*) Alternations of mobility (time and flow sequences) with stability (weight and flow) need mastering—together with central body awareness of strength and control.

(*d*) Time rhythmic sense is extreme, and would benefit from mastery of more normal degrees—particularly suddenness.

(*e*) Shape awareness could be expected to develop after the above areas, but would need help.

(*f*) Development of the weight/flow combinations, through artistic and creative work. Movement particularly would help this hyperactive boy.

The inconsistency and variability is typical of his coping attitude to life. The above areas where he needs help could not be tackled over a long period, and perhaps with limited hope of success, unless such therapy could be integrated with other forms of help.

3. Josie: age: 8 years 2 months; I.Q.: S–B 116; Scale B score: 10 (antisocial 3; neurotic 0)

From assessment through movement	Class teacher's report	Comments from B Scale
RELATIONSHIPS Quite outgoing personality, possibility for positive co-operative work, only hindered by her sometimes impatient and sudden unpremeditated actions. She can make quick decisions, and her friendly open attitude would indicate capacity for leadership—perhaps at present rather dictatorial, but could develop more sensitively as she gets older. She usually carries through an action once started, and this will help to inspire confidence, but on some occasions she can lose confidence and withdraw suddenly. This latter action	Generally co-operative and gregarious. Takes the lead with others in class, and sometimes with older children also. Leads by dominating rather than unobtrusively. Content to follow lead of adults and older children—not very much with others of own age. Makes easy contacts with both children and adults and has many friends. Is popular and not shy.	**Q's. 1 and 3.** Very restless, squirmy and fidgety child. **Q.6.** Is liked by other children. **Q.8.** Is not solitary.

From assessment through movement	*Class teacher's report*	*Comments from B Scale*
could occur if ideas other than her own rather forthright ones are introduced when once started on a project. Human contacts straightforward, though hastiness will hinder real understanding. Happy to follow firm lead of adults. Likes to work with others.	Confident in both work and play. Not aggressive—rather spiteful to other children if her plans are upset. Averagely sensitive to others. Not often upset by others. Generally emotionally stable and consistent.	**Q.5.** Frequently fights with children.

General agreement on relationships—the frequent fighting as reported on Scale B report should be balanced by report from teacher—"not aggressive—sometimes spiteful"—also relates to movement assessment of loss of confidence and withdrawal if her predetermined plans are upset.

ADAPTABILITY		
Adaptable in practical actions, but more limited in adapting to new ideas once a decision has been made. In coming to decisions, good mental adjustability and ability to adapt, *i.e.* good with general ideas. Will enjoy new situations.	Is adaptable.	

Movement assessment qualifies the statement in relation to decisions already made.

WILL-POWER AND DRIVE		
Strong-willed both in practical situations and in relation to other people. Nevertheless, has occasional weakenings which would make for unexpected "giving up."	Strong-willed—mainly when dealing with children of same age.	**Q.15.** Sometimes disobedient.

Movement assessment qualifies general statement.

From assessment through movement	Class teacher's report	Comments from B Scale
ALERTNESS AND PRACTICALITY Alert and bright and decisive in practical everyday situations. Quite efficient in handling materials, and has a good range of manual dexterity. (Sensitivity in relation to people needs developing with her quickness.)	Practical about everyday happenings and handling objects. Seldom dreamy.	
Agreement.		
DREAMY ATTITUDE Very little dreamy side to her nature is revealed—either passively (as day-dreaming) or actively (as creative drive). Occasionally appears as fearfulness and inturned withdrawal. She is therefore probably not entirely as secure as she might superficially appear to be. This anxiety might account for her sudden withdrawals from a situation.	Seldom dreamy. Anxious very occasionally.	**Q. 12.** Frequently sucks thumb or finger. **Q. 7.** Sometimes worried, or worried about many things. Q. 17. Not fearful of new situations or new things.
Agreement.		
REACTIONS Quick reactions—sometimes over-hasty; at other times she shows a good considered response.	Quick and alert. Apt to make mistakes because she is too quick.	
THINKING AND REASONING ABILITY She is a practical rather than an abstract thinker. Tends to be pinpointed and accurate rather than contemplative and seeing all round a problem. Accuracy can	Tends to be pinpointed in her thinking.	

From assessment through movement	Class teacher's report	Comments from B Scale
be spoiled by over-hastiness and jumping to a conclusion. Has a certain degree of independence. Probably just above average I.Q.		

Agreement: seems to work to her capacity. (N.B.—S–B I.Q. 116.)

| ABILITY TO INVENT, CREATE OR MAKE ORIGINAL CONTRIBUTIONS
    Not essentially very creative in her attitudes, though shows good ability for inventiveness and ability to manipulate materials—probably also words. Has wide range of openness to aural, visual and touch sense impressions. | Inventive and original in attitude to practical things, stories, sound, drama, paint and clay. Not so with numbers. Prefers to work with others. | |

General agreement: movement comment was based on the fact that her ability to invent is rather a manipulation, than from a weight/flow inner surging.

| TOLERANCE
    Not very tolerant at present, but has latent capacity to develop this to a greater degree. | Leans towards intolerance. | |

Agreement.

| ENTHUSIASMS AND CONTINUITY OF ATTENTION
    Sudden strong bursts of energy show that she works rather from repeatedly charged enthusiasms than from a sustained or regular even drive.
    Attention is directed and retained for periods when strong drive persists—there is sufficient long-term stability for her to return and rework an idea. | Is enthusiastic and is able to pay attention if really interested. Recharges enthusiasms in short bursts. Interested in anything new. Does not gradually build up energy, tends to be erratic, not complacent. | Q.16.
Has good concentration. |

From assessment through movement	Class teacher's report	Comments from B Scale
She has a fairly wide range of interests, and would enjoy most new activities—with possible exception of figures and abstract ideas.		
Agreement.		

ATTITUDE TO AUTHORITY, DIRECTION, ORDERS AND ORGANISATION
    Neither subservient nor resentful of being organised if she respects person and can see the point of it all.
    Independent to a fair degree, and self-contained attitude (though with reservations, already mentioned, of insecurity).
	Resents it from children. Will accept from adults.	Q.15.
		Sometimes disobedient.

Agreement.		
GENERAL COMMENTS Bodily compact and small—well controlled, with ability for mobility and stability. Uses centre of levity easily and frequently but not entirely secure always in elevation. Good body awareness, stressed practically. Good rhythmic awareness. Mainly outgoing —reasonably self-aware and confident, though occasional fears show through. Good range of capacities, not yet all developed. Reasonably harmonious development generally, though frequently over-hasty. Needs help in some directions as above.	Josie is a sharp quick little girl. Often leads the other children. Fairly self-confident. Apt to make mistakes because she is too quick. Gets enthusiastic and loves talking, which she does very well.	

There is almost complete agreement between the two assessments —both indicate the over-sudden and precipitate actions, and the apprehensions which sometimes show through her normal liveliness and self-containment.

Josie's drawings and paintings show an expected lively use of colour and pattern (*i.e.* expected because of her lively rhythmical ability). Writing is practical and relatively efficient.

C.A.T. findings

Efficient, average length stories, with predominantly literal interpretations of domestic happenings. Josie was agreeable to make up stories, and enjoyed her session, speaking with liveliness and fluency (this relates to rhythmic sense, and flow ability). No outstanding conflicts were revealed—she identified mainly with children in the stories, and in different situations they behaved well—naughtily—spitefully—cleverly—defiantly, or were unfortunate ... the full range perhaps of her personal experience. Parents seemed generally to combine authority with justice—she made one oblique attack on their going out and leaving children. Generally the family appeared stable—a stranger might be a threat—but parents protective if sometimes severe—in fact, varying between lenient and friendly, and dominating.

In general, a picture of a realistic, reasonably happy child, with clear thought processes, and only minor disturbances of growing up.

General conclusions

All the questionnaires and tests, therefore, seem to support the results obtained through movement. The high(ish) score of 10 on Scale B does not mean that the child is necessarily maladjusted—in any case, a borderline score.

In addition to the comments above, we can see certain areas of movement development which will help Josie. From the assessment she does not appear to be maladjusted or anxious or anti-social in any serious sense. Any help which can be given can well be done through the general educational system—and the following comments on special movement help should be incorporated within the class lesson of movement and all creative work in the school.

(*a*) Build on her capacity for rhythmical awareness to help mastery of greater range of suddenness (*i.e.* she needs the intermediate range as well as excessive) with directness in responses.

(*b*) Development of greater flexibility with free flow—especially within body attitude.

(*c*) Development of central body grip with strength rather than bound flow—this will increase stability.

(*d*) Development of light sustainment—to help sensitive fine touch in relationships—at present latent.

Most of the above suggestions could be developed in and through group work, which would also help her to develop more sensitive awareness of others. There is no indication that she requires any therapeutic help. By a generally more confident and sensitive development, many other minor areas of tension or distortion will fall into place.

4. Brigit: age: 8 years 4 months; I.Q.: S–B 134; Scale B score: only 7 (with 5/8 neurotic tendencies). (*See* comments, pp. 151 and 178.)

From assessment through movement	Class teacher's report	Comments from B Scale
RELATIONSHIPS Relationships will be difficult because of her extreme inward bound flow. Gentle sensitivity makes her extremely aware of other people, and her tentativeness means that she is happier with a few people rather than crowds or large numbers. Timidity and withdrawal is excessive so that any opposition or aggression will upset her. Tends to be isolated. Obviously she has no leadership ability and she will be relieved and content to follow, and avoid friction—to remain unobtrusive. Normal aggressiveness has been suppressed, so that a tight rigidity takes hold of her instead of a healthy strength of resistance.	Is co-operative generally. Isolated most of the time, especially in large group activities. Plays with others at play time. Never takes the lead. Content to follow lead of other children and adults. Does not make easy contacts with children or adults. Accepted by others rather than popular. Shy and timid in most circumstances, even with adults she knows. Not aggressive. Sensitive to others.	**Q.8.** Does things alone—rather solitary. **Q.5.** Does not fight with other children. **Q.26.** Does not bully other children nor **Q.4.** Destroy their property.

Agreement between assessments clearly shown.

From assessment through movement	Class teacher's report	Comments from B Scale
ADAPTABILITY She has considerable potential or latent capacity for adapt-ability, but cannot utilise it—the extreme inhibition of bound flow tension stops any lively adapt-ability. (This is different from a rigidity of resistance which is positive and anti-change.) (*See* Cheryl.) Lack of rhythmicality also supports this.	Is "carried along" rather than adaptable.	**Q.1.** Is not restless. **Q.3.** Is not squirmy or fidgety. **Q.17.** Tends to be afraid of new things or new situations.
Agreement.		
WILL-POWER AND DRIVE Cannot utilise her strength of movement, because it gets diverted into bound flow, in-wardly directed (as previously discussed). Isolated body move-ments reveal lack of central will-power—very narrow holding of hips and shoulders—shallow breathing.	Is not strong-willed.	**Q.15.** Is not dis-obedient.
Agreement.		
ALERTNESS AND PRACTICALITY A large range of externalised drives (contrast this with Lenny), and an alert, practical combina-tion of space/time, reveals her good manual and practical abili-ties—almost as though she has taken refuge in at least doing something well. Her rhythm of rather dull evenness means that she works persistently and routinely—but she has a great	Is practical about everyday happenings and situations and about handling ob-jects. Rather formal.	

From assessment through movement	Class teacher's report	Comments from B Scale
deal of latent vitality and rhythmicality which is unable to be utilised.		

Agreement.

From assessment through movement	Class teacher's report	Comments from B Scale
DREAMY ATTITUDE Weight/flow attitude is mainly excessively bound and inwardly orientated—revealing anxiety, fear or inhibition, rather than a flowing day-dreaminess. Attention could wander because of this, but in practical situations, the security of action will give her necessary support.	Rather dreamy outwardly but practical if called for. Shy and anxious at times.	Q.7. Often worried—worries about many things. Q.10. Sometimes appears miserable, unhappy, tearful or distressed. Q.17. Tends to be fearful or afraid of new things or new situations.

Agreement.

From assessment through movement	Class teacher's report	Comments from B Scale
REACTIONS Quick reactions to direct stimulus contrast with her considered judgments—both within her range. Very little spark and vitality shown in group situation where she is unobtrusive—occasionally her shadow movements show her potential (but crushed) liveliness and charm, i.e. when specially stimulated. Practically efficient.	Considered reactions to situations and to people. Quick reactions to direct orders.	

Agreement.

From assessment through movement	*Class teacher's report*	*Comments from B Scale*
THINKING, REASONING ABILITY More precise than flexible—quite able to use both when necessary. Clear spatial sense and awareness of self in space indicates clear ability for thought. This is frequently clouded by emotional tightness and therefore she is probably working well below her mental ability. Probably well above average I.Q.	Rather pinpointed—difficult to judge because she rarely can be drawn into discussion—individual or group.	

General agreement. The class teacher was surprised at her high I.Q. S–B I.Q. 134.) This was expected from the movement assessment because of her clear spatial ability, together with richness of movement combinations—both twos and threes.

ABILITY TO INVENT, CREATE OR MAKE ORIGINAL CONTRIBUTIONS All her creative or inventive capacities are so crushed under a flat, routine, defensive inhibition that no positive sign of them is likely to be seen. (This area is a possible way in which to relieve the excess tension.)	Not inventive or original in attitude to materials, sound, drama or colour, clay. Rarely so to stories and number. Prefers to work alone without help.	

Agreement.

TOLERANCE Tolerant in a passive way in everyday life—is probably bottling up resentments at a deep level towards near contacts, *i.e.* family, etc.	Tolerant, not necessarily open-minded.	

Agreement (not necessarily open-minded relates also to her narrowness of movement and lack of outward flow).

From assessment through movement	Class teacher's report	Comments from B Scale
ENTHUSIASMS AND CONTINUITY OF ATTENTION Would never dare to be enthusiastic—lack of buoyancy and enterprise is shown consistently. Evenness of rhythm is routine—good concentration usually.	I have rarely seen Brigit get enthusiastic about things. She "plods." Even on our trip to the Zoo there was very little display of excitement.	**Q.16.** Concentration and attention span normal.

Agreement.

ATTITUDE TO AUTHORITY, DIRECTION, ORDERS AND ORGANISATION Obedient, complying with all rules and organisation. Responds to direct orders efficiently and almost gratefully.	Accepts direct organisation from adults and older children and her peers. Responds willingly to direct orders from adults. (Impression is she has been brought up to be "an obedient child.")	**Q.15.** Is not disobedient.
GENERAL COMMENTS All the main movement patterns which Brigit uses are coloured by bound flow, inward and narrow movements of the body and isolated body actions. She has a good range of inner attitudes and drives, which implies a good intellectual ability and range of gifts—but they well may not be useful or used by her as she is so reserved and held back. A very disturbed child, showing acute signs of repression, fear and isolation ... this situation should be helped now.	Brigit is a very quiet withdrawn child. She copes well with work in class, but never appears to relax. I have found difficulty in making contact with her. She practically loses her voice with shyness. She is a sensible child. She lives with a large family in two rooms on a very busy main road. (Third of five girls.)	

N.B.—Brigit is a child who would not have been picked out by the Maudsley B Scale questionnaire, having less than 9 points (7), and I am quite sure that she is a very disturbed child (from the movement assessment). (This is an instance in which the B Scale seems to be better at sorting out the aggressive, or obviously neurotic, than these quiet, repressed children, as previously mentioned.)

The example of writing from her book shows the expected efficiency and evenness. Her drawings of family and her man and woman reveal exactly the shoulder tension and tightness in the upper part of the body which she experiences. The out-turning of the hands away from the arms held close to the sides of the body is a typical gesture of hypertension and inward-bound flow—facial expressions are glowering and discontented—the eyes of the *woman* (separate drawing) show apprehension, even fear.

C.A.T. findings

Throughout the first half of the session, Brigit rocked continuously forward and backward. She spoke in a flat, light voice, without much intonation—with long pauses (this would be expected, as these rhythms are her basic movement patterns, as shown above).

The main theme throughout was the relationship of child (or children) to parents—mainly mother (father only as "mother and father" or often shown as weaker than mother). The child needs and wants mother's love and attention—is resentful towards mother as it is not received—wishes death to mother—goes away from home (? in order to hurt and provoke love). Frequent reference also to death of children or child. Her own identification is with a child (either sex) against the mother's neglect (or against outside danger, fox, lion, etc.)—sometimes she dies—sometimes secure in mother's love. Inadequate to cope with others of varying attitudes. Pathetic last story of daughter dog who has to go away and physically damage herself in order to win mother's sympathy.

Her obvious main needs are for love and affection. She always introduces mother/father and outer danger. Frequently a punishment situation, and jealousy of others. An all-round conception of an insecure environment, where parents show preference for younger child (or physically damaged child)—jealousy towards younger children—friendliness to contemporaries.

Conflicts are in wanting love and affection from mother—hating harsh treatment and neglect—"some mothers look after their children" (piglets).

Anxieties about physical harm, about death of self and parents—lack and loss of love, of being deserted, being helpless, being locked away or sent to a "home." Running away, death wish—day-dreams of close love.

Altogether, the C.A.T. shows a supporting picture of an unhappy child in what she feels to be an unloving and insecure situation. She is tight, inhibited, shy and fearful.

General conclusions

Movement assessment shows her present state of being, her ways of coping with her problems—her use of efficient practical action for security—her obedience to avoid conflict—her withdrawal from others in fear, etc. Although working therapeutically in movement would not affect the basic problems, Brigit could be helped to cope with herself to some degree. If, of course, this could be part of a whole treatment, including the family (mother particularly), there could be great influence in this situation. Suggested areas which could be helped through movement both group and individual:

(*a*) The intense bound flow needs some releasing—probably initially by breathing and rhythmic help.

(*b*) A balancing of the inward flow by outer integration of isolated movements—the relationship of body parts to the centre, and to the centre of gravity.

(*c*) Encouragement of greater rhythmical excitement.

(*d*) Development of turning action.

(*e*) General integration of phrases, and transitions between phrases.

Any development and self-mastery in one area will affect the whole pattern, and I would suggest that for the best results, Brigit should work in a small group to start with. Certainly, she will not achieve her own potential either academically or in social and emotional integration, if nothing is done to help at this stage, as she is trapped in this tight cage of inhibition—all creative work in every medium would help.

5. Patrick: age: 7 years 9 months; I.Q.: S–B 104; Scale B score: 33 (antisocial, 8/8; neurotic, 5/8)

From assessment through movement	Class teacher's report	Comments from B Scale
RELATIONSHIPS Relatively non-existent at any level. His alternations of withdrawal and aggression typify his relationships, and his unpredictability is constant! He can barely co-operate, though given a sympathetic adult, he does respond somewhat. (By the time I had been visiting this class some months and he knew me, I found him co-operative enough to give S–B I.Q. test and C.A.T.) His movement patterns show such extremes that he is at the mercy of his inner moods, and lacks transitions from one to another. (*See* full assessment in Chapter 13.) Cannot lead others—nor willing to follow. Isolated. Aggressive at times.	Not co-operative with other children—only co-operative with myself on occasions. He will play sometimes in the playground, usually aggressively. Never co-operates in group work. Seldom takes the lead, then only in fighting. Does not follow others. No friends. Not popular. Withdrawn. Isolated —seldom varies though will now sit in circle for story at end of day.	**Q.4.** Destroys own and others' property. **Q.5.** Frequently fights. **Q.15.** Often disobedient. **Q.26.** Bullies other children. **Q.6.** Not much liked by other children. **Q.8.** Does things on his own—solitary.

Complete agreement.

ADAPTABILITY Patrick is too inturned and withdrawn to be readily able to adjust to new circumstances. His static holding of a position is one way in which he copes—a partial cutting off—another way is by aggressive lashing out, lacking control. (*See* general assessment.) He has infrequent moments of relative calm between these two extremes.	Not adaptable. He is open to persuasion sometimes.	**Q.1.** Very restless. Hardly ever still. **Q.3.** Often squirmy and fidgety.

Agreement—class teacher agrees that the restlessness alternates with withdrawn staticness.

From assessment through movement	Class teacher's report	Comments from B Scale
WILL-POWER AND DRIVE Extremes of alternations. Can be unmovable and ignore outer stimulus entirely—or can be actively resistant and stubborn and aggressive. However, none of this is positively used will-power to a purposeful end.	Can be strong-willed if he doesn't want to do something.	**Q.15.** Frequently disobedient.

Agreement.

ALERTNESS AND PRACTICALITY He can handle materials quite adequately, having a certain manual dexterity, when focused on an activity. His undeveloped shaping awareness, however, would preclude him at present from being really efficient in practical manipulation of materials—equally in manipulating ideas and thoughts. He has a fairly clear directional sense which saves him from completely submerging in feeling.	Practical about everyday happenings and situations. Tends to be clumsy sometimes in handling things.	**Q.18.** Fussy and over-particular.

General agreement.

DREAMY ATTITUDE He is frequently in a "timeless" situation—when he is almost hypnotised from inside—his dreaminess is not an indulging flow, but an inturned, excessive bound flow (also body shape concave) or erect, excessive bound flow (body shape convex).	Not balanced between dreamy and practical attitudes. Not dreamy in a positive creative way. Withdrawn and guarded. In the main, he finds difficulty in expressing himself	**Q.7.** Often worried —worries about many things. **Q.10.** Sometimes appears miser-

From assessment through movement	*Class teacher's report*	*Comments from B Scale*
Fearful, restrained, withdrawn (nightmarish) on some occasions. Never creatively free-flowing.	verbally, or with materials. Never gets enjoyment from music or singing. He will show originality sometimes in number.	able, unhappy, fearful or distressed. **Q.17.** Tends to be fearful of new things and new situations. **Q.22.** Sometimes complains of pains and aches.
Agreement.		
REACTIONS Extremes of (*a*) withdrawal and blankness, (*b*) excessively sustained and restrained, and (*c*) normal, direct, quick (in response (rare); in withdrawal (frequent)). Lacks any mastery over his reactions—no rhythmical alternations, nor transitions.	His reactions are quick if he feels he is being attacked. Otherwise tends to think about things.	
Movement assessment gives details of kind of responses and extremes—general agreement.		
THINKING, REASONING ABILITY Mostly these capacities are not utilised by him—they are latent and certainly available if not overwhelmed by his emotional conflicts. Space awareness and shape awareness could then develop. Attention is mainly direct, flexibility appears in body attitudes and as compensation—therefore they could be	He will see another point of view if explained to him. Cannot read or write. (six months later he was just beginning to read: age 8·3).	

From assessment through movement	Class teacher's report	Comments from B Scale
developed towards positive application. Certainly he cannot be using what mental ability he has and is no doubt very backward. Could well be above average I.Q. judging from his range of movement combinations.		

General agreement. N.B.—S–B I.Q. 104. (But it should be noted that I believe he could score much higher, as in the questions when encouragement and questions were allowed, he frequently gave the correct responses after first saying "Don't know." When this was not allowed—or a time limit was given, "don't know" meant that he had withdrawn. I am sure he often knew the answer.)

ABILITY TO INVENT, CREATE OR MAKE ORIGINAL CONTRIBUTIONS Lack of controlled or free outward flow will make him unable to participate well in creative work. Nevertheless, this is one way in which he could get some breakthrough for acceptable emotional outbursts—particularly in colour and clay. His stammer and general problem of speaking should improve with building of confidence (he spits as he talks and hangs his head down self-consciously), *i.e.* bound flow, inner tension prevail.	Finds difficulty in expressing himself verbally or with materials. Never gets enjoyment from music or singing. Sometimes original in number. Works alone, not with a group—is just beginning to ask for help.	

The assessment and the teacher's reports were done simultaneously—*i.e.* the child was at the same stage. Since these reports Patrick has developed a good deal, due to the class teacher's help and support, and also some speech therapy. He still basically has the same problems, but not so extreme when with this one teacher. With others, there is little change.

TOLERANCE Both tolerant and intolerant according to mood and moment,	Neither tolerant and open-minded nor in-	

From assessment through movement	Class teacher's report	Comments from B Scale
though tolerance is perhaps too positive a word for his passive acceptance.	tolerant and narrow —it depends upon his feelings at any given time.	

Agreement.

ENTHUSIASMS AND CONTINUITY OF ATTENTION Short-lived absorption . . . generally not enthusiastic— rather passive but all the forceful energy which is at present channelled into destructive aggression against himself and others, could gradually be diverted into interesting activities . . . *i.e.* he is not without good potential. Attention is often sustained, from a detached watching position. His whole diversified body/mind will have to be integrated before he can utilise his gifts.	On few occasions in class when his interest *is* caught, his enthusiasm dies away quickly. I have rarely seen Patrick get enthusiastic about anything. I think he considers himself a non-starter. He has sustained a desire to read to me since the beginning of the year when I took over the remedial readers. This may of course be only because of the attention received (written while he was still a non-reader).	**Q.16.** Has fairly poor concentration or short attention span.

General agreement. His persistency and general development have meant that he can now begin to read—very simply—which pleases him immensely.

ATTITUDE TO AUTHORITY, DIRECTION, ORDERS AND ORGANISATION He is too disturbed and disorganised in an active, fighting way to accept outside discipline	Mainly resents direction from anyone. Rarely responds will-	**Q.15.** Is often disobedient.

From assessment through movement	Class teacher's report	Comments from B Scale
easily. Will resist direct orders almost automatically.	ingly—especially to strangers.	

It was a measure of Patrick's progress that some months later he was willing to come alone with me to "help" me—with stories (C.A.T.) and to answer questions (S–B. I.Q.).

GENERAL COMMENTS		
Patrick shows his disturbances in extremes—as stated in his assessment. A breakthrough to some degree has been achieved by the class teacher during this year—but the basic patterns are still the same. Nevertheless, he has gained some confidence—begins to read and speak out. His elder brother in the class above is very aggressive and anti-social in a forthright way (*i.e.* not withdrawn or hesitant)—always on the verge of delinquency. Patrick reverts to very young child movements and habits to gain stability—in addition to his dispersed lack of cohesion bodily and mentally.	One older brother—twins of three years. Patrick is a very withdrawn child most of the time. Refusing absolutely to cooperate a lot of the time with adults and children. I personally find him a likeable child and he does respond to attention. He doesn't sulk so much as visibly detach himself from the situation/environment.	

There is agreement between the teacher's report and the movement assessment. The teacher knows this boy very well, having given him a great deal of special attention and help. This assessment was in fact done over two sessions (instead of the usual one) because during the first, Patrick sat cross-legged, body curled up, elbows on knees, gazing at the floor. In the second session he joined in for ten minutes, until a stimulus was too difficult for him—and he immediately sat down and withdrew again.

Patrick's writing is all copied, and shows lack of flow and consistency. Drawings are variable according to mood and day—his two men look like robots (he refused to draw a woman). His family drawing is interesting—he did this as a special gift for me, and was delighted when I accepted it and complimented him—he coloured one twin, and not the other (is he fonder of one than the other?). Style of drawing very young (done at 8·3 years).

C.A.T. findings

Throughout, Patrick was sitting quietly, never touched the pictures, spoke hesitantly and stared at the pictures all the time. No real stories—very withdrawn and non-committal—many "don't know" responses. After too long a pause I would ask a question, or try to encourage some involvement—without success. He made factual descriptions of the drawings—objects and animals—and withdrew at any question of emotion or involvement of characters.

Main theme was one of protestation of everything being all right —"They are happy"—or withdrawal—"I don't know." Little was given away—he identified perhaps with little ones—avoiding trouble (mouse) or getting sent away (monkey)—monkey escaped major hazard of tiger eating him—the dog was smacked although not guilty. Nothing introduced into the story not in the picture. The world is a problem—but nothing much revealed about how to cope with it (*i.e.* withdrawal).

Parental figures—father—strong—mother—not quite sure if she'll come—punishes without reason . . . but little real indication.

Nature of anxiety? Not revealed.

Defences—clearly repression—avoidance—denial.

All communication was delayed, slightly muffled . . . no real outcome of any action—frequent withdrawal.

It may be that there is more revealed in the stories than I have seen—but the picture of withdrawal from life is the basic one . . . As far as I can see, there is little revealed of the basic causes—every response is very guarded. Sometimes he makes conflicting statements—usually if I have asked a question—and then "Why?" Often his logic is obscure!

General conclusions

All the questionnaires and tests support the results obtained through observing Patrick's movements. This is particularly supported by the teacher's report—and she knows him more than usually well—and appears to understand his needs.

The kind of "therapy" which she is giving, *i.e.* a "holding" and supporting of his childishnesses, while encouraging progress and self-awareness, can only be commended. I would think that the boy will need some continuation after he leaves her class ... I would believe a good claim for psychotherapy could be made here, judging by his progress in the last months. Movement therapy, and all art forms, could help tremendously in integrating his dispersed attitudes. The list of his movement "needs" is of course, as stated before, a purely academic one—in the actual situation, all kinds of methods and mixtures and routes towards these ends would be made. I would start with individual therapy with Patrick—he needs the one-to-one relationship for quite some time—later bringing him into a small and then larger group. Movement aspects to be taken into account:

(a) Alternation of extremes—with transitions—at first a *pause*—then intermediate shapes, as he could cope.

(b) Gradual toning down of extremes towards more normal range—*i.e.* contrasting grades within same effort.

(c) Linking and joining of outward and inward flow.

(d) Practice and experience of body shapes—developing awareness of body image.

(e) Gradual introduction of rhythmical alternations and patterns—at first simple personal ones, gradually extending the range.

(f) Development of richer directional awareness, particularly balancing downward with upward, and opening, as well as forward.

(g) Shaping awareness—a later development (which could well develop of itself as other distortions become more balanced).

I should probably use percussion, which he could play at the beginning—to work from his practical ability—one of his few *active* gifts.

6. Arnold: age: 7 years 11 months; I.Q.: S–B 77; Scale B score: 15 (with neurotic tendencies 4/8)

From assessment through movement	Class teacher's report	Comments from B Scale
RELATIONSHIPS For all the reasons stated in his full assessment, Arnold has no real possibility to relate	Not co-operative with others—with teachers, in so far as he	Q.4. Never destroys property.

From assessment through movement	Class teacher's report	Comments from B Scale
positively to others (*see* p. 136). He can neither lead nor really follow. Lacks the positive drive necessary to make and maintain relationships. Isolate. Not aggressive—only very rarely is there any movement resembling a normal, strong outgoing action. Under strong provocation, he might react with some momentarily stronger (but mainly bound flow) force—but it quickly dies.	is able to remember what has been told him. Isolated—occasionally makes some contact in playground (short-lived). Never takes the lead. Does not even follow. Does not make easy contacts with anyone. Has no friends. Is unpopular. Is withdrawn most of the time—timid, not aggressive.	**Q.5.** Never fights with other children. **Q.8.** Tends to do things on his own—solitary. **Q.26.** Does not bully others. **Q.6.** Not much liked by other children (they ignore him).

Complete agreement that this child makes no contacts—is isolated and withdrawn.

ADAPTABILITY		
Unadaptable because of inner staticness—also because adaptability requires some co-ordinated adjustment which he lacks. Lacks rhythmical alternations between qualities which might have been positive adjustments, but which are so subdued that they are purposeless.	Not adaptable. Rigid outlook.	**Q.3.** Squirmy and fidgety.

Agreement.

WILL-POWER AND DRIVE		
No strength—undirected—no consistency.	I think he can be strong-willed on occasions.	**Q.15.** Never disobedient.

The class teacher agreed that Arnold never shows any strong will or drive to action in school . . . she has heard from his mother that he can be awkward at home.

From assessment through movement	Class teacher's report	Comments from B Scale
ALERTNESS AND PRACTICALITY Not alert. Practical only in minimal way. Can slowly dress, pass materials, etc.—but needs reminding.	Dreamy, not alert and practical.	

Teacher says, "I gather he is practical about everyday happenings at home" (from mother). This seems unlikely—probably very little is demanded.

DREAMY ATTITUDE Very frequent escaping into neutral weight/flow—only used positively when stronger/tense-bound flow, inwardly orientated, takes over (fearful, apprehensive, inhibited).	Often dreamy. Withdrawn, anxious and fearful—all three on occasions.	Q.7. Often worried, worries about many things. Q.17. Tends to be fearful or afraid of new things or new situations.

Agreement. Regularly wets the bed (never wets or soils at school).

REACTIONS Reactions vary between non-existent; very slow, but without considering; immediate response (automatic) and direct order.	Delayed reaction but not considered.	

Generally agreed—though movement assessment gives more detail of contrasts of response.

THINKING, REASONING ABILITY Very limited indeed—concentration poor in quality and soon veers away—energy weakens. Frequently shows phrases of complete illogicality and irrelevance to situation. Al-	Not intellectually able.	

From assessment through movement	Class teacher's report	Comments from B Scale
most no awareness of self in space or of spatial directions—shaping ability poor. Frequent split between directness/flexibility of one part of body and another. Likely to have low I.Q.—and he cannot easily use what abilities he has.		

Agreement—during the I.Q. test period, Arnold was occasionally quite coherent—showed some pattern awareness and interest—but this quickly faded and had to be recaught. Verbally, very illogical. (N.B.—S–B I.Q. 77.)

ABILITY TO INVENT, CREATE OR MAKE ORIGINAL CONTRIBUTIONS Not possible.	None. "Works" alone —will not ask for help.	
TOLERANCE Ignores others mainly.	Generally tolerant because he doesn't participate.	

Agreement.

ENTHUSIASMS AND CONTINUITY OF ATTENTION "Enthusiasm" is too strong a word for anything which catches his attention—he lacks the strength and suddenness to be enthusiastic. Any momentary drive fades rapidly and loses focus—except a strange kind of routine and mechanical persistency in his rhythms—repetition of an almost hypnotic type was seen.	Has no bursts of enthusiasm. Whatever there occasionally is quickly fades. Fairly even in attitude to life. "Accepts the role he thinks he has."	Q.16. Has poor concentration and short attention span.

General agreement.
Some months later I happened to see Arnold in the classroom, and he was

persistently weighing parcels on the scales—everything always dropped off, and he could not judge sizes and balance . . . this continued with a backward and forward walking to the parcels across the room for a long time—quite meaninglessly and to no apparent purpose. (This illustrates the mechanical repetition noted in movement phrases.)

From assessment through movement	Class teacher's report	Comments from B Scale
ATTITUDE TO AUTHORITY, DIRECTION, ORDERS AND ORGANISATION Cannot take an intelligent part. Responds mechanically to direct orders—ignores most other suggestions. Agreeable to react when he happens to tune into the situation. Wants to be left alone.	Responds willingly to direct orders, as a rule, usually from adults. Can resent direct organisation.	**Q.15.** Is not disobedient.

The resentment referred to by the teacher was, she said, more because it interfered with his isolation and inner activity than not wanting to participate. *See* also assessment comment under "Relationships": "under strong provocation, he may react with some momentarily stronger force, but it quickly dies." This seems to relate to the teacher's remarks.

GENERAL COMMENTS Arnold is pathetic, cowed, weak and small. His split attention, disconnected effort rhythms, irrelevant phrases (occasional focused attention) sum up his present position. He has just enough awareness to carry out the routine tasks of life and get himself to school, where he likes to be. His lack of body awareness and his unrelated movements give a clue to his dispersed and split mental/emotional life.	Arnold was at the beginning of the year completely isolated from the rest of the class. He has improved sufficiently to complain if others interfere with him. He is an enuretic and wets himself continually. He smells too. He is practically unable to concentrate at all. He reads the Ladybird reading scheme, but is unable to recognise words out of context.	

Since I made these observations, the educational psychologist has tested him, and says there is nothing wrong and no need for treatment—he is just a below average intelligence child, not quite E.S.N. Nevertheless, I would hold to my view that this boy is very deeply disturbed and in great need of help. (Scale B score of 15—as stated previously, this score seems low when the extent of his illness is seen.) Some examples of his writing show repetitive meaningless copying—his figure drawings are interesting and have a certain liveliness, with a fair degree of clarity of outline.

C.A.T. findings

All Arnold's responses were made in a flat voice, lacking dynamic —with broken phrases—long silences. Quite able to identify the animals. Sat passively through the session—frequently his attention wandered away. The full record of his stories shows his attitudes clearly.

His main theme was the danger from "outside." Relative security "inside" (house, room, ?self)—endings in death—stressing the finality of death. He also refers to food burning the chicks, which supports the view of an alien environment—?lack of security and love.

Usually he gave a detached chronical of events, without clear hero identification (once as small monkey or small dog).

His main needs:

(a) To be secure—either stay indoors, in a room, or be killed.

(b) Figure of hunter frequently introduced—leading to the death of the animal. Picture of death repeatedly. Once introduced "I" who was antagonistic to brothers and sisters, killed them and committed suicide. Once the hunter was killed (only after the question "Which would you prefer?" as the ending to a story when two alternatives were given).

He has a picture of an unfriendly alien world outside—always a hunter waiting to kill, usually successfully. Quite matter-of-fact tone of voice in reporting these deaths. He completely accepted the inevitability of these situations.

Parental figure—father seen as inadequate, he showed little concern. One story of children in parents' bed led to suicide in the dark. Never any rescue by parents. His anxieties were shown to be with death, with lack of love—injury (not deformity)—being overpowered and helpless (related to death)—frequently of being killed and eaten.

His main defences are complete submission to circumstances. Many times, the severe penalty of death was quite unrelated to crime. Death is the only possible future—a detached acceptance of the fact. Thought sequences muddled.

General conclusions

All the questionnaires and tests, therefore, combine to show a deeply disturbed child, with fairly low I.Q. (certainly at present, what mental ability he has is not adequately used). I do not believe in this situation that any one therapy—say, movement—alone will have any great influence. If any help can be given it would seem necessary that combined medical, psychological and environmental approach be given. Within such teamwork, movement therapy could help to stabilise, intensify and clarify his "coping" behaviour. Certain movement phrases and combinations which are at present so reduced could be encouraged, and some degree of integration might be achieved. However, this child seems to me to be outside the range of the "normal" neurotic or maladjusted group of children.

If some therapy were to be given, the following aspects of movement would be considered:

(a) Gradual integration of action in the body/mind—united action.
(b) Increase intensity in all effort elements (except bound flow).
(c) Balance of bound and free flow.
(d) Transitions developed between one action and another.
(e) Simple body awareness.
(f) Later, the development of space and shape aspects.
(g) Later, rhythmical alternations.

Probably at first, individual help should be given—or perhaps working with one other child, and later in a small group.

7. Richard: age: 8 years 4 months; I.Q.: S–B 119; Scale B score: 17 (with neurotic tendencies 6/8)

From assessment through movement	Class teacher's report	Comments from B Scale

RELATIONSHIPS
    As stated in the main assessment (Chapter 13) Richard is retiring and withdrawn, isolated rather than gregarious, and will be able to co-operate better with those in authority than in a mobile changing situation with other children. He could not lead a group—probably prefers to be alone than follow. Contacts of a normal kind are difficult for him.
    Nevertheless, he has all the potential or latent capacities for a co-operative group member—rather as an equal than a leader, and certainly could become less isolated . . . and should be helped to do so.
    Not aggressive or destructive towards people or material—timid and retiring—also anxious.
	Co-operative when necessary. He doesn't look for situations calling for co-operation. Mainly isolated all the time. Never takes the lead. Remains outside the group, rather than follow other children. Makes no easy contacts—these have to be worked for by the other party.	Q.5.
		Does not fight with other children.
		Q.8.
		Tends to do things on his own—solitary.
		Q.26.
		Does not bully other children.
		Q.4.
		Does not destroy own or others' property.

Agreement—movement assessment gives indication that this state of isolation can be remedied within the school situation.

ADAPTABILITY Not really unadaptable, but probably doesn't welcome change too easily. Has latent gift of mobility (which at present is wasted in a kind of personal discharge of energy—frequent fidgeting, touching face and head, body shrugs, etc.). This can	Not particularly rigid or unadaptable. No visible resistance to change.	Q.3. Squirmy, fidgety child. Q.17. Tends to be fearful or afraid of new things or new situations.

From assessment through movement	Class teacher's report	Comments from B Scale
become a positive adaptability with greater security.		**Q.11.** Has twitches, mannerisms of face or body. **Q.13.** Bites nails.

Agreement.

WILL-POWER AND DRIVE		
Unlikely to be strong-willed, because of absence of strong, held movement ... it usually fades. Practically, he has such resistant movement patterns, and it seems likely that he could develop this side of his make-up much more. He needs greater intention and drive in outward flow—a latent capacity.	Not strong-willed in school.	**Q.15.** Is not disobedient.

Agreement.

ALERTNESS AND PRACTICALITY		
His alertness is either active, or just "below the surface"... again, as a latent capacity, it could be greatly developed to his advantage. His security in practical action brings out his alertness most clearly. Good range of practical and manual ability—usually will work in short periods, with pausing for checking and reassurance (rather than long continuous enthusiasms).	Rather dreamy. Practical about everyday happenings and situations, and about handling objects.	

Agreement.

From assessment through movement	Class teacher's report	Comments from B Scale
DREAMY ATTITUDE Withdraws (inward flow, and concave body backward). His range of weight/flow combinations shows that he has both inturned, fearful withdrawal states, as well as more outgoing, inventive. Not likely to be highly creative, but perhaps has potential which could develop further.	Rather dreamy when should be alert. Withdrawn and anxious. Inventive and original with stories, drama and number.	Q.7. Often worried, worries about many things. Q.10. Often appears miserable, unhappy, fearful or distressed. Q.17. Tends to be fearful of new situations or new things. Q.11. Has twitches and mannerisms. Q.13. Bites nails.

Agreement.

| REACTIONS
Reactions can be both delayed (with withdrawn attitude) or fairly alert and quick. The latter in practical situations where he is secure and bodily able. | Reactions delayed but not considered.
Reacts to direct orders, not necessarily quickly. | |

No mention made by the teacher of his immediate responses in practical situations (*i.e.* this was very evident in the movement class, where he felt secure when given direct guidance. When choice was asked for, he dithered, unable to make up his mind, and showed all the rhythms and signs of withdrawal and anxiety).

| THINKING, REASONING ABILITY
Is essentially a practical thinker—has some latent capacity for | Not answered. | |

From assessment through movement	*Class teacher's report*	*Comments from B Scale*
developing ability for abstract thought ... can at present think through a problem, and see more than one practical solution.		

Certainly not working at full capacity, because of emotional inhibition and withdrawal from situations. Frequent absences from school. (N.B.—S–B I.Q. 119.)

| ABILITY TO INVENT, CREATE OR MAKE ORIGINAL CONTRIBUTIONS
    As stated above, could probably develop much greater originality and creative work in varied spheres. | Inventive and original in words, drama and number. | |

See later comments from teacher at end of this report.

| TOLERANCE
    Friendly and tolerant when not isolated. | Tolerant. | |

Agreement.

| ENTHUSIASMS AND CONTINUITY OF ATTENTION
    In action rhythms show variety and vitality for short periods —sometimes fading (particularly in body attitudes). Recharged so that he can continue over a period, but not with evenness and consistency.
    General attitude is flatter and more subdued and lacking vitality. | Sometimes shows bursts of enthusiasm —not lasting over long periods—but recharged at short bursts, *e.g.* when he is discovering something, when learning new words, etc. | |

Agreement.

From assessment through movement	Class teacher's report	Comments from B Scale
ATTITUDE TO AUTHORITY, DIRECTION, ORDERS AND ORGANISATION Security gained from direct orders (when choice given, he is afraid). Enjoys direction and being organised.	Enjoys direct organisation from adults. Responds willingly.	**Q.15.** Is not disobedient.
Agreement.		

GENERAL COMMENTS
  Richard is slightly overweight and "pasty"-looking—as though he does not get enough air or robust activity. His range of "semi-latent" abilities cannot fully develop because of this withdrawal and timidity. Seems highly over-pampered. Needs help to develop now, before these attitudes become too established.
  (The Headmistress tells me that the mother is "overwhelming.")
	Richard has spent almost half the time I have been in the school off sick. He now has his tonsils out. He is a retiring child who responded to a different classroom atmosphere to that he had before. Rather sensitive and tentative still although he is getting bolder. He doesn't romp with the other children, maybe because he can hardly know them. He has very bad eyesight and nearly always forgets his glasses. This has had its effect on him as well.	

Three months after the assessment and report were completed the teacher told me that she thought there had been such a change in Richard that I asked her to complete a new questionnaire, without reference to her first one. The alterations from one to the other are:

(*a*) Generally "yes" to co-operativeness with others (the qualification has gone), but still isolated rather than gregarious and doesn't take the lead.

(*b*) "Yes," he likes to follow the lead of other children (previously he had remained withdrawn), but still does not make easy contacts.

(*c*) Now has a few friends (previously had none).

(*d*) Not unpopular (previously "He is just there")—still shy in new situations, particularly. Still timid most of the time.

(*e*) Much more adaptable.

(*f*) A good balance of dreamy and practical attitude.

(*g*) Reactions—quick and alert—to situations, people and direct orders. This is quite a new comment from last time, when he was delayed and hesitant.

(*h*) Able to see more than one point of view.

(*i*) Inventive in sound, practical things, paint and clay (as well as previously in words, drama and number).

(*j*) Still prefers to work alone, but will now ask for help.

(*k*) Enthusiasms last over longer period (about practical things).

(*l*) Not complacent in attitude to life (previously was complacent "because I suspect he feels it's no good fighting life").

(*m*) Enjoys organisation now by other children as well as adults.

These are interesting developments in Richard. They bear out entirely the suggestions which were made regarding "latent" capacities in the movement assessment, and it is greatly to the teacher's credit that she has been able to supply the right environment and help for this boy. His mother still comes each morning and afternoon to bring him to and collect him from school—and in this area he must be the only child in the school to receive this treatment! He is the youngest of five children, and absent as much as present.

Richard's writing and drawing are well below the average for an eight-year-old, and considering his I.Q. of 119 he is very backward. His colour sense is very pleasant, and his family drawing shows a good sense of organisation—he is separate from the rest of the family—Dad is pretty small and insignificant (though drawn first) and sister and Mum are bigger. His view of his teacher is interesting!

C.A.T. findings

Generally his stories were slowly delivered, and with not much interest—very matter of fact and practical. Descriptive of picture—difficult to get him to make a story (in spite of teacher's statement of his originality with words!). Perhaps it was his lack of confidence in me, as he had not seen me as often as the other children had because of his frequent absences from school.

Generally the scenes are domestic situations, with pleasant endings and logical happenings. In story 5, it appeared that Richard sleeps in the same room as his parents. His sisters share a room, and the two brothers "sleep downstairs."

Practically, he talked of his operation and his stay in hospital—his parents' visits, gifts, etc. Generally a scene of a friendly family setting. Richard was much more interested to talk to me about his own life than about the pictures, which obviously did not interest him at all! No special areas of tension, or fears, or interests were revealed. Perhaps this supports my general view that there is not a great deal wrong with Richard—he just needs to develop greater independence and self-assurance. Or does it mean that any conflict is much too deeply hidden to be revealed by this means?

General conclusions

Richard can be, and is being (luckily, because of this teacher), helped greatly by the present situation at school. Movement sessions were a great delight to him, and he would gain tremendously from them if they were provided regularly and with special understanding of his needs—preferably group work—both small and large.

Movement aspects to be considered:

(a) The increasing use of strength, and its retention over a period, particularly in body attitude changes.

(b) Based on his rhythmical ability, a development of purposeful and decisive action—particularly by giving him simple choices, and progressing to more complicated ones.

(c) Working with others in creative work, where he had to contribute, and sometimes initiate.

(d) Vigorous, active agility, controlled and mastered to a good standard.

(e) Gradual extension of ability in those elements which are "reduced" in degree.

(f) General creative atmosphere, with opportunities for both individual and co-operative work.

8. Katie: age: 7 years 10 months; I.Q.: S–B 120; Scale B score: 10 (with high 6/8 anti-social and 2/8 neurotic tendencies)

From assessment through movement	Class teacher's report	Comments from B Scale
RELATIONSHIPS		
Good—generally spontaneous and genuine, with a natural resiliency.	Makes easy contacts with others. Is co-operative generally, and gregarious. Takes	**Q.5.** Fights with other children.
Able (and willing) to stand up for herself, and enjoys the challenge.	the lead in group situations with children of own age.	**Q.9.** Quick to fly off the handle.
A good leader in a forceful way—needs to develop greater sensitivity outwardly orientated (at present it is frequently inwardly focused) in order to be as aware of others as herself. Can be dogmatic and domineering if challenged but also flexible and adjustable. If circumstances became too oppressive, she would probably respond by being negative and strongly anti-social. At present this is not so.	Tends to domineer. Follows the lead of older children and adults—sometimes of children of same age. Can be aggressive, particularly to the other leader of the girls, Josie. Friendly with most of the children in the class. Is popular, and not shy. Sometimes sulks.	**Q.15.** Is often disobedient. **Q.26.** Bullies other children.
Content to follow lead of adults and probably older children—no doubt she resents challenge from an equal.		
Bound flow exaggeration is used sometimes as an escape from a challenging situation—this causes withdrawal.		

Generally agreement in all aspects—Katie is a forceful character with contradictions in her relationships—but she is, in spite of her weaknesses, popular and friendly.

ADAPTABILITY		
Is adaptable—either with liveliness and freedom, or with caution. Enjoys new situations and challenges.	Yes, is adaptable. No, is not rigid.	

Agreement.

From assessment through movement	Class teacher's report	Comments from B Scale
WILL-POWER AND DRIVE Very energetic, has strong will-power and drive—hard-working and forceful. Inevitable that she will sometimes cross authority!	Strong-willed when she wants something done her way.	**Q.15.** Often dis-obedient.

Teacher agrees that she is not unmanageably disobedient—but she needs careful handling to provoke the best attitude.

ALERTNESS AND PRACTICALITY Is quick, alert and vital. Very practical. Enjoys doing.	Quick and alert. Prac-tical and efficient.	

Agreement.

DREAMY ATTITUDE Not essentially a "dreamer," much more stressed practically. Her tensions, fears and anxieties are shown in strong/bound com-binations. She has a very small range of other weight/flow com-binations, but these aspects could well be developed to give greater balance to her natural extrover-tion. Not really creative in other than practical things, but prob-ably very inventive and original in manipulation particularly. Can work equally well alone or with others—probably enjoys group work.	Inventive, and origin-al in all spheres, but particularly in hand-ling practical things.	**Q.7.** Sometimes worried. **Q.10.** Sometimes appears miser-able. **Q.17.** Certainly *not* afraid of new situations.

Latent capacity for richer development of weight/flow should be noted.

REACTIONS Lively, thoughtful and appro-priate. Absorbs impressions easily and reacts spontaneously	Quick and alert.	

From assessment through movement	Class teacher's report	Comments from B Scale
(good rhythmical awareness—this could develop into real intuitive perception if circumstances favour it).		
Agreement.		
THINKING, REASONING ABILITY Good. Uses her probably above average intelligence well. Able to see through a problem logically—also to appreciate more than one viewpoint.	Able to see more than one point of view.	
Agreement. (N.B.—S–B I.Q. 120.)		
ABILITY TO INVENT, CREATE OR MAKE ORIGINAL CONTRIBUTIONS Katie has this ability and interest and curiosity: in all spheres, but mainly practically.	Inventive and original.	
Agreement.		
TOLERANCE Generally tolerant in a positive way. No doubt she can be intolerant in some circumstances.	Tolerant.	
Generally agreed.		
ENTHUSIASMS AND CONTINUITY OF ATTENTION Very enthusiastic—can maintain interest and concentration over a long period (shows in good sustainment, carried through a phrase, as well as a natural resilience and buoyancy).	Energy and enthusiasm lasts over a long period in relation to most activities.	Q.16. Has good concentration and attention.
Agreement.		

From assessment through movement	Class teacher's report	Comments from B Scale
ATTITUDE TO AUTHORITY, DIRECTION, ORDERS AND ORGANISATION Probably varies according to (*a*) person, and (*b*) method of giving instructions. Those which are understood and reasonable are probably accepted willingly —others perhaps are resisted.	Enjoys direct organisation from me. Can resent it from other adults and some children. Responds willingly to direct orders from me.	**Q.15.** Is often disobedient.
Agreement.		

GENERAL COMMENTS
    Generally well-adjusted child with strong personality. Weaknesses appear to be:
(*a*) an overdeveloped self-control sometimes;
(*b*) over-strong and intense force (slashing action) when emotionally disturbed;
(*c*) inturned bound flow revealing anxieties, and fears.
 	
    Katie needs a great deal of creative opportunity for outlet of her drive and energy, and her mental gifts. She has a good wide range of abilities which will make for an interesting life. If seriously frustrated, she will fight back aggressively.
	Second child of three. Eldest child hates her. Youngest is a paraplegic of eight (as a result of an accident). Katie presents a bright, eager appearance. She came up with a reputation for being difficult, but I have not found this so. Vivacious and interested sums up her general attitude. She talks well.	

There is agreement between the reports as above. Katie's needs for development from the school point of view are being well catered for—sufficient leadership, with enough freedom to explore and experiment creatively. Movement lessons are a great source of enjoyment and opportunity for integration and development for her. Although she scored 10 on the Scale B, and 6/8 anti-social, I do not believe that these figures are in fact a true reflection of any maladjustment—although it is possible to see the potential for it if the environmental support broke down. The hidden anxieties and insecurity might be cause for concern and attention.

C.A.T. findings

Katie enjoyed her opportunity to make up stories, and did not hesitate, showing good ideas, mainly based quite practically on the illustrations. In general, the stories were very like fairy-tales—with the villain dying—danger to the small creatures, but usually a happy ending for them. The strangest story was of a "strange thing" which attacked the whole community—a reaction to the kangaroo picture —and gradually all of them died . . . this seems to reflect a different fantasy from the other more conventional fairy-tale ones—a fear of unknown outside forces, at whose mercy we all are, and no doubt based on her own insecurity previously mentioned in the movement assessment—no particular emotional accompaniment was observed though she was intensely serious about it.

Fears of the unknown, and of outside forces, were balanced by stories of the little one beating the older and bigger—*i.e.* mouse and lion; monkey and tiger.

Katie appears to be a reasonably balanced child, developing her gifts well and actively, but carrying with her anxieties and conflicts which could be disturbing to her progress.

General conclusions

It is uncertain whether the generally supportive atmosphere of the school and class will be sufficient to help this child to carry her anxieties without too great a conflict.

9. Tom: age: 8 years 5 months; I.Q.: S–B 101; Scale B score: 23 (antisocial 6/8; neurotic 4/8)

From assessment through movement	Class teacher's report	Comments from B Scale
RELATIONSHIPS		
Unpredictable alternations and extremes will make his relationships chancy—lack of fine touch indicates insensitivity, and he therefore will not be able to	Sometimes co-operative with children of own age—stands and watches those older, and co-operative in	**Q's. 1 and 3.** Somewhat restless—squirmy and fidgety child.

From assessment through movement	Class teacher's report	Comments from B Scale
develop contacts very deeply. He will be easily led by a stronger character—though not always reacting in the same way. Cannot lead others, and tends to work alone rather than as a group member.	an apathetic way with people in authority. Tends towards isolate. Follows the lead of particular children of own age group or older—not authority. Does not lead others. Has few friends, not necessarily chosen. Not particularly popular. Aggressive on occasions—mainly to children who need my extra attention—in class and at play.	**Q.15.** Often disobedient. **Q.26.** Bullies other children. **Q.8.** Tends to do things on his own—sometimes solitary. Does not destroy own or others' belongings.
His undoubted aggressive actions fade fairly quickly, but he is probably quarrelsome.		
His body attitude often shows apathy, but shadow movements of flexible suddenness (face) reveal inner agitation and fears —leading to avoiding action or withdrawal (sometimes hitting out).		**Q.5.** Frequently fights with other children. **Q.9.** Irritable—is quick to "fly off the handle." **Q.11.** Has twitches, mannerisms or tics of face or body. **Q.13.** Bites nails.

General agreement.

ADAPTABILITY

| His ability to adapt is latent rather than active. He is restless but not positively able to adjust to new situations. His rigidity comes from tense stiffness, especially when insecure—and a different kind of staticness is | Emotionally changeable if things do not go his way. Can be easily upset. Not adaptable—rather rigid and unadaptable. | **Q.9.** Irritable. **Q.17.** Fearful or afraid of new things or new situations. |

From assessment through movement	Class teacher's report	Comments from B Scale
revealed in heavy placement of body. Lack of central body control makes real mobility and adaptability, as well as adjustable stability, impossible for him. Nevertheless—they are both latent and capable of development. (Shown in neutral state.)		

General agreement.

| WILL-POWER AND DRIVE
Has force of will, but it is rarely maintained to carry through a phrase. This means that sustained and concentrated will-power is unlikely. He substitutes tense bound flow, which makes for a stubbornness, rather than positive, active will-power exertion. This contrasts with weakness and apathy ... unpredictable in extremes. | Can be strong-willed | **Q.15.**
Often disobedient. |

General agreement.

| ALERTNESS AND PRACTICALITY
He is a mixture of confidence in some aspects (mainly practical) and great insecurity in others. His physical daring has not been channelled and developed sufficiently.
Shadow movements of eyes and face can be quick and direct, showing alertness, but simultaneously his body is flexible, and even other parts of face. (Shows conflicts.)
Fairly practical generally, but not outstandingly efficient. | Tends to be cut off sometimes but can be practical—about handling objects. Sometimes dreamy when should be practical. | |

Agreement.

From assessment through movement	Class teacher's report	Comments from B Scale
DREAMY ATTITUDE He shows two aspects of this attitude: 1. Withdrawn, neutral passivity —an escape from active participation. 2. Active strong free flow, outwardly orientated, which could indicate a latent capacity for imaginative work, though this would not be manifest in his alternations of attitudes and his insecurity with lack of central control.	Not dreamy in a positive, creative way. Withdrawn and I suspect anxious, he hides it.	Q.13. Bites nails. Q.7. Often worried, worries about many things. Q.17. Fearful of new things and situations.
General agreement.		
REACTIONS His reactions are averagely bright, alert and spontaneous, and he has the ability to consider the problem at hand.	Quick and alert reactions—considered.	
Agreement.		
THINKING AND REASONING ABILITY Mental action is direct rather than flexible, but a fairly good balance is achieved. Uses his mental capacity quite sensibly— about average ability—his weakness is in following through a decision.	Tends to be pinpointed in his thinking.	
Agreement generally. (N.B.—S–B I.Q. 101.)		
ABILITY TO INVENT, CREATE OR MAKE ORIGINAL CONTRIBUTIONS Insecurity and withdrawal and lack of central stability from	Not inventive or original, refuses to	

From assessment through movement	Class teacher's report	Comments from B Scale
which to launch any creative endeavour will inhibit what latent powers he has. Through creative activity, he could be helped towards integration.	join in some activities (music particularly). I think he is afraid of failure/embarrassment. Beginning to be more inventive in number work.	

Generally supporting statements.

TOLERANCE Too involved with his own inner conflicts to be very tolerant of others. Also his lack of light sensitivity will limit his tolerance.	Narrow—tolerates children with problems seldom.	

Agreement.

ENTHUSIASMS AND CONTINUITY OF ATTENTION The same general weakness of lack of co-ordination, lack of adaptability and stability, together with a weakening of strong intention, and a not very highly developed sustainment, indicates that although enthusiasms are probably strong they are not maintained. Short-lived concentration.	Has sudden bursts of energy and enthusiasms dying quickly away—about most things.	Q.16. Has poor concentration and short attention.

Agreement.

ATTITUDE TO AUTHORITY, DIRECTION, ORDERS AND ORGANISATION Contradiction of attitudes— between agreement (especially seen when stimulated towards	Veers towards resentment when directly organised by most	Q.15. Often disobedient.

From assessment through movement	Class teacher's report	Comments from B Scale
physical activity) reluctance, and defiance.	children and adults. Does not respond willingly.	

Agreement.

GENERAL COMMENTS Tom shows in his movement patterns the clear contradictions and problems which reflect his insecurity and lack of confidence. Many capacities are latent and may be able to grow if and when he can master the more fundamental lack of central co-ordination. He already is quite adept at hiding his insecurity and fears—his aggressiveness is often an attempt to establish himself from a position of insecurity. Easily knocked off balance, and needs frequent outside stimulus to action.	Fourth of four children; late child and aware mother is forty-eight, making the point often. Tom's next brother is eighteen and mentally retarded and at a training centre. Two older brothers are married and away from home. He will not compete for attention with the rest of the class, preferring to wait until he can get me alone. He rocks occasionally. Tends to follow Sam, showing initiative seldom in class or play.	

Tom's writing and drawings are a bit messy, with beginnings clear and neat but fading away. Little content, showing lack of concentration.

C.A.T. findings

These findings in general support the view that Tom feels inadequate in face of outside forces and powers. He tries to be astute and agile (usually physical action ideas) and in one story (monkey and tiger) he is successful—otherwise he is killed or eaten, or, once, rescued by parents. No indication of emotion from parents except that they punish fairly severely. "Hit him" if he doesn't behave.

General conclusions

There is a fairly strong inadequacy in his body, and this parallels with his lack of integration and central co-ordination. He is basically rhythmical and agile—much could be done through movement to help him, as he feels secure in this field.

(*a*) Lots of practice of mobility and its contrasting stability—particularly stressing the need for central grip in moments of stopping. Develop this into rhythmical action alternations.

(*b*) Gradual development of transitions of different kinds between extremes of behaviour.

(*c*) Holding of strength with sustainment over a gradually lengthening period.

(*d*) Development of resilience in coming from height.

(*e*) Contrasting strength with sensitivity in many combinations, as an active force (at present it is mainly seen in preparations only).

(*f*) Above will help towards the pursuing of an aim once decided upon—all kinds of creative work should be encouraged.

Not very rich variety of movement combinations, but what he has could gradually be used much more efficiently.

10. Jane: age: 8 years 4 months; I.Q.: S–B 100; Scale B score: 18 (neurotic tendencies 6/8)

From assessment through movement	Class teacher's report	Comments from B Scale
RELATIONSHIPS Jane will be as co-operative as possible—and she is acutely aware of other people's responses and attitudes. Too much, so that she tends to "tune in" and adapt to them rather than be herself. She is an active follower—not a leader, and anxious to conform to others in most circumstances. She will not be very popular, but not actively dis-	Co-operative with other children and adults. At play, gregarious, but frequently isolated in school. Does not take the lead and is content to follow lead of both children and adults. Does not make easy contacts with older chil-	Q.26. Never bullies other children or Q.5. Fights with them. Q.8. Tends to do things on her own—solitary.

From assessment through movement	Class teacher's report	Comments from B Scale
liked, I think. Although she likes to co-operate she will frequently be on her own. Not disobedient or aggressive. Movements revealing her anxiety appear all the time.	dren or adults— easier with children younger or same age. Few friends—chosen. Shy, but not with-drawn. Always on edge. Trying to please.	**Q.6.** Not very much liked by other children. **Q.10.** Often appears miserable, un-happy, fearful or distressed. **Q.7.** Often worried, worries about many things. **Q.12.** Sucks fingers. **Q.15.** Never dis-obedient.

General agreement—anxious to please others, and fearful and anxious generally.

ADAPTABILITY

Although Jane lacks the true mobility of flow/time, *i.e.* able to change in a fluid way, she com-pensates with body attitude flexi-bility. This is a much more con-scious way of adapting to outer circumstances. Her personal stability becomes strained and rigid when required to maintain a position—anxiety always as to whether this is acceptable. Rarely at ease. The non-time movement combinations are outstanding in her make-up—a kind of spell or trance-like state—at the mercy of outer and inner forces. Does not exert her own influence.	Adaptable because she is trying to please.	

Agreement.

From assessment through movement	Class teacher's report	Comments from B Scale
WILL-POWER AND DRIVE Persistent and persevering rather than strong will-power in active sense. Control from body centre becomes weaker under pressure from outside ... shows lack of self-confidence. Occasional moments of strong-held position show potential gift.	I think she is strong-willed in relation to her mother, and on one or two occasions in school, but not as a rule.	**Q.15.** Never disobedient.

General agreement. On the questionnaire the teacher tends to comment on "will-power" as negative and resistant opposition or stubbornness. (A wider interpretation was intended.)

ALERTNESS AND PRACTICALITY Practical within a limited range—rather routine and pedestrian. General attitude is slow rather than lively, but would make every effort to be quick if required from her ... she has sufficient capacity to do this, but needs outer stimulus. Under anxiety, might become inefficient and "flapping about."	Towards alert and practical—in everyday happenings and handling things. Sometimes dreamy when should be practical.	**Q.18.** Fussy and over-particular child.

General agreement.

DREAMY ATTITUDE Her main use of weight/flow takes the form of strong bound movement—indicating driving pressure. When directed inwards, it can become nightmarish, or it loses strength and is just tight apprehension—withdraws also when too severely challenged. Not really dreamy in a creative sense—would need to balance with active free flow to	Tries to be imaginative—not withdrawn with me now, but can be with other teachers. She is anxious. Fearful of her father.	**Q.7.** Often worried. **Q.8.** Rather solitary. **Q.10.** Often appears miserable, unhappy, fearful or distressed. **Q.11.** Twitches and

From assessment through movement	Class teacher's report	Comments from B Scale
be effective (at present latent). Sometimes momentarily gives up in hopeless heaviness.		mannerisms of face. **Q.12.** Sucks thumb. **Q.17.** Afraid of new things or situations.

All kinds of "freeing up" work is necessary for Jane—but primarily to get to the cause of her excessive anxieties—note teacher's comment "Fearful of her father."

REACTIONS Jane's reaction pattern is sustained into quicker movement—that is, she overcomes her initial hesitation and hurries into action.	Quick and alert mainly if she understands.	

Jane does not appear very lively and alert—there is always this rather held, questioning look of apprehension—but she gets on with life. Never fully at ease to react freely.

THINKING, REASONING ABILITY Not a very wide range of capacities—probably average but variety and imagination will be lacking because of her continuous apprehension and fear. Not clearly developed directness or flexibility in shadow movements, and lacking alternations.	She tries to see other point of view—not always successfully.	

General agreement. (N.B.—S–B I.Q. 100.)

ABILITY TO CREATE OR MAKE ORIGINAL CONTRIBUTIONS Not at all—as previously indicated, too routine and afraid.	Not inventive or original in any activity. Tends to copy because she is still not confident.	

Agreement. A great deal of help and guidance necessary to lead her to creative work, where some form of *herself* could be expressed.

From assessment through movement	Class teacher's report	Comments from B Scale
TOLERANCE Anxious to please, and to be accepted by others. Tolerant.	Generally tolerant.	
Agreement.		

ENTHUSIASMS AND CONTINUITY OF ATTENTION Persistent and routine rather than enthusiastic for the job's sake.	Can pay attention for long period—not necessarily because of enthusiasm. Sometimes has sudden burst of enthusiasm and energy, which dies away if and when she feels relaxed ... mainly tries to please adults.	**Q.16.** Has poor concentration or short attention span—applies somewhat.

The seeming contradictions here are in Jane's varied responses to situations. Not enthusiastic about what she is doing for its own sake or her interest—always half an eye on the adult to see if approval is being won. Pathetically anxious to please, even to driving herself too hard. (N.B.— Main assessment: works often "as if under a spell.")

ATTITUDE TO AUTHORITY, DIRECTION, ORDERS AND ORGANISATION Welcomes all kinds of direction and organisation, as it makes her feel accepted. Her lack of personal integration might make her resentful if she dare. (A hint of a "break-out" occasionally.)	She wants to develop her initiative, but is only able to do so now and again. Usually responds willingly to direct orders from adults.	**Q.15** Not disobedient.
Agreement.		

General comments

All Jane's actions are coloured by her fears and apprehensions. They are not so crippling that she cannot be effective at all, but they limit the development of her capacities. All the movement signs of lack of integration and harmony are shown (*see* under *General conclusions*). She needs help to face her problems. As yet, there is still some spirit of resistance remaining in her—but she rarely dares to use it, and smothers it down.

Her writing is strong, restrained and fairly well formed and even. Her drawings simple and small.

C.A.T. findings

Jane talked incessantly in an even flow, handling and turning the cards over and over all the time (a transcript of her stories is given in Appendix II). She frequently introduced the figure of father into her stories—he showed no emotion, but pictured as giving presents—as returning from absences and giving presents to a baby. (She is an only child—her father is not in fact away from house, and this seems like a wish story.) She wants his love and approval—tries to appease adults—"don't argue." Identifies herself with the child or new baby being "good," winning affection, or at the receiving end of gratuitous affection. Feels rejected and lost. She shows her need of:

(*a*) presents (affection)—through illness, being helpful or being a new baby;
(*b*) father figure.

Other themes ignored. Environment is chancy—insecure and not very loving. Parents are "*father*" mainly—mother plays domestic practical role.

Contemporaries are shown as vindictive. Her conflicts and anxieties are lack of affection, and she tries to imagine situations where she would receive it. She fears disapproval, and defends herself by regression. Punishments are too severe for minor crime. Her hero figure is inadequate, wanting to be happy, and unrealistic . . . a picture of her own situation.

General conclusions

As it seems unlikely that her domestic situation will change—the very strict religious atmosphere of Plymouth Brethren—every opportunity should be taken in school to build up her own resistance and buoyancy, and to give her an opportunity to experience some degree of personal achievement and affection. Movement and drama would help a great deal, where she can physically experience situations of stress, and the resolving of them. The following aspects of movement would be taken into account if special work could be done:

(a) The split between the upper and lower parts of the body—as if there is no integration between her two aspects of mental/ emotional and down-to-earth physical life.

(b) The development of alternations of opposite capacities—in flow—time—space and weight. Her lack of rhythmical alternations makes for "sticky" transitions and strain.

(c) Encouragement of resilience, and a balancing recovery use of high as well as deep movement.

(d) Encouragement of asymmetric movement, and help towards a greater mobility and adjustability.

Her overweight is probably psychological—she is very well cared for from the dress and cleanliness point of view—she needs warmth and love and spontaneity.

11. Sam: age: 8 years 5 months; I.Q.: S–B 129; Scale B score: 14 (antisocial 5/8; neurotic 2)

From assessment through movement	Class teacher's report	Comments from B Scale
RELATIONSHIPS Generally difficult, because of his tension and withdrawn attitude. More co-operative when he is confident. Desires to participate, but often held back by insecurity. His weak endings to phrasings (reduced lightness with bound flow) and his inability to hold a really stable position show his lack of a stable centre—easily disturbed, but covers this frequently by an aggressive-type action rather than giving in. Probably likes to play with	Sometimes co-operative with other children of same age group; more often with older children; never with adults unless he happens to approve of something. Isolated in classroom. Gregarious at playtime—with older boys. Sometimes takes lead with children of same age, by making good sugges-	Q.5. Frequently fights with other children. Q.6. Not much liked by other children. Q.8. Tends to do things on his own—rather solitary. Q.11. Has twitches,

From assessment through movement	*Class teacher's report*	*Comments from B Scale*
older children, with whom he can well hold his own. Resistant to organisation—often immediate avoidance and resistance is followed by acquiescence. Works best alone—would be stimulated by good partner relationship. Lacks sensitivity to others—may bully a bit—weaker children.	tions. Sometimes content to follow lead of others—though not "content." Resists adults. Contacts are never "easy"—it depends upon the activity. Few chosen friends rather than many. Not popular. Over-confident — almost to aggression. Is aggressive on occasions (with words also).	mannerisms or tics of the face or body. **Q.15.** Is often disobedient. **Q.26.** Sometimes bullies other children.

General agreement.

ADAPTABILITY

| Although Sam has a latent capacity for adjustability, he does not always achieve this now (time rhythms are even and restricted) and he is usually slightly behind a rhythm. His ability for intuitive perception is inhibited by his emotional feelings which are bound and inward-flowing. Transitions poor. | Not very adaptable, but not entirely rigid, there has been a change during the time I have known him. | |

General agreement.

WILL-POWER AND DRIVE

| Very strong-willed, particularly in how he presents himself to the world—but often his strong movement is associated with bound flow, or fades into weakness. This strength of will is probably his main way of coping with his problems—sometimes it seems almost desperation. | Is strong-willed in most circumstances. | **Q.15.**
Often disobedient. |

Agreement.

From assessment through movement	Class teacher's report	Comments from B Scale
ALERTNESS AND PRACTICALITY Is very bright, alert, "cheeky" (face often bound and twisted showing anxieties). Quite practical and efficient manually. Thinks in practical way—down-to-earth facts and information (preponderance of action drives).	Is practical about everyday happenings and situations, and in handling objects. Rarely dreamy.	**Q.18.** Not fussy or over-particular.

Agreement.

From assessment through movement	Class teacher's report	Comments from B Scale
DREAMY ATTITUDE Rare—but when he is inturned and withdrawn, he is strong bound—revealing greater inner tension—face is already quite lined. Too tied up in himself to be very creative, but there is a definite latent capacity—probably for words and movement rather than visual medium.	Rarely dreamy. Not anxious, withdrawn or fearful.	**Q.7.** Often worried. Worries about many things. **Q.9.** Irritable. Is quick to "fly off the handle." **Q.11.** Has twitches, mannerisms or tics of face and body.

Teacher's remark "not anxious" is not supported by the assessment or by the Scale B comments—she says that she was trying to show that Sam is not a withdrawn, anxious child, but an anxious extrovert! This I agree.

From assessment through movement	Class teacher's report	Comments from B Scale
REACTIONS Bright and alert, aware of what is going on—spontaneously avoids challenge from authority—often changes that reaction, after consideration, to agreement (though carry through not necessarily consistent). Generally reacts quickly.	Quick reactions to situations— considered to direct orders.	

Agreement.

From assessment through movement	Class teacher's report	Comments from B Scale
THINKING, REASONING ABILITY Good mental ability—probably well above average . . . inner conflicts might well inhibit full use of his gifts. Well able to appreciate problems and situations. Uses both directness and flexibility effectively and in relation to each other—frequently, flexibility directness.	More pinpointed in thinking.	

Appears quite straightforward—enjoys intellectual challenges. (N.B.—S–B I.Q. 129.)

ABILITY TO INVENT, CREATE OR MAKE ORIGINAL CONTRIBUTIONS Is very practical and down to earth, not given to imagery and fantasy—nevertheless, has some latent capacity—particularly in words. Also in movement. This needs great encouragement.	Not creative. Formal and rigid. His God is 007 and he will write pages recounting all the films he has seen —but none of it is original.	

Agreement.

TOLERANCE Unlikely to be tolerant (minimal use of fine touch in shadow movements).	Mainly intolerant. Will sit in silence during class discussion, giving the impression he is "above it all." Intolerant towards other children who he thinks are not as "clever" as he is— and towards those in trouble.	

Agreement.

From assessment through movement	Class teacher's report	Comments from B Scale
ENTHUSIASMS AND CONTINUITY OF ATTENTION Can sustain interest over a long period—if uninterested, withdraws. Can have bursts of enthusiasm and hard work when absorbed.	Yes—has bursts of enthusiasm and energy if interest is aroused —if not keen—no enthusiasm.	**Q.16.** Good concentration and attention span.
General agreement.		
ATTITUDE TO AUTHORITY, DIRECTION, ORDERS AND ORGANISATION Generally against authority—but not unbearably so—has a mind of his own, and needs "handling." A rebel with enough intelligence to see the implications of what he does.	Resents direct organisation most of the time from adults. Never seen him respond willingly to a direct order—at the same time he is not surly, but just ignores the order!	**Q.15.** Often disobedient.
General agreement.		

Teacher's comments

Sam's personality has been affected by his medical history—he has had asthma rather severely—three years on cortisone—this stunted his growth, I am told. Having had to fight for his breath and for his position with earlier adult contacts, he tends to be rather insular and independent. He is an extremely good reader (12·8) but as a result of earlier experiences doesn't like number work. He wants to do what he wants—he is improving, but doesn't yet take the full part he could in the class social structure.

General comments

Sam's struggles and problems are mirrored in his tensions in the face and body. He frequently shows conflicting movement phrases in different body parts at the same time. He appears all the time to be fighting—inwardly or outwardly. His writing is fluent, and his drawings efficient and detailed.

C.A.T. findings

Sam was lively and amusing while telling stories, and in between —asking questions, amused at the whole idea. Highly dramatic use of voice.

He identified himself with male child of same age, or baby, and the main theme was pitting his wits against authority—good sense of humour and of the ridiculous—not always scrupulous. All was action.

The child was always astute, physically agile, very adequate in action. One direct and simple identification was shown in his story of the kangaroo who learned, after much practice, to jump higher than teacher. He caught a robber, tricked a tiger and escaped punishment by avoidance—when caught said, "Ouch."

Didn't mind if someone else got the blame.

A challenging picture of his environment was painted—the need to fight—either seriously or jokingly—and aware of the need to practise things to gain a standard.

Parental figures—father strong, mother and father fair game to be tricked—aunt, teacher, all to be beaten if possible. Punishment accepted if caught. Contemporary figures were allies in this conspiracy against adults.

Most conflicts shown in his relationships with adults, and his fears and anxieties seem to revolve round being helpless and overpowered if he doesn't fight.

Avoids anxiety by aggression and fooling; *i.e.* in action. Prefers to avoid punishment and let others take blame—if punished, it is usually appropriate—*i.e.* having lost the battle of wits.

Hero is adequate and successful, realistic, and triumphant—no doubt his own striving to be this.

General conclusions

Aspects of personality which could be helped through movement:

(*a*) Transitions between movements—at present jerky or non-existent. Extremes of behaviour appear violent.

(*b*) Lack of integration of movement in different parts of the body.

(*c*) Development of balancing non-fighting attitudes (*i.e.* opposites of fighting).

(*d*) Specific development of higher, lighter movement, particularly in elevation.

(*e*) Development of rhythmical alternations in time.

(*f*) Central body weakness.

(*g*) Development of wider range of externalised drives (three elements together).

In discussion later with the teacher, she revealed that Sam's mother is very aggressive, always visiting the school and claiming her rights, and her children's rights. Note Sam's asthma—no doubt he has been under considerable strain to live up to a fight against life—also drugs may have affected his attitudes. I would put the statement of class teacher the other way round—not "Sam's personality has been affected by his medical history," but "Sam's personality and physical illnesses are interrelated," and the present result of tensions on his development can be seen in the above report.

12. Edith: age: 7 years 11 months; I.Q.: S–B 119; Scale B score: 1

From assessment through movement	Class teacher's report	Comments from B Scale
RELATIONSHIPS Friendly contacts, easy relationships, must be well liked and generally amenable. Not a leader, but willing to co-operate and to follow others. (Confident use of horizontal plane, good alternations of free with bound flow—good sensitivity and awareness of others—rhythmical ability). Ability to work alone or in a group situation—unobtrusive and consistent.	Co-operative with others—children and adults. Gregarious—does not take the lead herself but follows others—preferably adults or older children. Makes easy contacts and has many friends. Popular. Quietly confident most of the time. Not aggressive. Sensitive to others.	**Q.8.** Sometimes does things on her own.

Agreement.

From assessment through movement	Class teacher's report	Comments from B Scale
ADAPTABILITY From her poised and balanced security, she can adjust other situations and people. Greater mobility could be developed, particularly if the slightly over-stressed bound flow is released a little, and greater use made of her time/flow sequences.	Is adaptable, not rigid.	
Agreement.		
WILL-POWER AND DRIVE Edith has quite firm and strong actions when required —mainly peripheral—though strength tends to become tight and bound, or is used in lessened degree. Would not be described as "strong-willed"—but also not "weak-willed" and has quite sufficient determination to achieve her objects. Works more from sensitivity.	Not particularly strong-willed.	
General agreement.		
ALERTNESS AND PRACTICALITY Very balanced in attitudes to alertness and dreamy state—can be extremely alert and bright, and is practical, particularly good at small delicate actions. Astute in everyday activities, and quietly confident. Some timidity and shyness might appear in strange situations, but not excessively.	Practical in everyday happenings and handling things. Only anxious when she doesn't understand. (Shy meeting strangers.) Quietly confident most of the time.	
Agreement.		

From assessment through movement	Class teacher's report	Comments from B Scale
DREAMY ATTITUDE Lacks swing and resilience, but has good range of weight/flow combinations—but very often the order of use is limiting—*i.e.* from strong/free to light/bound. This is an area which could be developed to her great advantage.	Is dreamy in a positive way, imaginative, and creative. Tends to be rather formal and finds difficulty in accepting informal suggestions.	

The two statements of the teacher which appear to contradict are perhaps both appropriate here—she has ideas and starts well, but limits and does not develop them . . . definitely a latent capacity for creative work.

From assessment through movement	Class teacher's report	Comments from B Scale
REACTIONS Direct, quick and light . . . pays attention and reacts spontaneously.	Quick and alert most of the time to situations and people.	

Agreement.

From assessment through movement	Class teacher's report	Comments from B Scale
THINKING, REASONING ABILITY Good ability—probably above average, and working to capacity. She will never be a highly intuitive or original thinker, but is practical, very adequate and lively. Direct rather than flexible.	Tends towards a pinpointed way of thinking.	

Agreement. (N.B.—S–B I.Q. 119.)

From assessment through movement	Class teacher's report	Comments from B Scale
ABILITY TO INVENT, CREATE OR MAKE ORIGINAL CONTRIBUTIONS Latent rather than active powers, though not outstandingly creative . . . rather self-contained and composed—lacks exuberant resiliency and "flair" to be really original in large way.	Tends to be formal. Prefers to work with others, and likes guidance.	

Agreement.

From assessment through movement	Class teacher's report	Comments from B Scale
TOLERANCE Is sensitive to others and actively tolerant.	Generally tolerant and open-minded.	
Agreement.		
ENTHUSIASMS AND CONTINUITY OF ATTENTION Good persistency and continuity of attention. Enthusiasm is contained eagerness rather than exuberant explosions!	Sometimes bursts of energy—enthusiasms last over long period. Good attention span for most things. Fairly even in attitude to life, but not complacent.	
General agreement.		
ATTITUDE TO AUTHORITY, DIRECTION, ORDERS AND ORGANISATION Sense of tidiness and care, with agreeable attitude to life and people. Accepts happily organisation and direction.	Responds willingly to direct orders from teachers and some older girls. Accepts organisation of authority.	
GENERAL COMMENTS Small, angular and bright. Absorbs herself in activity, and is gay, charming and contained. Occasional anxieties are coped with sensibly, and she rarely exhibits any real distress. Quiet and unobtrusive. A "light" personality in a sensitive attractive way. Lacks robustness and buoy-	Second of five children. Daughter of Greek-Cypriot parents. Appears to be reasonably stable. Happy child who laughs often, enjoys what she is doing and is fairly confident.	

From assessment through movement	Class teacher's report	Comments from B Scale
ancy. In her present situation, all seems to be well with her. (*See* General assessment.)	Quick in reactions and gets on well with her peers. She is understanding with less able children and will help them.	

The absence of comments in column 3 is because the answers, with the exception of Question 8, were "doesn't apply." Even Question 8 (Tends to do things on his own, rather solitary) was only "applies somewhat"—and can be, after all, a positive attribute of independence.

Edith's style is light and bright—she lacks the robust surging kind of activity, but it is pleasing to find in this group and area such a relatively well-balanced child, seemingly working well and to her capacity. She is obviously secure and happy at home, and the school presents no problem of adjustment.

Her writing and drawing seem adequate, though figure drawings are rather immature.

C.A.T. findings

Edith handled the cards naturally, pointing or touching occasionally.

Her main themes were of domestic situations—quite satisfactory ones, confidence in mother, good food, enjoyment.

She identified with animals of same age, or "baby." No particular sex identification. Amenable to situations which were reasonable ones. Body images clear.

General contentment shown—nothing introduced or omitted—unoriginal stories, not imaginative.

Her world is a warm friendly place.

Parental figures were portrayed as good (once father seemed pretty weak), uncle more important in giving advice. Contemporary and junior figures friendly.

Anxieties and conflicts seemed minor and of childish situations easily dispersed—crying in the night, "being caught"—all well under control of family security.

Her defence is—caution. Hero is adequate, happy and realistic. Thought processes unoriginal, slight, logical, complete and concrete.

General conclusions

Her I.Q. was a bit higher than I should have expected, though the movement assessment shows quite a good range, much of her ability still latent, and open to development. The C.A.T. findings support all the rest of the assessments and reports.

Within the educational setting, Edith could be helped through movement and other creative activities to enlarge her mastery of her capacities, and to develop those aspects still latent:

(*a*) more resilience and swing;

(*b*) shaping ability;

(*c*) alternations of elevation and buoyant resilience in recovery;

(*d*) extension of movement in other planes as well as horizontal;

(*e*) dramatic ability of projection (this was seen as a possibility through movement lesson).

CONCLUSION TO PART THREE

I think that a fair case has been made out for the accuracy of assessment through movement. Within its own limitations, that is, commenting on the present state of the person, it compares well with the teachers' reports.

As a tool for diagnosing and advising, it can be used to great advantage, especially if it is one of a group of diagnostic techniques. As a therapeutic medium, movement has already been used for many years in clinics and special schools as well as with private patients.

I see the special value of movement as a therapy, in that it can assist the psychological and physical growth of a child according to the stage of development which he has reached; it can help the gradual unfolding process of differentiation and self-realisation, according to his own capacity. The aim is not towards any "ideal" or "average" person, and therefore there is no "norm." Every human being reacts in his own way to the challenges of life, and is in a state of continual change, though the most obvious changes occur in children and adolescents. The growing awareness of being "oneself" and the subtleties of action and reaction which occur in this development can be experienced in movement situations, and harmonious and disharmonious solutions or tensions worked out. Movement therapy is an artistic medium, and, as all therapy, needs an experienced and sensitive therapist, able to guide when necessary, and able to leave alone when necessary. Although there are basic principles which should be understood, no set system of rules is given which should be followed.

Appendix I: Effort

MOTION FACTORS AND ELEMENTS OF MOVEMENT

Quantitative and qualitative aspects of movement

Laban discerned four motion factors which are common to all movement.

Quantitatively, the motion factors can be described as:

The amount of *space* (the measurable degree of angles of movement).

The amount of *weight* (the measurable degree of strength used in the action).

The amount of *time* (the measurable length of time taken to make a movement).

The amount of *flow* (the measurable degree of continuity or pausing in the movement).

The quantitative measurements of movement have mechanical interest, and may be relevant in practical action; if I want to lift a very heavy weight, I need a high degree of muscular strength, or if I want to win a race, the measurable time taken for each step becomes significant.

Qualitatively, the motion factors can be described as the moving person's "attitude towards":

Space (*e.g.* the flexibility or directedness of attention).
Weight (*e.g.* the sensitivity or forcefulness of intention).
Time (*e.g.* the leisureliness or urgency of decision).
Flow (*e.g.* the ease or restraint of the action).

The qualitative aspects of movement have special significance in personality assessment, as they reveal the mental/emotional relationships to the body movement. Qualitative movement can be understood in analogy with music—a conductor conveys not only measurable beat, phrasing and strength, but the quality of the music, the inner content which colours the technical skill. Beethoven indicates this "quality" when marking a section to be played with *Innigkeit*.

The effort graph

Motion factors

Both the quantitative and qualitative aspects of movement are conveyed in the notation system originally devised by Laban. Any later modifications of the original signs are of detail and do not make fundamental changes.

The *accent* sign / is central to the notation, *i.e.* some *effort* is present.

The sign for *space* is

The sign for *weight* is

The sign for *time* is

The sign for *flow* is

The combined signs give the *effort graph*:

Elements of movement

The attitude of the moving person towards each motion factor is a discernable and classifiable fact. Either the factor is "indulged in," "yielded to" or it is "fought against," "resisted." The resulting movement is described as an *element* of movement.

THE MOTION FACTOR OF SPACE is notated

and each *element* takes half of the symbol, thus:

flexibility (which is yielding the body to space, or indulging in space), or

directness (which is fighting against the body using space).

How the effort element is seen and recognised cannot easily be described in words. It is impossible to use photographs to illustrate, although film sequences could be used.

Flexibility

There is flexibility (indulging in the use of space) as the common factor in such practical actions as twisting a corkscrew, wringing a cloth.

Similarly the flexibility can be recognised in non-practical movements such as: a body twisting (in embarrassment or avoidance); a floating gesture of a meandering pathway (in explanation) or a swaggering walk.

Directness

This can be described as fighting against the body using space. There is directness as the common factor in such practical actions as precise placement of an object (such as a key in the latch); aiming an object at a target (a ball game, archery or shooting) and in making precise incisions (such as those a surgeon or dressmaker makes).

Similarly, the directness can be recognised in non-practical movements such as a penetrating look (seeking attention or in response); a purposeful walk (straight to destination); a pinpointing gesture (indicating a position or place, or as though trying to penetrate the mind of the listener).

It has been observed that the motion factor of space occurs in relation to inner attitudes of paying attention (*e.g.* directedly or vaguely); mental activities of thinking, cognition (*e.g.* pinpointing an idea, seeing around a problem); and the ability for patterning and organisation (*e.g.* planning and organising a scheme of work, project or campaign).

Visually, it can be recognised that there are two opposite attitudes towards any factor: both are positive and active and demand a good deal of measurable energy. In the central, "neutral" state, there is little energy, and little attitude towards the factor.

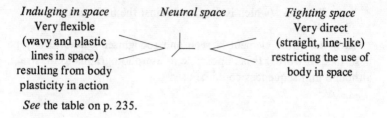

Indulging in space	*Neutral space*	*Fighting space*
Very flexible		Very direct
(wavy and plastic		(straight, line-like)
lines in space)		restricting the use of
resulting from body		body in space
plasticity in action		

See the table on p. 235.

The alternating appearance of directness and flexibility in a movement phrase or series of phrases would indicate well-developed thinking ability, attention and organisational powers. In practice, this ability might be rendered useless if the space factor were associated with other factors which did not support, or it might be a positive attribute given supportive associated elements.

In making observations of space elements, it will soon be recognised that certain elements often appear in a more natural combination. For example, the exaggerated form of flexibility is frequently associated with free flow and lightness and sustainment (*see* later comments):

The exaggerated form of directness is frequently associated with bound flow, strength and suddenness:

Later interpretations will make these comments clearer.

THE MOTION FACTOR OF WEIGHT is notated

and each element is written thus:

> *lightness or fine touch* (which is overcoming the weight of the body), and
>
> *firmness or strength* (which is resisting or fighting and utilising the body weight).

Various degrees between neutral and extremes can be discerned

+		–	neutral space	–		+
Excessive flexibility, inability to keep to any point	Normal all-round flexibility—several parts of the body going to different places at the same time	Lessened flexibility—slight roundaboutness	Aware of body and self in space—"present"	Lessened directness and sharpness, deflecting from straight	Normal direct, sharp—all body parts "lining-up" towards same aim	Very narrow, limited and pinpointed, very restricted use of space
Exaggeratedly deviating and avoiding	Generous all-round attentiveness	Widening of vision		Less accurate in thought	Keeping to the point or following a fixed line of thought	Exaggeratedly holding on to a point (of view) (?obsessional), narrow-minded

Lightness ↙

There is lightness as the common factor in such practical actions as tapping gently (on an electric typewriter), manipulating tiny pieces of material (in watchmaking or repairs), handling delicate objects (such as glass, china, flowers).

Similarly, the lightness or *fine touch* can be recognised in non-practical movements, such as a caressing gesture, a small tapping of finger or foot, while thinking, or a gesture of blessing.

Strength ⌜

There is strength or force as the common factor in such practical actions as: pushing or lifting a heavy weight; forcing or opening a tightly closed container; throwing a heavy object; or punching or hammering a resisting object.

Similarly, the strength can be recognised in non-practical movements as gripping and clenching the facial muscles (often accompanied by a tensing of shoulders and general body attitude, as though fighting against a heavy weight—maybe an opinion or a feeling); a violent gesture of head and shoulders, as in defiance, similar to getting rid of an object, or removing oneself from the offending object; a repetitive stamping of the foot and a threatening gesture of the fist as in attacking a person, or an idea—or hammering an idea into someone's head!

The motion factor of weight can be associated with, or appears in relation to, intention, will-power and sensation (that is, perception through conscious sensory processes).

Yielding	Neutral	Fighting
Very fine touch, sensitive, lighter tension in the body		Very strong, forceful, firm grip in the body

See the table on p. 237.

The alternating appearance of firmness and sensitivity in movement phrases has some connection with well-developed intentions, firmness of purpose and type of will-power. (This will be positive or of little practical value to the person, according to other associated

Various degrees between neutral state and extremes

			neutral weight			
Excessive "airiness"	Light, slight tension of airborne, buoyant	Lessened – lightness	Heavy, lacking the tension of fine touch or firmness	Lessened or weakened strength— reduced firmness	Strong, forceful, energetic, firm action or position	Very rigid, tense and cramped
Exaggerated delicacy, superficial, shallow	Sensitive, fine, delicate	Blunted sensitivity	Can be sentimental if with flow	Weakening of will-power	Resolute, strong-willed	Exaggerated stubbornness, crude (perhaps brutal)

motion factors.) The exaggerated forms of strength have frequent associations with bound flow, directness and suddenness.

The exaggerated forms of fine touch have frequent association with free flow, flexibility and sustainment.

THE MOTION FACTOR OF TIME is notated ／

and each element is written thus:

／   *sustainment* (which is indulging in time), and

／   *suddenness* (which is fighting time).

Sustainment   ／

There is sustainment as the common factor in such practical actions as the gradual guiding or feeding of material into a machine; the edging or crawling along a small tunnel.

Similarly, the sustainment can be recognised in non-practical movements such as a gradual smile, as if an idea slowly dawns; a slow calming gesture, towards an agitated group; a loitering, dawdling walk, indulging in time and no hurry.

Suddenness ／

There is suddenness as the common factor in such practical actions as darting away from an object or place, when in contact with a hot object, or a sprint start in athletics; snatching objects—from a conveyor belt as it passes; quick passing of an object, such as a ball; or using the fingers, for plucking strings or using castanets.

Similarly, the suddenness can be recognised in non-practical movements such as the agitated excitement of body-jumping (a child

Various degrees between neutral state and extremes

＋／—	／—	／—	／／ (neutral time)	／—	／—	／—＋
Hardly moving, very sustained	Leisurely, lingering, waiting, smooth, prolonged, gradual, slow	Less sustained	Neither urgent nor lingering	Reduced urgency	Brisk, sudden, staccato (particularly in repetition), urgent, immediate	Jerky, excessively sudden
Exaggeratedly lingering—lazy indulgence, hesitation	Ability to sustain over a period	Reduced enjoyment of leisurely movement		Less lively—blunted reactions	Animated, instantaneous (reactions), vivacious. Shivering, fluttering, vibrating, excited (in repetition)	Hasty, over-excitable, jerky, especially in repetitions (may be hysterical)

waiting for a promised event); a turn or jump in response to a loud, unexpected noise; the twitches of fingers or facial movements (in impatience or irritation); and the jittery transfer of weight from one foot to another (in agitation).

The motion factor of time is associated with, or appears in relation to, decisiveness, and intuition (perception by way of unconscious content and connections).

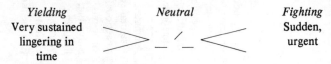

Yielding	*Neutral*	*Fighting*
Very sustained lingering in time		Sudden, urgent

See the table on p. 239.

The alternating appearance of suddenness and sustainment in movement phrases is rhythmical, indicating some intuitive and decisive quality (positive or of little practical use according to other associated motion factors).

The exaggerated forms of suddenness have frequent associations with bound flow, directness and strength.

The exaggerated forms of sustainment have frequent associations with free flow, flexibility and lightness.

THE MOTION FACTOR OF FLOW is notated ___╱___

and each element is written thus:

___╱ *free flow* (which is yielding to the flow of movement), and

╱___ *bound flow* (which is resisting the flow of movement).

Free flow ___╱

There is free flow as the common factor in such practical actions as the throwing of a net or line in fishing; running in rugby or soccer;

swinging an object to a high ledge (such as throwing heavy tyres on to a hook above head).

Similarly, free flow can be recognised in non-practical movements; such as the outgoing hearty gesture of greeting, perhaps to an old friend; wild slashing out in anger; blustering gestures, in an argument; a young child's rush towards his mother; the loose-limbed free-swinging walk of negro races; the swaying of the body to a waltz rhythm; and the easy breathing of contentment.

Bound flow

There is bound flow as the common factor in such practical actions as the careful winding of thread; the guiding of a machine in cutting out an intricate pattern; cautious stepping (on to insecure boards or on stepping stones); or the restrained jabbing at an object.

Similarly, bound flow can be recognised in non-practical movements, such as the cautious advance towards an adversary; a restrained or reluctant gesture of agreement; the inhibited walk towards an admonition; the held, caught breathing in fear of apprehension.

The motion factor of flow is associated with precision, emotional feeling and relationships.

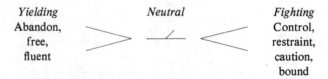

Yielding	Neutral	Fighting
Abandon,		Control,
free,		restraint,
fluent		caution,
		bound

See the table on p. 242.

The alternating appearance of bound and free flow in movement phrases has some connection with a well-balanced emotional life and ease of relationships (provided that no opposite influence is introduced by associated motion factors).

The exaggerated forms of free flow have association with flexibility and lightness and sustainment.

Various degrees between neutral state and extremes

				neutral flow			
+							+
Uncontrolled outpouring	Fluent, easy, free	Reduced fluency	Neither restrained nor free	Reduced control	Controlled, restrained	Cramped, "sticky," limited, withheld
Exaggerated, free, abandoned	Whole-hearted	Less easy-going			Slight restraint	Caution, care	Inhibited, repressed

The exaggerated forms of bound flow have frequent association with directness and strength and suddenness.

Associated movement elements

Although the generalised statements of associated movement components can be justified through observation, this does not mean that the stated relationships between elements invariably, or even usually, appear together. For instance, exaggerated sustainment frequently appears with neutral weight or heaviness giving a general lethargic content. Also, it is often, as previously stated, free-flowing, and flexible, indicating a weak, floppy, easy-going wavering attitude. There could, however, appear a combination of the exaggerated sustainment with exaggerated directness and restraint and cramp (excessive strength) which would be tense, tight, narrow and yet lazy action. This is a more conflicting state of mind (as anyone practising this movement will experience), as it mixes the laziness of exaggerated indulgence in time with the fighting attitudes of weight, space and flow. The more natural associations might be expected in situations not requiring or stimulating any special tension, even to the substitution of one element for another of a similar kind, such as sustainment in place of flexibility or free flow. Special note is made of any cross- and counter-tendencies in the relationship of elements.

For instance, it is not surprising if exaggerated suddenness which becomes hasty in repetition is associated with cramp, restricted flow and direct narrowness, *i.e.* a fighting attitude to all the elements. But hasty fine touch with free flow gives a special mixture to be noted; it indicates a "flipperty," "butterfly" kind of movement and attitude.

Another interesting association can often be noticed, namely that time is often excluded altogether in movements where there are excessive or exaggerated movement elements. This is understandable if one realises that time—decision and intuition—has a tendency to be pushed away in extremes. A kind of hypnotic or spell-like attitude can result from many extremes; extremes of rhythm, fear-inspired fixation, cramp, indulgence in trance-like whirling or ecstatic daydreaming; these are timeless states.

The normal range of movement indulgence or fighting is not excessive, except in special circumstances or in necessity. If excess and exaggeration occur habitually when those extremes have no obvious value, one is immediately alerted as to whether this indicates some kind of maladjustment, slight or intense. Equally, a habitual indulgence in the neutral states when a more active attitude is required by circumstances will reveal a lack of adaptability. An excessive use of one element at the expense of a natural balance or release attitude will reveal a one-sided and therefore limited development or adaptability.

Two of the most easily recognisable movement patterns revealing lack of adaptation, therefore, can be summarised as *exaggeration* and *excessive use of a limited range of elements*. No human being is evenly balanced but a reasonably developed child or a mature adult will have a natural access to all elements as appropriate to whatever situation occurs. The special personal "flavour" will always be present, according to the way in which these elements are combined. Educationally, teachers try to help children to retain and gain mastery over their natural effort range; therapeutically, it may be necessary to help them (or adults) to regain this range and remaster the subtle combinations of movement.

Objective or subjective movement?

The significance of the accent sign, to which all the symbols of active elements are related, is the indication that some kind of accent, stress or effort is present in any given movement.

For the purpose of describing the elements so far, the simplified form alone has been used. In practice, when observing and notating movement, it is necessary to differentiate between two kinds of movements:

(*a*) Movement which is at the service of a *practical or externally functional action*, without any particular stress of mental or emotional significance. (A straightforward working action may be almost devoid of mental significance, though of course it could equally be highly emotionally charged. The more mechanical the movement is, the less actual emotional content is involved, though again there may be strongly stressed "emotional" movement in another part of the body at the same time, and even the most mechanical movement has an individual flavour to some small degree—watch a well-drilled group of soldiers!)

(*b*) Movement which is not related to any external or objective aim, and is therefore serving an *inner-emotional* or *mental function*, such as an expressive gesture, a facial expression and so on.

Objective, functional movement is usually notated ╱, and *subjective* movement ✕. Frequently, it is necessary to write two lines of observation relating to the same movement pattern, thus:

The upper line describes pushing away an object; and the lower line the accompanying facial expression.

There may be an interspersing of functional and non-functional movement, as here:

The movement starts as a practical action, in, say, the right hand, but a cramped, intense, bound flow movement of the hand interferes with the action, but then releases into sudden tightness. The ease is also reflected in an accompanying shadow movement of sudden free flow—perhaps in the face.

Boredom, annoyance or gaiety can all influence the performance of practical action, and detract from or add to its effectiveness. All of these can be observed in the movement patterns—in children, usually in their whole body, and in adults, very often in a small isolated part of the body, such as:

tapping of foot in annoyance, or

fingers tense or gripping.

SECTION B

TWO ELEMENTS OF MOVEMENT APPEARING SIMULTANEOUSLY IN A COMBINED WAY

Combinations of movements

It has been suggested in the previous section that the significance of any element of movement can be modified by its accompanying element of a different motion factor. That is, lightness, sensitivity or fine touch will be modified if they appear with, let us say:

(*a*) *bound flow*, when it becomes tentative and delicate, cautious and restrained, or

(*b*) *free flow*, when it has then an ease, freedom and buoyancy accompanying the sensitivity, or

(*c*) *suddenness*, when it becomes lively, bright, gay and so on.

In fact, single elements of movement rarely appear over a prolonged period of time, and most of the words we use in everyday life to describe actions and feelings have a combination of two or more elements of movement. This is one reason why it is so difficult to describe isolated elements in words. Isolated elements often appear momentarily as one kind of preparation or recovery movement: thus, lightness can be a preparation for a slashing action; the lightness written in brackets indicates a preparation or transitional movement:

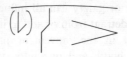

Incomplete efforts and inner attitudes

These combinations of two elements are called *incomplete efforts*, and they reveal inner states of mind which are referred to here as *inner attitudes*. Many sequences and series of them occur in all our movement phrases used in everyday life, and they form the basis of dance movement.

Incomplete efforts can appear as a substitute for a *basic action* which is a combination of three elements (*see* Section C), and in

these cases where a practical physical action is required, the movement may well become less appropriate to the job in hand. For
instance, if an action of *punching* ⌐‾‾ is necessary:

the man using only   lacks the necessary   ╱
strength and directness   suddenness   ‾
                              (which is essential in a punch)

or if he uses only   he lacks the necessary __╱
sudden strength   directness

or if only direct   ╱‾‾   he lacks the strength   (
and sudden   ‾

In this sense then, an incomplete effort is really a depleted external
action. As mental or emotional *inner attitudes*, these combinations of two elements are not depleted actions, but complete states
of mind. For example: a flexible sustained movement can reveal a
state of slow mental consideration.

There are six possible combinations of motion factors:

weight and flow __⊥__ and its opposite *space and time* ⊥

weight and time __⊥__ and its opposite *space and flow* __⊥

flow and time __╱__ and its opposite *weight and space* ⊩

Relationships of inner attitudes

The relationship of one inner attitude to another is shown visually
in Diagram 1. It is necessary to see this as a three-dimensional
model, with three axes:

weight/flow ....space/time ⎫ opposite
weight/time ....space/flow ⎬ inner
flow/time..................................weight/space ⎭ attitudes

All six inner attitudes have equal though differing significance.
This is shown visually by the equal lengths, or distances, between

two neighbouring inner attitudes. There is no significance in the order of discussing these inner attitudes (*see* Diagram 2).

Interrelationships are shown visually. Each inner attitude has a close relationship, which means that it shares a common factor with four of the other inner attitudes, and is completely opposite to only one (as previously stated in Diagram 1).

For example, as shown in Diagram 3, weight/flow has a relationship with space/flow and time/flow (because of the common element of flow) (shown by solid line); and with weight/space and weight/time (because of the common element of weight) (shown by dotted line).

Diagram 4 shows relationships of inner attitudes (combinations of two factors) to movements which comprise a combination of three factors. The significance of this diagram will be evident in Section C.

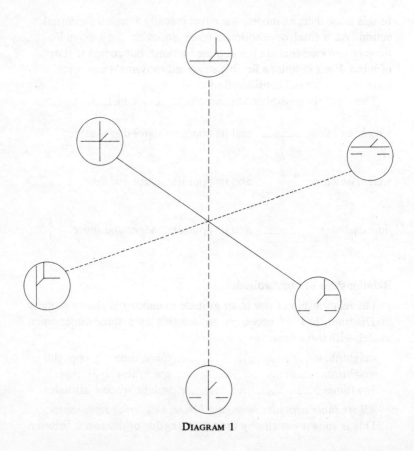

DIAGRAM 1

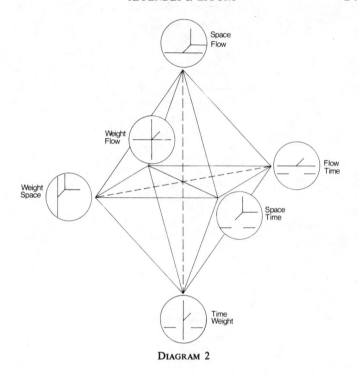

DIAGRAM 2

Variations of inner attitudes

Each motion factor has its alternative of yielding or fighting element, and this obviously gives four possible combinations of two elements—or four variations of each inner attitude. (In addition, of course, there are the varied degrees between exaggeration and lessened attitude, but for this particular explanation, these various degrees will mainly be ignored.)

WEIGHT AND FLOW

Associated with a less conscious inner attitude, it can be dream-like and creative, or doubting and restrictive (this inner attitude is dominant in the waltz). It combines emotional feeling with the dynamic of sensation, and excludes thinking and intuition:

These latter two factors are in the background and one or other, or both, may appear as a recovery.

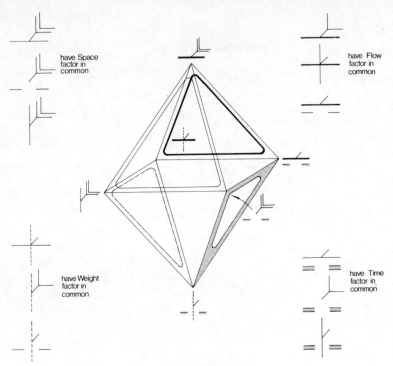

have Space factor in common

have Flow factor in common

have Weight factor in common

have Time factor in common

DIAGRAM 3

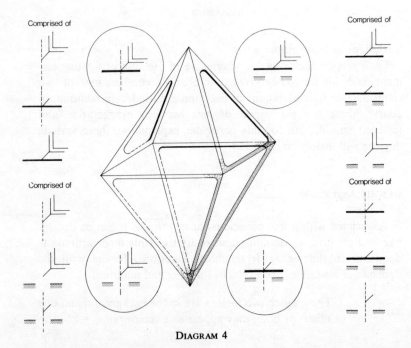

Comprised of

Comprised of

Comprised of

Comprised of

DIAGRAM 4

The four basic variations (ignoring, for the moment, most exaggerations) are as follows:

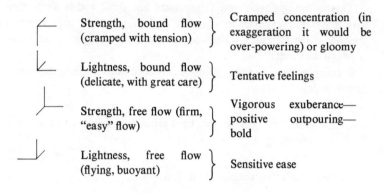

	Strength, bound flow (cramped with tension)	Cramped concentration (in exaggeration it would be over-powering) or gloomy
	Lightness, bound flow (delicate, with great care)	Tentative feelings
	Strength, free flow (firm, "easy" flow)	Vigorous exuberance— positive outpouring— bold
	Lightness, free flow (flying, buoyant)	Sensitive ease

SPACE AND TIME

The opposite state from weight and flow, the *space and time* combination, is associated with conscious awareness and practicality ("awake" attitudes—often one of the dominating inner attitudes in literal mime action).

It combines thinking and intuition, and excludes emotional feeling and sensation:

these remain in the background, and may appear as a recovery.

The four basic variations are given below:

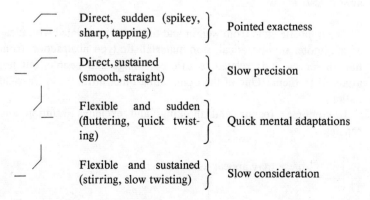

	Direct, sudden (spikey, sharp, tapping)	Pointed exactness
	Direct, sustained (smooth, straight)	Slow precision
	Flexible and sudden (fluttering, quick twisting)	Quick mental adaptations
	Flexible and sustained (stirring, slow twisting)	Slow consideration

WEIGHT AND TIME

This is the opposite state from space and flow, and is associated with rhythmic experience—human and materialistic attachments, down-to-earth attitudes. (Often one of the dominating inner attitudes of negro dancing.)

It combines sensing and intuition, and excludes thinking and emotional feeling:

these remain in the background and may appear as a recovery.

The four basic variations are as follows:

Strength and suddenness (vigorous rhythm in repetition)	}	Forceful, energetic (in extreme may be dogmatic, materialistic)
Light, sudden (bright, brisk)	}	Lively, delicate, gay, crisp (in exaggeration, superficial)
Strength, sustainment (powerful)	}	Slow persistency, concentrated perseverance
Light sustainment (quiet, peaceful, soothing)	}	Lingering sensitivity, unruffled delicacy

SPACE AND FLOW

The opposite state from weight and time, and associated with ideas of a remote, non-practical, non-materialistic-type abstraction from human senses, it is related to external things and people, but not attached to them. (One of the dominating inner attitudes in classical ballet.)

It combines feeling and thinking, and excludes intuition and sensing:

these may appear as a recovery.

The four basic variations are given below:

⟋⎓	Bound direct (limited, restricted, controlled)	Precise, narrow, withheld, cramped
⟋⎓	Free direct (fluent, channelled)	Directed, purposeful ease
⟍⎓	Bound flexible (screwing, knotting, restricted)	Careful, all-round consideration
⟋	Free flexible (undulating, fluent, winding)	Carefree ease, dispersing

WEIGHT AND SPACE

The opposite state from flow and time, it is associated with unimaginative, unchanging stability, steadfastness. (One of the dominating attitudes in dimensional movement of dances like those of Pueblo Indians.)

It combines sensing and thinking, and excludes intuition and emotional feeling:

⟋⎓   these may appear as a recovery.

The four basic variations are as follows:

⌐	Strength, directness (firm, directed, solid)	Stolid, commanding, resolute, powerful (in extreme, stubborn)
⟨	Strength, flexibility (lithe, sinuous)	Striving (in extreme, tortured)
⌐	Lightness, directness (pointed, threadlike)	Gentle and direct, straightforward, sensitively receptive
⟩	Lightness, flexibility (gentle, spiralling, roundabout)	Sensitive, all-round awareness (with flexibility extreme, vague)

FLOW AND TIME ___/___

The opposite state from weight and space, it is associated with change, adaptability, mobility and variation—a less conscious attitude. (One of the dominating attitudes in, for instance, a dance drama depicting agitation, change and fluidity.)

It combines emotional feeling and intuition and excludes sensation and thinking:

⊦— these may appear as a recovery.

The four basic variations are given below:

⟋—	Bound, sudden (jerky spurts of action) ⎱	Restless or abrupt withholding
—⟋	Bound, sustained (cautious stalking, controlled adjustment) ⎱	Measured, cautious, controlled withholding
—⟋	Free, sudden (bouncy, urgent or abrupt) ⎱	Excited (in repetition), agitated change
—⟋	Free, sustained (lazy, unhurried) ⎱	Leisurely ease

Application to movement observation of the individual

In any movement, it is always possible to discern to some degree the moving person's attitude to all four movement elements. That means that a reply could be given in every case to "how does he move in relation to the weight factor, time factor?" and so on. The subtlety of observation, however, is not to progress in this mechanical way, but to discern what movement elements are used predominantly at which moment and in what order. The remark that certain elements or motion factors are "excluded but may appear as a recovery" in fact means that they are there in a kind of inner, shadow balance, and are acting as a "regulating" force, ready to be called upon in recovery or preparation for a new positive action. It is often in a lack of this natural recovery action that disturbances are revealed.

It should be noted that this is yet another kind of recovery from that noted in Section A, when the opposite element was kept in reserve as a recovery, for example, lightness in recovery for strength or the recovery referred to at the beginning of this section, when one element alone balances and acts as recovery for two or three combined.

SECTION C

THE ASSOCIATION OF THREE MOTION FACTORS

Working actions and mental, emotional actions

Basic effort actions

The most efficient working actions are performed in a rhythmical phrase of preparation, action and recovery. The action itself is most often a combination of three elements—of weight, time and space— at various degrees of intensity according to the particular job. An inefficient action can often be recognised as using inappropriate intensity, or an inappropriate combination of elements.

Working actions are related to external objective activity (often handling or manipulating materials), and can be very simply grouped into *eight basic effort actions*:

Thrust		*Float*
direct		flexible
strong	and its opposite	light
sudden		sustained

Press		*Flick*
direct		flexible
strong	and its opposite	light
sustained		sudden

Glide		*Slash*
direct		flexible
light	and its opposite	strong
sustained		sudden

Dab		*Wring*
direct		flexible
light	and its opposite	strong
sudden		sustained

Externalised drives

When these same combinations of three elements appear not as functional, working action, but as mental, emotional "action," they are called *externalised drives*, and would therefore appear having a different significance. Various examples are listed below:

Working action

Thrusting, hitting or jabbing action, knocking in a nail, punching a punchball.

Mental action or externalised drive

Hitting or thrusting gesture (perhaps in support of a dogmatic statement, or banging a table, as though trying to hit an idea into someone's head—a frequent gesture at political meetings!)

Working action (W.A.)

A mixture, floating or stirring action, as if mixing together light, fluffy powders.

Mental action (M.A.) Externalised drive

An all-round floating gesture (perhaps while describing a peaceful, relaxed time spent in the sun, or a lightly considering winding of the head or eyes).

W.A.

Pushing or lifting or pressing action; lifting a heavy weight, or pushing away a heavy object or squeezing together a resistant material such as clay.

M.A.

A pressure (of eyebrows, as in frowning, or a whole body movement of "pulling oneself together").

W.A.

A flicking, brushing-off action, such as removing a speck of dust from material, or flicking aside a light object.

M.A.

A flicking, casual or flippant gesture (accompanying a laugh, or a slight shrug of the shoulders in a flirtatious or irritated way).

W.A.

A gliding, smoothing action—smoothing out a piece of tissue paper, or testing along the edge of a delicate piece of glass.

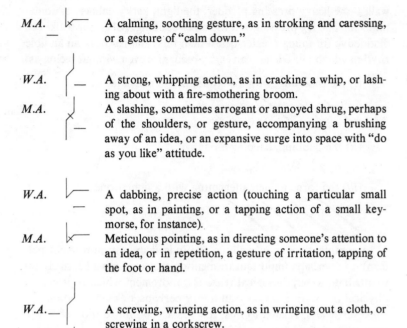

M.A.   A calming, soothing gesture, as in stroking and caressing, or a gesture of "calm down."

W.A.   A strong, whipping action, as in cracking a whip, or lashing about with a fire-smothering broom.

M.A.   A slashing, sometimes arrogant or annoyed shrug, perhaps of the shoulders, or gesture, accompanying a brushing away of an idea, or an expansive surge into space with "do as you like" attitude.

W.A.   A dabbing, precise action (touching a particular small spot, as in painting, or a tapping action of a small key-morse, for instance).

M.A.   Meticulous pointing, as in directing someone's attention to an idea, or in repetition, a gesture of irritation, tapping of the foot or hand.

W.A.   A screwing, wringing action, as in wringing out a cloth, or screwing in a corkscrew.

M.A.   A winding, wringing gesture—"wringing of hands" in agony—writhing of the body in avoiding an issue, screwing up the face in distaste.

Of course, few functional actions or *externalised drives* are limited to a single simple action in the phrase or sequence; usually there is a change from one to another in fairly quick succession. Also it should be noted that the very superficial interpretations given above regarding the externalised drives are generalisations for the purpose of illustration.

Application to observations of individuals

To consider generalising about people from the observation of basic actions alone is very crude. For instance, no person is ever a "thruster" or a "wringer" or a "dabber" alone, although any one action may be repeatedly observed in a person's individual movement pattern. It is, nevertheless, only significant in relation to how the person goes into the movement and recovers from it, and to a whole series of other related aspects of spatial patterns and body attitudes. Some people have very easily observed basic actions in, for instance, their walk—the heavy pressing plodder, the light, perky dabber, or sometimes the one leg pressing and the other dabbing. All of our walks are distinctive (in much greater detail than this) and result in an audible rhythm which our friends can easily recognise even without seeing us:

(*i*) the plodding, with a slight stress to one side,

(*ii*) the dabbing, tripping along,

(*iii*) the forceful step alternating with a lighter one,

In commenting upon walking (or indeed on any movement pattern) it is perhaps important to mention that care must be taken not to attribute to psychological reasons a movement which is primarily physical in origin caused by an injury perhaps, or malformation.

Nevertheless, related to this, there is a good illustration of how a repeated practical action can induce an experience through which the mood of the action is felt in the body. A woman had both knees stiff and rigid after surgery, and was thereby extremely limited in movement especially in changing positions from standing to sitting and vice versa. The resulting body movement for a purely functional purpose of sitting and standing was a strong *wringing* action. This was habitual and frequent, and it was interesting to observe that she developed after some time an increase of the use of a *dabbing* action in her *shadow* movements of fingers and face, clearly a compensatory movement of the body and mind mechanism.

The changes from one movement phrase to another

Greater subtleties are observable in everyday movement phrases, when the changes from one, two or three elements in all possible combinations are used. Some of these changes are abrupt and jarring, some are fluid and harmonious. Changes between those actions which are akin to the other actions make for smooth transitions while changes between opposites make for abruptness. When there is a necessity to change from one movement combination to a distant or opposite mixture, we frequently incorporate transitional movement elements to ease the change, to make it a "natural" transition. Awkward or clumsy transitions usually reveal a lack of inner mastery; a person jerking from one attitude to another causes tension and discomfort. Quick or immediate transitions can also be mastered through resilient buoyancy, when there is little transitional sequence, but rather a rebound action.

The relationships between the eight basic effort actions can be seen in the cube in Diagram 5.

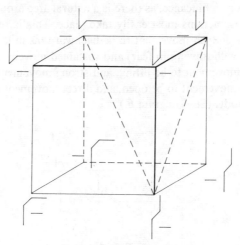

DIAGRAM 5 *The effort cube*

Those effort actions which are akin are separated only by an edge, for example, between light, flexible sustained and light, flexible sudden; those slightly more distant, by a plane diagonal, for example, light, flexible sustained and flexible strong sudden; those opposite by the cube diagonal, for example, light flexible sustained and strong direct sudden. In different terminology, the akin actions have only one element different and two the same, the slightly akin have two different elements, and one the same, the opposite have all three elements different, *e.g.*:

press / glide / float / flick

press / flick

It can be seen that the first phrase alters only one element at any time and makes for a smooth and developing sequence, while the second phrase gives an abrupt, sudden and alternating sequence (in repetitions) which may be either jerky and uncomfortable, or resilient and bouncy, according to the individual tiny transitional movements between the two.

The placement of the eight actions in their particular corners of the cube has a significance, as there is a natural area around the body in which these actions most easily take place. This is related to the tendency for sudden movement to be backward (as in leaping out of the way, or withdrawing in fear) and sustained movement to be forward; light movement to be lifting, and strong movement to be sinking; flexible movement to be open, and direct movement to be closed across the body. (See Diagram 6.)

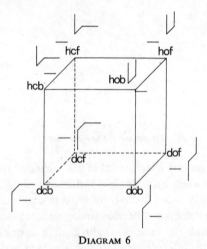

DIAGRAM 6

So we see that *pressing* is deep, closed, forward, and its opposite, *flicking*, is high, open, backward and so on.

Each of the eight basic actions has three variations: one spaceless, one weightless and one timeless, while flow is substituted for the element held in the background.

Imagine a body standing inside the cube. (Closed action is to the left of the body (when the right side is active) and open action is to the right.)

In giving an example of a possible interpretation of an externalised drive, it is suggested that frequently a gesture or shadow movement supports a verbal statement. However, when a shadow movement, gesture or body attitude is not supporting what is being said, this gives a clue to the speaker's intention; a crude example of this would be "I shall tell you all about it"—verbally an open statement of intention to share an idea. The accompanying movement to this statement was a crossing of arms tightly (narrow), a slight rounding of the spine (closing) and a backwards pull so that the head was dropped and the chin withdrawn. Clearly, the speaker did not really mean to tell very much. Usually, signs would be much more subtle than this.

Flow as an alternative factor

Still in the realm of externalised drives, there is a whole new range when we consider the *motion factor of flow* as a possible alternative to one of the other factors.

We have said previously that the combination of weight, time and space gives:

An action-like drive:

It lacks flow, which remains in the background as a balancing factor, and is frequently used in preparation and recovery.

If we substitute flow for space effort we have:

An emotional stressed drive:

It lacks space effort, which remains in the background, and may well be used as a recovery; for instance, when "coming back to reason after an emotional outburst." The observed movements might change from wild, free flow—strong, urgent repetitive actions, into more directed, controlled (more bound) sequences.

If we substitute flow for time we have:

A timeless, spell-like drive:

It lacks time, which remains in the background and may be used as a recovery, as when "coming back to a sense of time after being spellbound by something or someone" (this seems timeless while it affects us). For example, the timelessness is experienced in extreme fear or terror of seeing a snake, or an aggressive beast, or imaginary witch-like creature with power over you.

	weight space	weight time	time space	weight flow	flow time	space flow
Action-like drive, combines:						
Emotional stressed drive, combines:						
Timeless, spell-like drive, combines:						
Weightless, visionary drive, combines:						

If we substitute flow for weight we have:

A weightless, visionary drive:

(not necessarily of a high level!).

It lacks weight, which remains in the background and may be used as a recovery, for instance, "coming down to earth after a wonderful vision of what we might do."

Combination of three elements

I have said previously that combinations of two elements (inner attitudes) appear very frequently in our normal movement patterns. Combinations of three elements (externalised drives) are also frequently observable in phrases which are more active and indicate a carrying through of an inner attitude into practice. The relative number of drives to inner attitudes will be different in every person, and leads to a different interpretation of the patterns; a man of action may have many more drives, fully externalised, than perhaps a creative artist, and they will be of a different type.

Each type of externalised drive carries within it *three* inner attitudes (*see* Diagram 4 on p. 250).

Now the significance of Diagrams 3 and 4 in Section B can be seen. The changes from one drive to another, through various inner attitudes, can be simple and "akin," or difficult and uncomfortable. Also the relationships between near or akin inner attitudes and drives can be followed.

Selection from possible interpretations

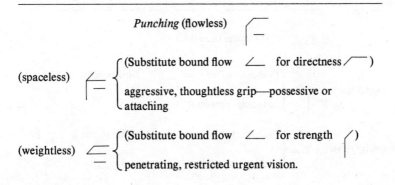

(timeless)

　　(Substitute bound flow ∠— for suddenness ╱ —)

　　hypnotic cramp, concentration, domination

Slashing (flowless)

(spaceless) —

　　(Substitute free flow —╱ for flexibility ╱)

　　uncontrolled, wild, thoughtless—careless

(weightless)

　　(Substitute bound flow ∠— for strength ╱)

　　controlled, sudden avoidance

(timeless)

　　(Substitute bound flow ∠— for suddenness ╱ —)

　　restricted, assertive influence

Pressing (flowless)

(spaceless)

　　(Substitute bound flow ∠— for directness ╱⌐)

　　restrictive, powerful pressure

(weightless)

　　(Substitute bound flow ∠— for strength ╱)

　　slow penetration of restricted idea

(timeless)

　　(Substitute free flow —╱ for sustainment ╱ —)

　　resolute drive for power, surging.

Wringing (flowless)

(spaceless)

　　(Substitute free flow —╱ for flexibility ╱)

　　outgoing, powerful ease

(weightless)

　　(Substitute bound flow ∠— for strength ╱)

　　cautious, considered comparison

(timeless) ⎰ (Substitute free flow ___/ for sustainment ___/)
         ⎱ generous outpouring, influencing

Dabbing (flowless)

(spaceless) ⎰ (Substitute bound flow ∠ for directness /‾)
          ⎱ niggling, narrow irritations

(weightless) ⎰ (Substitute free flow ___/ for lightness ↓/)
           ⎱ lively ideas and reactions

(timeless) ⎰ (Substitute bound flow ∠ for suddenness /)
         ⎱ tentative, restrictèd influence, meticulous

Flicking (flowless)

(spaceless) ⎰ (Substitute free flow ___/ for flexibility ↗/)
          ⎱ flippant, off-hand

(weightless) ⎰ (Substitute free flow ___/ for lightness ↓/)
           ⎱ sudden imaginative ideas

(timeless) ⎰ (Substitute bound flow ∠ for suddenness /)
         ⎱ uncertain restraint

Gliding (flowless)

(spaceless) ⎰ (Substitute bound flow ∠ for directness __/)
          ⎱ hesitant, restrained (? shy)

(weightless) ⎰ (Substitute free flow ___/ for sustainment /)
           ⎱ continued pursuance of clear aim.

(timeless)   ⌐ (Substitute free flow ＿／ for sustainment ／)
         ⌊ open to clear direction and guidance

Floating (flowless)   ⱱ

(spaceless)   ⌐ (Substitute free flow ＿／ for flexibility ⌐)
         ⌊ formless, indulging

(weightless)   ⌐ (Substitute free flow ＿／ for lightness ⌐)
         ⌊ imaginative indulging

(timeless)   ⌐ (Substitute free flow ＿／ for sustainment ／)
         ⌊ yielding to influence

Any exaggeration or diminishing of intensity will swing the interpretations from those associated with "normal" to either:

(*a*) a more obsessional degree of indulgence or opposition (written as +) for instance:

     becomes brutal instead of firm if exaggerated

or:

(*b*) a lessened degree of intensity (written as) for instance:

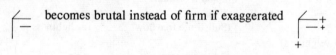

     becomes sentimental if reduced

SECTION D

SEQUENCES OF MOVEMENT

Attention, intention, decision and action (precision or relationship)

It is necessary to distinguish between different mental attitudes, as they appear in a phrase of movement preceding action, or as they appear almost simultaneously with the action. The build-up of phrases was discussed in Chapter 4, but a simplified form of movement sequence as shown here is fairly typical of a normal sequence of mental activity (though the appearance of these motion factors is not limited to this order).

Space   *Weight*   *Time*   *Flow*

Variations, reversions and complications on this basic phrase are normally observed in an individual's personal movement pattern.

Attention always contains some *spatial* effort, but can be varied and given shades of meaning according to the factors with which it is associated (as well as where it appears in the phrase). Similarly:

Intention always contains some *weight* effort;
Decision always contains some *time* effort;
Action (or resulting *precision* or relationship) always contains some *flow* effort.

If we look at each aspect of mental attitude in turn, and see which movement associations are possible, some of the nuances of each become clear. These nuances are more subtle than words can describe, so that the interpretations often seem to lack the very differences which we are seeking, but a person who has some mastery over his own movement can easily be brought to experience these differences.

The use of the dot symbol after a particular element is to denote its primary importance in the combined movement, and therefore the lesser importance of the supporting element or elements.

Attention ⊥

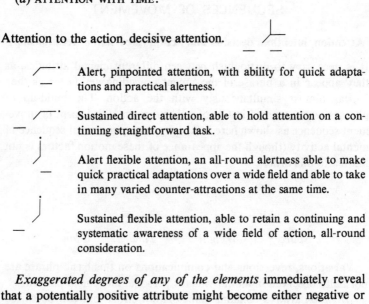

(*a*) ATTENTION WITH TIME:

Attention to the action, decisive attention.   ⊥

Alert, pinpointed attention, with ability for quick adaptations and practical alertness.

Sustained direct attention, able to hold attention on a continuing straightforward task.

Alert flexible attention, an all-round alertness able to make quick practical adaptations over a wide field and able to take in many varied counter-attractions at the same time.

Sustained flexible attention, able to retain a continuing and systematic awareness of a wide field of action, all-round consideration.

Exaggerated degrees of any of the elements immediately reveal that a potentially positive attribute might become either negative or futile, thus:

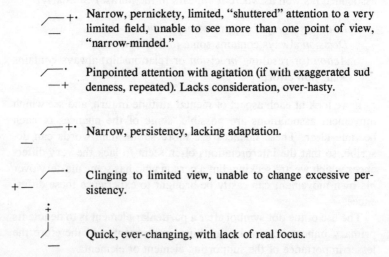

Narrow, pernickety, limited, "shuttered" attention to a very limited field, unable to see more than one point of view, "narrow-minded."

Pinpointed attention with agitation (if with exaggerated suddenness, repeated). Lacks consideration, over-hasty.

Narrow, persistency, lacking adaptation.

Clinging to limited view, unable to change excessive persistency.

Quick, ever-changing, with lack of real focus.

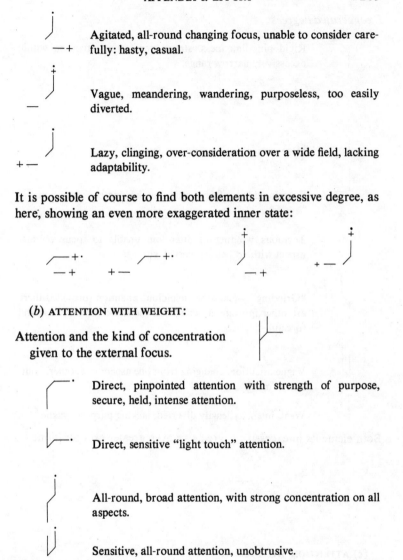

Agitated, all-round changing focus, unable to consider carefully: hasty, casual.

Vague, meandering, wandering, purposeless, too easily diverted.

Lazy, clinging, over-consideration over a wide field, lacking adaptability.

It is possible of course to find both elements in excessive degree, as here, showing an even more exaggerated inner state:

(*b*) ATTENTION WITH WEIGHT:

Attention and the kind of concentration given to the external focus.

Direct, pinpointed attention with strength of purpose, secure, held, intense attention.

Direct, sensitive "light touch" attention.

All-round, broad attention, with strong concentration on all aspects.

Sensitive, all-round attention, unobtrusive.

The overall characteristic of attention with weight is stability; it is reliable and unalterable, compared with the alert, bright practicality of attention with time.

Exaggerated degrees:

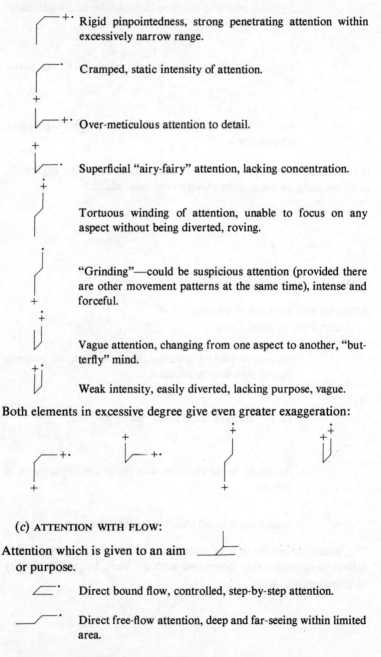

Rigid pinpointedness, strong penetrating attention within excessively narrow range.

Cramped, static intensity of attention.

Over-meticulous attention to detail.

Superficial "airy-fairy" attention, lacking concentration.

Tortuous winding of attention, unable to focus on any aspect without being diverted, roving.

"Grinding"—could be suspicious attention (provided there are other movement patterns at the same time), intense and forceful.

Vague attention, changing from one aspect to another, "butterfly" mind.

Weak intensity, easily diverted, lacking purpose, vague.

Both elements in excessive degree give even greater exaggeration:

(*c*) ATTENTION WITH FLOW:

Attention which is given to an aim or purpose.

Direct bound flow, controlled, step-by-step attention.

Direct free-flow attention, deep and far-seeing within limited area.

Flexible bound flow, controlled attention to wider range, or varied aspects.

Flexible free-flow attention, broad and varied, open to impressions, far-seeing.

The overall characteristic of attention with flow is related to the ability to envisage, foresee and to some degree to plan towards a future aim.

Exaggerated degrees:

Paying cautious attention to one step at a time, over-limited vision, very narrow view of problem.

Over-cautious, controlled, restrained or inhibited attention (can also be withdrawing), reluctant facing of situation.

Area of attention too narrow, unable to take more than one idea into account, follows line of attention to its limit, "blinkered," misses related facts.

Follows freely line of attention (without caution), over-emotionalising, lacks discretion.

Tries to cope with too many aspects at the same time and thereby loses focus, restrained and cautious and ineffectual.

Cramped, inhibited and restrained, attention is tortured and changing from one aspect to another.

Generous and open attitude becomes undifferentiated in focus, cannot stick to the point, vague and undefined.

Attention swamped by feelings, lacks any caution and discrimination in all-round awareness of problem.

Both elements in excessive degree give even greater exaggeration:

Intention

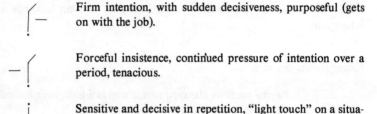

(*a*) INTENTION WITH TIME:

The strength of intention related
to the way of action.

Firm intention, with sudden decisiveness, purposeful (gets on with the job).

Forceful insistence, continued pressure of intention over a period, tenacious.

Sensitive and decisive in repetition, "light touch" on a situation.

Light sustainment, handling of people and situations, sensitive and "relaxed" over a period.

The overall characteristic of intention with time is related to a person's attitude of will-power, sense of purpose and drive, and his ability to carry this out rhythmically.

Exaggerated degrees:

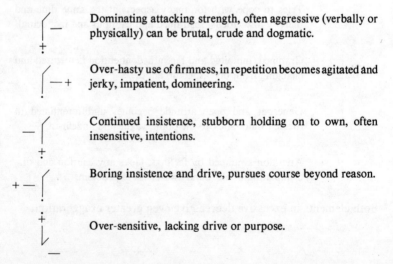

Dominating attacking strength, often aggressive (verbally or physically) can be brutal, crude and dogmatic.

Over-hasty use of firmness, in repetition becomes agitated and jerky, impatient, domineering.

Continued insistence, stubborn holding on to own, often insensitive, intentions.

Boring insistence and drive, pursues course beyond reason.

Over-sensitive, lacking drive or purpose.

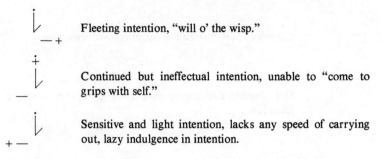

Fleeting intention, "will o' the wisp."

Continued but ineffectual intention, unable to "come to grips with self."

Sensitive and light intention, lacks any speed of carrying out, lazy indulgence in intention.

Both elements in excessive degree give greater exaggeration:

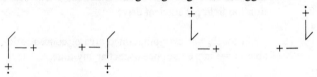

(*b*) INTENTION WITH SPACE:

The strength of intention related to external focus.

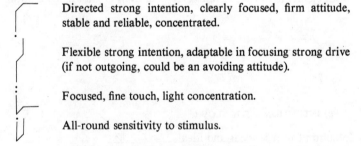

Directed strong intention, clearly focused, firm attitude, stable and reliable, concentrated.

Flexible strong intention, adaptable in focusing strong drive (if not outgoing, could be an avoiding attitude).

Focused, fine touch, light concentration.

All-round sensitivity to stimulus.

The overall characteristic of intention with space is stability, reliability and "taking an attitude" to a situation.

Exaggerated degrees:

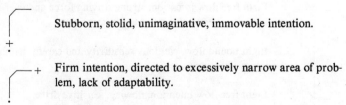

Stubborn, stolid, unimaginative, immovable intention.

Firm intention, directed to excessively narrow area of problem, lack of adaptability.

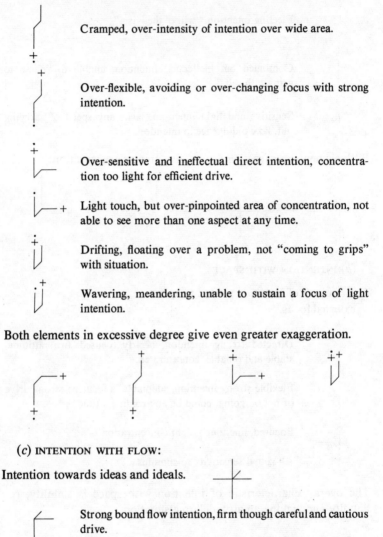

Cramped, over-intensity of intention over wide area.

Over-flexible, avoiding or over-changing focus with strong intention.

Over-sensitive and ineffectual direct intention, concentration too light for efficient drive.

Light touch, but over-pinpointed area of concentration, not able to see more than one aspect at any time.

Drifting, floating over a problem, not "coming to grips" with situation.

Wavering, meandering, unable to sustain a focus of light intention.

Both elements in excessive degree give even greater exaggeration.

(c) INTENTION WITH FLOW:

Intention towards ideas and ideals.

Strong bound flow intention, firm though careful and cautious drive.

Firm free flow intention, strong driving force and energy, if outgoing, persuasive to others, enterprising.

Light bound flow, cautious sensitivity and careful withholding of intention.

Light free flow intention, flowing, sensitive drive.

The overall characteristic of intention with flow is a less conscious, more feeling, state of intention and drive.

Exaggerated degrees:

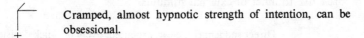

Cramped, almost hypnotic strength of intention, can be obsessional.

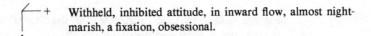

Withheld, inhibited attitude, in inward flow, almost nightmarish, a fixation, obsessional.

Bulldozing, overbearing force.

Unthinking, surging energy, lacking consideration and discernment, reckless.

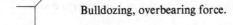

Over-sensitive and delicate relations to situations or people.

Hesitant, over-cautious restraint with sensitivity.

Drifting in over-sensitivity, almost fainting in weakness of intention.

Dreamy, even ecstatic, indulgence in impractical dreams, unfocused drifting.

Both elements in excessive degree give even greater exaggeration.

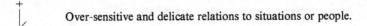

Decision   ╱

(*a*) DECISION WITH SPACE:

Decision about the way of action,
reactive to inner or external stimulus.

Direct suddenness, clearly focused, lively or quick decision.

Flexible suddenness, quick, adaptable lively decision, taking in many points of view immediately.

Direct sustainment, clearly directed, considered decisions.

Flexible sustainment, all-round contemplation and gradually achieved decision.

The overall characteristic of decision with space is related to the focus of decisiveness, an alert practicality.

Exaggerated degrees:

Hasty decisions, in repetition agitated.

Over-pinpointed focus to decision, narrow, limited awareness of implications.

Hasty, flexible action in decision, shrugging reaction.

Quick decisions and reactions, lacking clear focus.

Exaggerated slowness and sensitivity in decision, though aware of straightforward problem.

Slow decisions, with very limited awareness of situation.

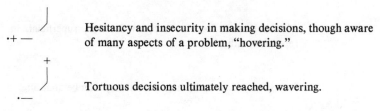

Hesitancy and insecurity in making decisions, though aware of many aspects of a problem, "hovering."

Tortuous decisions ultimately reached, wavering.

Both elements in excessive degree give even greater exaggeration.

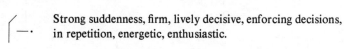

(b) DECISION WITH WEIGHT:

Decision which has a rhythmical, dynamic excitement.

Strong suddenness, firm, lively decisive, enforcing decisions, in repetition, energetic, enthusiastic.

Light suddenness, sensitive and delicate with decisiveness.

Strong sustainment, forceful continuance of a policy decision, or a reaction.

Light sustainment, sensitivity in gradually developing decision.

The overall characteristic of decision with weight is the driving power behind the decision, the energy or sensitivity to express or support an intuitive decision.

Exaggerated degrees:

Hasty, reckless reactions and decisions.

Dogmatic, brutal drive in decision.

Agitated, light decisions, in repetition, vibrating, oscillating.

Almost lacking force to support decision, superficial, in repetition, dithering.

Excessively slow and ponderous, dreary, can be doubting.

Ruthless, over-forceful, pedantic.

Lingering indulgence, never coming to the decision.

Afraid to enforce own drive, hovering.

Both elements in excessive degree give even greater exaggeration.

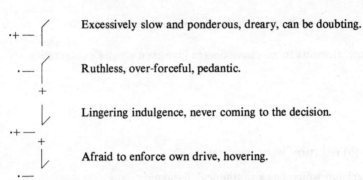

(c) DECISION WITH FLOW:

Decision regarding the aim or ideal.

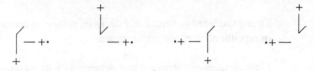

Bound flow suddenness, restrained, careful decisiveness.

Free flow suddenness, lively, far-envisaging, daring, audacious decisions.

Bound flow sustainment, careful and controlled decision slowly reached.

Free flow sustainment, easy, relaxed, slowly coming to decision.

The overall characteristic of decision with flow is the possibility of fluidity and adaptability (mobility) within the decision.

Exaggerated degrees:

    Jerky (particularly in repetition), hasty jumping to decision.

    Restricted, inhibited, withdrawn, reluctant decisions which shoot out.

    Over-hasty, rushing at decision.

    Reckless, overwhelming involvement in decision.

    Hesitant, over-slow caution in decision.

    Cramped, inhibited, over-cautious decisions.

    Over-indulgence in time, often loses the opportunity for making a decision.

    Excessively sentimental, drifting along towards a decision.

Both elements in excessive degree give even greater exaggeration.

Action: the flow of the activity or relationship (its precision or its progression)

It is concerned with the carrying out of the previously made decision, that is, how the action or relationship develops and the kind of attention paid to it.

(a) PRECISION WITH SPACE (RELATIONSHIP WITH SPACE):

    Direct bound flow, limited to one aspect, pinpointed cautious action, formal.

    Flexible bound flow, all-round awareness with care and restraint.

Direct free flow, surging, easy, relaxed, directed focus in carrying out action.

Flexible free flow, uninhibited, wide view and sweeping surge of activity, exploratory.

The overall characteristic of precision and relationship with space is its focused awareness of the activity and its problems or related aspects.

Exaggerated degrees:

Inhibited, over-cautious self-restriction, can lead to lack of action, coldness.

Narrow-minded, over-limited view of action with caution.

Cramped, inhibited meandering, often inability to deal with problem, although recognised.

Cautious but too easily diverted to different aspects, misses the point.

Over-enthusiastic, overwhelming, uncontrolled activity on limited action.

Narrow-minded, failing to see more than very limited aspect, surging on with enthusiasm.

Uncontrolled meandering, "heart more than thought."

Losing way in over-flexibility, leads to lack of focus.

Both elements in excessive degree give even greater exaggeration.

(b) PRECISION WITH WEIGHT:

Concerned with the force or drive connected
with the carrying out of action.

Strong bound flow, cautious, forceful progression (if outward flow).

Light bound flow, delicate restraint and care in carrying out
action or in relationship.

Strong free flow, energetic and forceful purpose, emphatic,
influencing (if outward flow).

Light free flow, delicate, fine touch with ease and freedom in
carrying out action.

The overall characteristic of precision with weight is its less conscious, less analytical sensing and feeling for the activity.

Exaggerated degrees:

Gripping restriction and restraint, holding back, often associated with fear and nightmarish sensation.

Over-forceful, often to cramp and tenseness, making action
ineffectual.

Over-cautious, restricted with sensitivity.

Excessive sensitivity, superficial, lack of drive with cautious
approach.

Strong over-emotional, lack of control, often dissolves into
weakness or changes to cramp, fury.

Overwhelming strength and power, drives forward without
sensitivity, brutal, crude, aggressive (if outward flow).

Indulgence in sentimental attitude to action or relationship
(particularly if associated with   or   ).

Over-delicate and sensitive, easily discouraged.

Both elements in excessive degree give even greater exaggeration.

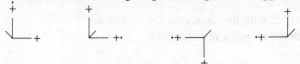

(c) PRECISION WITH TIME:

Concerned with the urgency of carrying out
the action or making a relationship.

    Sudden bound flow, controlled, lively carrying out of action.

    Sustained bound flow, calm, controlled action, leisurely.

    Sudden free flow, excited, lively outpouring of enthusiasm for action, spontaneous.

    Sustained free flow, calm ease and freedom of action, patient and gradual adaptations.

The overall characteristic of precision with time is seen in its quality of adaptability (mobility) towards the action, or making the relationship.

Exaggerated degrees:

    Inhibited jerky action, lack of ease and freedom.

    Agitated (particularly in repetition), restless but controlled.

    Over-restrained, over-cautious care and control of action.

    Exaggerated, slow, controlled action almost stops.

    Lively reckless changeability, can be irresponsible.

    Agitated and over-excitable, unstable.

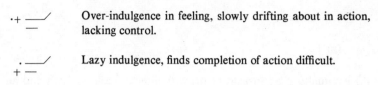

.+ ⎯⎯⁄ Over-indulgence in feeling, slowly drifting about in action,
⎯ lacking control.

. ⎯⎯⁄ Lazy indulgence, finds completion of action difficult.
+ ⎯

Both elements in excessive degree give even greater exaggeration.

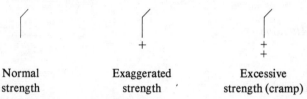

Exaggeration of elements

The above exaggerations of elements are, in practice, often described in greater subtlety of degree, for instance:

Normal	Exaggerated	Excessive
strength	strength	strength (cramp)

The descriptions above are really concerned with the excessive degree, rather than simple exaggeration. All of us can usefully call upon exaggerated degrees of movement elements in particular situations, either practical or non-practical, but the habitual use of exaggerations on occasions when it is inappropriate reveals the lack of balance in the personality. For instance, one of the typical exaggerations in many maladjusted children is in exaggerated bound flow and exaggerated strength (example (*a*)) which gives a tense, cramped attitude. It is also seen in some children that this swings in alternation with exaggerated free flow and exaggerated strength (example (*b*)) which is wild, uncontrolled and aggressive (if outward-flowing).

(*a*)   ⎡⎯ +   (*b*)   + ⎯⎤
⎸   ⎸
+   +

Lessened elements

In addition to the exaggerated degrees, we can also consider the lessened or weakened elements. Sometimes a personality pattern will reveal an under-use of nearly all elements (perhaps the quiet, crushed inoffensive, timid, weak child).

For instance:

(c) habitually used instead of (d) will show a weak strength and an inferior kind of control, neither actively controlled, nor positively free, easily led, easily influenced, lacking drive, determination and positive action. So for each area of attention, intention, decision and precision, similar charts for interpretation could be drawn, all showing lessened degrees.

Neutral states of motion factors

One other aspect which should be taken into account is the use of the neutral state of the motion factor:

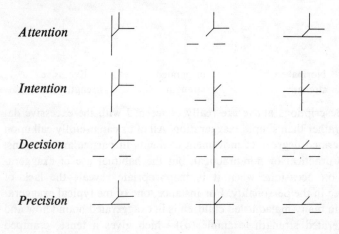

In the observations previously referred to, it will be seen that frequently neutral states are used, sometimes only of one motion factor, together with an active element of another, as, for instance:

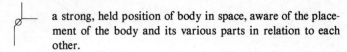

a strong, held position of body in space, aware of the placement of the body and its various parts in relation to each other.

Appendix II. Examples from C.A.T. Stories

Cheryl (Assessment 1)

Story I

Once upon a time there was a hen and she had three little babies, and one day they were eating their breakfast at the table, but the mother wasn't there eating it, she was doing the housework while they were eating. And then they got down and they went out and started playing while their mother was doing the housework. One of them saw a bird flying around and wanted to try to fly as well, so he tried but he kept on falling on his nose, and he had to go back in and go to bed. Another one saw a different bird and he wanted to try to fly, and he done the same thing—the same thing happened to him. But the other bird never, he just went in and didn't play at all. ("Which one would you rather be?") The one that didn't try to fly.

Story II

Once upon a time there were three bears, one was the mother bear, father bear, and the other was baby bear and they were playing— I've forgotten what you call it ("Tug of war?"). Yes—tug of war. And the baby was on mother's side, and her father was on his own. But the father fell on his back and the other two won, so they went home, and father went to bed, and then mother got some special stuff and made him some porridge. And they took it upstairs and the baby bear was telling him a story. ("Why did Daddy bear go to bed?") Because he fell—he hurt his back—medicine made him better. ("Not the porridge or the story?") They helped a bit. They bought the medicine in a chemists. ("Did they like playing tug of war?") I don't know. I think they did.

Story III

Once upon a time—I'm going to put a princess in it—there lived a princess and her father had a spell on him and it turned him into a lion. One day when he was looking into the garden, a mouse came along and bit his tail and the princess took him in, and then he went

out again and then something happened to his foot, and so she took
him back in again and got a walking stick for him. Then he went out
again, and she kissed him, then he changed back from a lion into the
king. ("And then?") He felt much better. ("And the mouse?") Before
he went out again, the mouse came and bit him again and the lion ate
it.

Story IV

Once upon a time there was a mother kangaroo and she had two
little children and they had to go to school. The mother went to
school with them. One of them rode a bicycle and they had to go
through a wood until they could get there, but she packed some food
and put on a hat and got a balloon for one of the babies. She put on
her hat and they got off, and there were tall trees there—one had a
lark in it which was singing. The baby on the bicycle stopped to hear
it but her mother was in front—she could not catch up with her, so
she got off the bicycle and jumped all the way there and when she got
to school she was late, and the teacher told her off, and she had to
stay in and do sums and then the mother kangaroo couldn't take her
home 'cos she had to stay a bit longer than the other baby. And that's
the end.

Story V

Once upon a time there was a mother bear and a father bear and
they had two twins. One night one twin got out of his cot and went
down the stairs quietly and peeped in the cupboard and got something to eat because he was hungry and then the other bear got up and
done the same, but he knocked a jam pot off and then mother bear
told them off and they had to stay in bed, and she made the cot higher
so they couldn't get out—and then she went to bed—father bear got
up and went to see what the baby bears had done, and he saw that the
pies had gone, so he went and told mother bear what had happened,
but mother bear said that she knew what happened, so she switched
off the light and went back into bed, but the other two little baby
bears were still awake and heard this, and got up and stood on
mother bear's bed and father bear's bed and then jumped up and
down. Mother bear felt this and woke up and told him off again. The
other bear got up but didn't wake mother bear or baby bear or daddy
bear up. He went to the window carefully, switched on the light and
peeped out. He saw there was a little girl coming in. He went and told
mother, and mother bear went downstairs and they ate the girl up for

supper. ("Where are the mother and father bears?") Mother and father bears are those two humps . . . ("Where did the little girl come from?") A little hut. ("Why did they eat her up?") Because they thought she was trespassing.

Story VI

Once upon a time there was a mother bear and a father bear and they had one baby around about. They all lived in a cave and they went out every day hunting. Once baby bear went out and found a rabbit and killed it and took it home. Father bear found a deer, killed it and took it home. Mother bear, all she found was a couple of leaves, but she took them home for the fire and some wood. The baby bear wondered what she had brought for them to eat, and then as she saw the mother bear hadn't bought anything except leaves and wood, she went out and got some feathers and some leaves and made a bed. Mother bear and father bear helped the baby bear and then baby bear after that went hunting again with her daddy and this time they found a deer, and they got the deer's antlers off and caught the deer before they did that. And then they took the deer home and put the deer's antlers on the chest of drawers for ornaments. They all went to bed—had their tea, and went to bed and slept.

Story VII

It's a fierce one. Once upon a time there was a lion who was fierce, every day he went out. The monkey went by and he heard him and the lion came roaring nearer and nearer. The monkey tried to jump up, but he was only a little baby one and his mother had to come down to help him up. He got up in the end, but the lion stayed down. He kept on trying and trying to go up the tree that the baby monkey went up, but he couldn't, so he changed his mind, and went back home, but before he could get near the house, the mother bear was pulling his tail and then he roared, fiercely and angrily and the mother monkey went home. Took the baby over to another tree and made another house there and then the lion kept on going to the tree where their house used to be and was waiting and waiting and waiting all day long for one of them to come down so he could catch it and then he realised that she had gone to another tree, so he kept on looking at the trees and kept on trying to find her, but then, all at once baby fell down. He had found the tree and caught the baby and took it home. And then he went hunting again, but before that he never done any harm to the baby because he knew that he must be kind to the babies, and then all the baby lions made friends with the monkey. If the monkey went home, then they went and followed him but he always stayed at their house because he thought it was a friendly home until one day the fierce lion got fierce again and ate the poor little baby and ate the mother. "Oh dear," the father one said, "I must save the mother before she gets eaten," and then he pulled his tail and he growled angrily and then he let go and jumped up in the tree nearby, and he got the other away, because that was one trick, but the baby was eaten and then they went to another tree and the mother had another baby but kept him up in the trees, so the lion would not eat him. When he was fully grown, he went out hunting with his father, but the lion was dead, so they had no more trouble after all that.

Story VIII

Once upon a time there lived three monkeys and they had a little baby and the baby was always getting told off—so one day, when the mother and father monkey was drinking a cup of tea, the auntie took the baby over to her place, and kept him there. The other monkeys were looking for him, but they did not know where the auntie was staying for a couple of days and weeks, and so they never found the baby monkey. And they stayed home—the mother one was crying her eyes out but father one comforts her, and then one day, auntie monkey came over there and took the baby as well. He never got told off that day, he just went straight to bed, and got a book out and was reading it in bed. And mother and father and the auntie was pleased, but the auntie went up there and said, "You must come again soon, my dear, because this might be the last time that you might be able to come." So the two monkeys were listening to this, so they tried to fight auntie monkey, and baby monkey came and bit them both, and then auntie took the baby monkey away and let him free and auntie went free and took her earrings off and left them behind. Other two monkeys were looking for her and the baby, but they could never find them, because they had left that world—to another land—to Africa.

Story IX

They are rabbits. Once upon a time, there lived a little baby rabbit who lived all alone. He kept the door open so he could see. One night he closed the door and heard footsteps coming flip-flap across the rooms. He went out and had a peep but there was a fierce animal—a gorilla—not actually a friendly gorilla, and he tried to get the rabbit but he closed the door, and closed every single door in the house, closed all the windows and had something by the side of his bed, and when he got in the room he was in, he picked it up, but he found out it was another rabbit, and then he got out of his bed, and went to see the rabbit and made friends and they both lived together very shyly actually, because they did not want to go out, and see the others, so they stayed in all the time playing with their toys. Then the gorilla came again but now he had two to fight, he went shy, and the others, they weren't shy any more. So they went out, and took the gorilla away and let him free in the world, and then the gorilla and the two rabbits lived happily ever after.

Story X

Once upon a time there was a dog and she had a baby dog. Baby dog always told mother dog where he was going. One day, baby dog did not tell mother dog that he was going to go to the toilet and he just went, and the mother dog came, picked him up and took him out again and said, "Why did you not tell me where you were going, because if you did not, I might have thought you went with a wolf or something—tell me always where you are going," and then he went back into the bathroom and washed his hands, and after that he had a bath and went to bed, but the mother dog wasn't quite sure what he had done, so she went into the bedroom and saw that he was fast asleep and then she went back down again and told her husband that he never had any tea, so father dog went up there and took some tea—woke the dog up and said to him, "You did not have your tea— why is this?" And the baby dog said, "I did not want any." "Oh, why is this?" the father dog said. "Well, you see, I went out hunting while my mother was sewing—I did not tell her this, and I went and got something that was lovely, and I ate it—and I never wanted any tea, so I just went straight to bed." "Oh, all right," said father dog—and then they went to bed, and in the middle of the night, the baby dog went out again—he just wanted to go to the bathroom 'cos he left some perfume in there—wrapped it up carefully 'cos it was his mother's birthday the next day and he gently creeped into the room and got the present and laid it on the foot of the bed and then the mother felt this—he ran quickly off—when he banged the door, mother knew it was a present, so she opened it and found it was beautiful perfume—perfume she always wanted to have—but she could never get it—father bear wondered what she was up for—she said, "I wondered where this present came from. I wonder if baby put it there and went back into his room" and she said, "Baby, did you put this present on the foot of my bed?" Baby said, "Yes. I wanted to put it there before you woke up in the morning"—"Oh but I felt it and woke up and thought it was a very beautiful present," and then mother bear went out and got a book for the baby bear, 'cos she wanted that oh so much so she thought she might give baby bear—dog—a reward.

Analysis of stories

1. *Main Theme*: Being at mercy of others; getting hurt; food; helping father.
2. *Main Hero*: Child—usually female, same age or baby—avoiding mother's domination—romanticised role—often fails—or is great success. No emotional feelings of father and mother expressed.
3. *Main Needs*: To avoid physical hurt; to escape mother; to help father; to pal up with another—when grown up, no more trouble.
   Introduced: princess (self)—friend into stories.
4. *Environment*: Troublesome—child hungry, in danger.
5. *Parents*:
   (*a*) Mother—domineering, though playing role of mother in family. Father—needing her care and help.
   (*b*) Once, wanting a friend—brothers and sisters accepted.
   (*c*) No real comment on younger ones.
6. *Conflicts*: Disobedience to mother—getting hurt, so plays safe.
7. Physical harm and punishment from mother—lack of love (?linked with food obsession).
8. Playing safe—withdrawal—or resisting mother without making it obvious—shy?
9. Punishment—just.
10. Unhappy, partially realistic—when grown up, no more trouble.
    Rambling thoughts—concrete.
    Appears dispersed and enjoys meandering.

Jane (Assessment 10)

Story I

Once upon a time there were three ducklings and a cock and one day, one of them got up and went downstairs to make some porridge before the cock crowed. The other two were in bed. They woke up and both said "We will not bother Mummy today, we will get ourselves dressed and washed." When Mummy got up, she found them gone from the bedroom, so she went round the house looking for them. Then she found them downstairs, eating their porridge. "Where have you been?" "We got ourselves dressed and didn't want to bother you." So they said "Shall we help you with the housework, because Daddy is coming home today?" And when they left the table, they said "Thank you very much for the porridge." Then they washed up— one washing, one drying, and then they both went out to play for a bit. Their Mum called them in to go shopping, so when they came back, they saw someone sitting in the armchair. They wondered who it was and said to Mummy, "Who is that person?" Mummy said "It's your Daddy, and here is a present to give him." And so they both went up to their Daddy and said "Here is a present for you," and after that they were always happy. He had been away for a long time.

Story II

One day a little bear went out to play with his two big sisters, and they were having a fight and so one of the sisters said "Come on my side, little bear"—so he did, and the other one said "It's not fair, you've got two, and I am on my own." And they were pulling the skipping rope, 'cos one wanted to play alone, and the others wanted to play together. So baby bear said "Don't argue, let's all play with it together." They said "Who is going to be enders—we are not"—and so baby bear was, and Mummy bear came out and said "I will be an ender for you for a little while."

While Mummy bear was outside, she forgot about the potatoes for dinner because they had been playing a very long time. She just remembered and ran indoors and the potatoes were burned, so they couldn't have any potatoes for dinner. When daddy came home, he didn't know about this, and he said "Where are my potatoes?" and baby bear said "Mummy burnt them while she was skipping with us—so we can't have any potatoes for dinner." So daddy didn't want his dinner, because he always wanted potatoes with it—so he went out and had a dinner at the café, and when he came back he went to bed.

Story III

One day a lion became king over England. And he was thinking what to do—to go up the road in his carriage?—No, I won't do that— shall I go into the garden?—No, I won't do that either. I will smoke my pipe indoors. A mouse was in the corner listening to him, and came up to him and said "How do you do? I will tell you a story while you smoke your pipe" First of all, the king didn't know who it was, and then he looked down and saw the mouse. And he said "What do you want?" "I was listening in the corner, and heard that you didn't want to do anything, so I thought 'Shall I tell you a story?'" So the king said "All right." The story was about a princess and a prince, and at the end, he was full of joy because they got married and lived happily ever after, and he said "I think I'll do that because I haven't been living happily." So every day the mouse used to sit in his corner, and when he wasn't busy, he used to tell him a story. So they became very best friends and often people in the palace used to come and listen to him, and used to get fond of the mouse and gave him everything he wanted.

Story IV

One day a mummy said to her baby kangaroo "We are going shopping in the market today." So she got the baby out of the cot, and put her in her pocket. He said to the brother "Would you like to take your bike" and he said "Yes" he would. And so baby got her balloon, and Mummy got her bag, and her hat and shopping basket. And so they all went off to market. On the way back, little baby bear fell out of Mummy's pocket, and Mummy didn't know this and went on home. When they got home, Mummy said to brother "Where is baby kangaroo, I thought she was in my pocket." And brother said "You dropped her on the way back." Mummy said "I would not do such a thing!" So she told brother to go and look for her on his new bike and bring her back in her shopping basket. When he had gone, someone was shouting "help"—He went over and saw it was his sister, and he said "Jump in, my little sister, I will take you home to Mummy." When they got home, Mummy said "Did you find baby?" "Yes I did, here she is."

Told me between the stories here:
No brothers and sisters.
No television—"I used to talk to myself and Dad will play Chinese patience, or I play with my dog. I used to go out, but I don't now as there are so many horrible children."

Story V

One day a man said to his wife "I am going away for a year"— packed up and went away. In December on Christmas day a baby was born in the lady's bedroom, and on Christmas day Daddy came home and he saw a new baby was born. He unpacked and went out to get some clothes and a present for the baby. On the next day, someone came to the door. The lady went to the door, gave the baby to the father for a minute—and he said "What do you want?" "Here is a present for you"—and she gave him some money and took in the present—and she unpacked it and put the paper in the dustbin, and there was a new pram for the baby. And then someone else came knocking at the door. But the lady didn't go, the man went, and he knew what it was, so he gave the other person some money and he took it indoors and he held the baby and let the lady unpack it—and it was a cradle, what you can rock with. She got the baby and put him in it, and when she put him in, and went to get his bottle, he started to rock the cradle and sang him a lullaby, and went to sleep and he didn't wake up till dinner time for his food.

Story VI

There was a cave near a village on the rocks, but the people didn't go near it because they were scared because there was a mummy bear and a little baby bear there. One day a man went in and saw them asleep—the mummy bear woke up, and started to talk. The man's eyes nearly popped out of his head. The bear said "What do you want? Do you want some food?" "Yes, I'd like some food—but people say they won't go near this cave because they think you would eat them all up." And mummy bear said "I'd do no such thing" and so the man said "Goodbye" and went home, but he didn't tell anybody because the bear had told him not to. If he did tell somebody he would be eaten up.

Story VII

In a jungle there were lots of animals—but the animals didn't like one animal because he was a tiger, and if you didn't say he was the prettiest, he would scratch you and eat you. One day a monkey was new to the jungle, but his mother forgot to tell him about this animal. The other brothers and sisters knew, and wouldn't tell him. When he was climbing a coconut tree, the animal came out and he was going to fall into his pitch, but before the tiger got him, and before he ate him, he said "Am I the prettiest of all?" And the monkey said "No" and the tiger started to eat him all up. The next day the mother got worried and they all went out to find him, and they saw the monkey's fur and knew that the tiger had eaten him. And they all took it home and buried the body in their front garden, and made a grave and put some leaves and a coconut on it. While this had happened, Daddy wasn't there and when he used to come home, baby monkey used to come running to him, but he didn't today and they all used to be sitting in the garden, and they wasn't, so he thought there must be something wrong—and he found them all crying— "Did you see the grave?" "Yes, what is it?" "Our dear little monkey is dead" and he said "How did it happen?" "Yesterday we went to the woods and saw his body and so we knew he was eaten up by the tiger, so we brought the body home and buried it and got a coconut and leaves."

Mother said "Let's all go to bed and get it over. Tomorrow we will go for a picnic." So they went to bed and the next day forgot all about it and had a happy day.

Story VIII

There was a mummy and daddy and a baby bear and they were all monkeys. One day, Mummy was doing the housework and was in a rush. "Why are you doing all the housework in a rush?" said baby— "Your uncle from the jungle is coming to see you." At night Daddy came home and said "Did you tell monkey-bear about Uncle?" She said "I forgot at first, but monkey saw me doing the housework so quickly, so I told him and so it was a surprise for him."

And at night, the uncle came and gave baby a present and it was a little pet monkey and he was really happy and Uncle gave him a cave for it. And Uncle said "I can stay the night with him."

Story IX

One day a little rabbit wasn't very well, and when mummy and daddy came up to get him up he didn't want to get up for school, so they got the doctor and he said "He is not well and he will have to stay in bed." So mother had to stay home, and daddy couldn't because he had to go to work. So he went to work and came home and gave little rabbit a present. It was a little doll. She was very happy and that's what she always wanted. Door open to bring fresh air in—also window—"I am not in here."

Story X

There were two puppies in this house a lady and man lived in. One day they crept upstairs and went to the bathroom. Mother bear sat on the stool, and baby bear nearly fell into the toilet and couldn't get out. And so mummy puppy went running downstairs, and told the lady and the lady said "What was you doing in the bathroom?" She pulled him out and put him in a kennel and didn't let him out for two days. So that was their punishment. On the third day the lady and man let them out and they went for a picnic. Before they went for the picnic, the two dogs had two tears coming out of their eyes and they said "We are sorry for doing what we shouldn't do."

Appendix III. Example of a Movement Report Sheet

NAME		AGE	/D/B	I.Q.
Phrases, transitions etc.	Body		Space	
Inward Outward Flow	Awareness		Shaping	
Length of phrases Long Short	⊙ ⊠ ●		Near, far, zones etc.	
Transitions			Planes & directions	
	Symmetry			
	Asymmetry			
Rhythm of phrases (Rebound etc.)	Body shape			
Pattern of phrases	Balance			
Increase/decrease	Manual dexterity			
Motion factors Weight Time Space Flow				

INDEX

UE

Jı